Memorial book
The Ritavas Community
A Tribute to the Memory of our Town
(Rietavas, Lithuania)

Original Book Edited by Alter Levite

Edited by Dr Dina Porat and Roni Stauber,
Published in 2000 in Cape Town, South Africa,
By The Kaplan-Kushlick Foundation

Published by JewishGen

**An Affiliate of the Museum of Jewish Heritage - A Living Memorial to the Holocaust
New York**

Memorial book
The Ritavas Community
A Tribute to the Memory of our Town

Copyright © 2019 by The Kaplan-Kushlick Foundation
All rights reserved.
Printed by JewishGen, Inc. March 2019, Adar II 5779

First published in Hebrew, Yiddish and English by the
Fellow Townsman Association of Ritavas in Israel and Abroad 1977

Revised English edition published by the The Kaplan-Kushlick Foundation,
Cape Town 2000

Cover Design: Rachel Kolokoff Hopper
Layout: Donni Magid

Published by JewishGen, Inc.
An Affiliate of the Museum of Jewish Heritage
A Living Memorial to the Holocaust
36 Battery Place, New York, NY 10280

"JewishGen, Inc. is not responsible for inaccuracies or omissions in the original work and makes no representations regarding the accuracy of this translation. Digital images of the original book's contents can be seen online at the New York Public Library Web site."

The mission of the JewishGen organization is to produce a translation of the original work and we cannot verify the accuracy of statements or alter facts cited.

Printed in the United States of America by Lightning Source, Inc.

Library of Congress Control Number (LCCN): 2019936582
ISBN: 978-1-939561-80-0 (hard cover: 302 pages, alk. paper)

JewishGen and the Yizkor-Books-in-Print Project

This book has been published by the **Yizkor-Books-in-Print Project,** as part of the **Yizkor Book Project** of **JewishGen, Inc**.

JewishGen, Inc. is a non-profit organization founded in 1987 as a resource for Jewish genealogy. Its website [www.jewishgen.org] serves as an international clearinghouse and resource center to assist individuals who are researching the history of their Jewish families and the places where they lived. JewishGen provides databases, facilitates discussion groups, and coordinates projects relating to Jewish genealogy and the history of the Jewish people. In 2003, JewishGen became an affiliate of the **Museum of Jewish Heritage - A Living Memorial to the Holocaust** in New York.

The **JewishGen Yizkor Book Project** was organized to make more widely known the existence of Yizkor (Memorial) Books written by survivors and former residents of various Jewish communities throughout the world. Later, volunteers connected to the different destroyed communities began cooperating to have these books translated from the original language— usually Hebrew or Yiddish—into English, thus enabling a wider audience to have access to the valuable information contained within them. As each chapter of these books was translated, it was posted on the JewishGen website and made available to the general public.

The **Yizkor-Books-in-Print Project** began in 2011 as an initiative to print and publish Yizkor Books that had been fully translated, so that hard copies would be available for purchase by the descendants of these communities and also by scholars, universities, synagogues, libraries, and museums.

These Yizkor books have been produced almost entirely through the volunteer effort of researchers from around the world, assisted by donations from private individuals. The books are printed and sold at near cost, so as to make them as affordable as possible. Our goal is to make this important genre of Jewish literature and history available in English in book form, so that people can have the personal histories of their ancestral towns on their bookshelves for themselves and for their children and grandchildren.

A list of all published translated Yizkor Books in the project with prices and ordering information can be found at:

http://www.jewishgen.org/Yizkor/ybip.html

Lance Ackerfeld, Yizkor Book Project Manager

Joel Alpert, Yizkor-Book-in-Print Project Coordinator

JewishGen
Yizkor Book Project

This book is presented by the
Yizkor Books in Print Project
Project Coordinator: Joel Alpert

Part of the
Yizkor Books Project of JewishGen, Inc.
Project Manager: Lance Ackerfeld

These books have been produced solely through volunteer effort
of individuals from around the world. The books are printed and
sold at near cost, so as to make them as affordable as possible.

Our goal is to make this history and important genre of Jewish
literature available in English in book form so that people can have
the near-personal histories of their ancestral towns on their bookshelves for themselves and for their children and grandchildren.

Any donations to the Yizkor Books Project are appreciated.

Please send donations to:
Yizkor Book Project
JewishGen
36 Battery Place
New York, NY 10280

JewishGen, Inc. is an affiliate of the
Museum of Jewish Heritage
A Living Memorial to the Holocaust

Acknowledgements

Special thanks to the National Yiddish Book Center in Amherst, Massachusetts and the New York Public Library for supplying the high resolution images used in this book.

Our sincere appreciation to Prof. Milton Shain and Romi Kaplan of the Kaplan-Kushlick Foundation for permission to allow JewishGen.org to use this material.

Our sincere thanks to Seth Morgulas who scanned the original English edition and edited the text, and to Helen Rosenstein Wolf for editing a considerable proportion of the scans, thus enabling us to facilitate the addition of all the text to this project.

Geopolitical Information:

Rietavas, Lithuania: 55°44' N, 21°56' E

Alternate names for the town are: Rietavas [Lith], Riteve [Yid], Retovo [Rus], Retów [Pol], Retowo, Rietevas, Riteva, Ritova

Period	Town	District	Province	Country
Before WWI (c. 1900):	Rietovo	Rossieny	Kovno	Russian Empire
Between the wars (c. 1930):	Rietavas	Telšiai		Lithuania
After WWII (c. 1950):	Rietavas			Soviet Union
Today (c. 2000):	Rietavas			Lithuania

Nearby Jewish Communities

Tverai 8 miles E
Kuliai 12 miles WNW
Žarėnai 12 miles NE
Kvėdarna 13 miles SSE
Plungė 13 miles NNW
Laukuva 14 miles SE
Veiviržėnai 16 miles SW
Varniai 17 miles E
Švėkšna 19 miles SW
Pajūris 20 miles SSE
Gargždai 21 miles W
Šilalė 21 miles SSE

Siauliai

Klaipeda

● **Riteve**

Lithuania

Taurage

Kaunas

Vilnius

Marijampole

Map of Lithuania showing Riteve

Cover Design by Rachel Kolokoff Hopper
Background Cover Photo: Wildflowers by Rachel Kolokoff Hopper

My town was a locked and enchanted garden.
Tzila Beirak (Linde)
From the Memorial Book, the Ritavas Community (page 77).

The Ritavas Community Memorial Book cover illustrations are two collages created from individual photographs from the interior of the book layered over a photo of dried wildflowers. The collages represent what the community once was, and the covers tell a visual story of the people and places from this lost place. On the cover, the people of Ritavas are forever interconnected and forever joined. More than a place on a map in the country of Lithuania, Ritavas was the soul of the people that lived there.

Once a living and thriving place of community, family, education, work, hardship, love, and joy, Ritavas and its people were wiped from the face of the earth during the Holocaust. But with the memories of the survivors, we can all remember what once made this Shtetl a home to so many of the lost.

My hope is that this cover evokes a deep, raw, and emotional response. It is painful to look at this collection of photographs and we cannot help but feel a sense of loss, longing, and then, horror. But we must look, and we must remember. We must remember the people of Ritavas. And we must never forget.

The faces and places on the cover:

- The teacher Alter Leveite with his students (Page 52)

- The two brothers, Alter and Zahnan Lab Levite (page 32)

- The senior class of girls at the Hebrew (Jewish) School with teachers Moshe Kos, and Alter Levite (page 39)

- The third graduation class of the 'Yavneh' School (Hebrew School) with teachers Izchak Paktor, Miriam Levite, Dr. Pirkin, and Miriam Rabinowitz (page 42)

- The firemen of Riṭeve (page 52)

- The Dramatic Circle in Riteve (page 75)

- David Salzman, Leib Katz, Eliezer Lande, Gutman Shmole and Asher Erman (page 91)

- Shalom Saks, Shmuel Peskin, Zvi Gillon, Moshe Ballin, Shlomo Babush, and Shlomo Jakov Salzman (page 99)

- Chone Babush, Shimon Friedman, Jehiel Tollman, Peskik, Baruch Strass, Chaim Itzkowicz, Ze'ev Heiman and Izchak Wolf (page 100)

- Gavriel (Gabriel) Ben–Ze'ev Grod (page 113)

- Rabbi Itzchak Ben–Nachum Menachem Ahronowitz (page 116)

- Rabbi Aron Zalmanowicz, (page 119)

Notes to the Reader:

.

Also please note that all references within the text of the book to page numbers, refer to the page numbers of the original Yizkor Book.

In order to obtain a list of all Shoah victims from Riteve, the reader should access the Yad Vashem web site listed below; one can also search for specific family names using family name option. These lists are continually updated by Yad Vashem, so it is worthwhile to periodically search these lists.

There is much valuable information available on this web site, including the Pages of Testimony, etc.

http://yvng.yadvashem.org

A list of this book and all books available in the Yizkor-Book-In-Print Project along with prices is available at:

http://www.jewishgen.org/Yizkor/ybip.html

Page from the original English translation

MEMORIAL BOOK

THE RITAVAS COMMUNITY

A Tribute to the Memory of our Town

That the generation to come might know them, even the children that should be born, who should arise and tell them to their children.

(Psams 78:6)

Editor ALTER LEVITE

Published by the Fellow townsmen Association of Ritavas
In Israel and Abroad.

This English title page of the original publication, written partly in English and Yiddish, but mainly in Hebew. The latter two languages have been translated for this new edition which has also been expanded with new chapters providing historical background and with reference notes.

Page from the original English translation

A YIZKOR BOOK TO

------RITEVE------

A JEWISH SHTETL IN LIHTUANIA

EDITED BY ALTER LEVITE

REVISED EDITION
EDITED BY DR DINA PORAT
AND RONI STAUBER

PUBLISHED BY THE KAPLAN-KUSHLICK FOUNDATION
CAPE TOWN 2000

A Yizkor book should not just be read – it should be studied:
One a day it should be taken off the shelf and kissed. And a
chapter read – the way a page of the Gemara of the weekly
Portion were once studied.

Haim Liberman, Forward, June 1959

DEDICATED IN GRATEFUL REMEMBRANCE OF
ALEXANDER JUDELIS AND HARRY SINGER, FORMERLY
OF RITEVE, FOR THEIR INTEREST AND ASSISTANCE IN
THIS NEW EDITION OF THE YIZKOR BOOK OF THEIR
SHTETL

Table of Contents

Family Notes

[Page 8]

Foreword

by Dina Porat

Riteve – a Jewish shtetl in Lithuania

This is a memorial (Yizkor) book, published in honour of a small town, a shtetl in Lithuania. The town is called Rietavas (or Ritavas) in Lithuanian, Ritova in Hebrew and Riteve in Yiddish. Let us call it Riteve, since most of its inhabitants were Yiddish–speaking Jews.

The first memorial book dedicated to Riteve appeared in Israel in 1975, written with some sections in Yiddish and Hebrew and a few in English. Every page vibrates with the love and nostalgia shared by all those who once lived there and with their desire to make the book a monument to their town. In this respect it is no different in any way from dozens of other Yizkor books, written by the townsfolk. In these books, repetitions, irrelevant material, rather ornate style and a somewhat exaggerated rosy picture of the place and the people who inhabited it are often the general rule. Inasmuch as this occurred in the Riteve material, out of respect to the work done before we began ours, careful editing was employed in order to preserve the original tone and spirit in which it was written. The life stories of some of the personalities who were connected with Riteve only briefly or indirectly were included, however, as long as they demonstrated the strength and values acquired through life in this little town.

Most of the Jews who left Riteve between the two world wars emigrated to South Africa, as did most Jews from other towns in Lithuania. Others went to the USA and to Israel. With the passage of time, new generations were born for whom the memory of the small, faraway towns is at best nothing but grandparents' stories. It is for them that this English edition of the memorial book has been prepared. And it is for their convenience that a glossary of Jewish terms and objects is included at the end of the book.

The text is based on the original 1975 edition, the Hebrew and Yiddish sections having been translated into English. However, the need was felt for introductory chapters in order to place the town in its historical and cultural context: 'The Jewish shtetl in Lithuania', 'The Jews of Lithuania in the inter-war period' and 'The Holocaust in Riteve'. We provided footnotes explaining events, names and locations. On second thoughts, because many general readers avoid foot-notes, and because some people may lack a background of Lithuanian history, particularly its Jewish history, many footnotes were incorporated into the introductory chapter written by Mendel Kaplan: "A background to the story of Riteve."

The introductory chapters and the illustrations evoke a vivid picture of a Jewish town. But it is perhaps the combination of personal memoirs, written by the townsfolk, added to the efforts of the historian to supply context and details, glossary and archival material, which offers a meaningful contribution to an understanding of one's roots. We hope that the combination presented here makes this book a unique Yizkor for a shtetl

Many thanks to Mendel Kaplan, whose roots are in Riteve and who initiated this work, and to his family The Singer family, Harry, Lily and Selwyn, were of great help, providing extensive testimony, photographs and a video cassette filmed during a visit to Riteve in June 1992. Sadly, Henry Singer died in 1998 before the book's publication. We also thank Sally Frankental, then of the Isaac and Jessie Kaplan Centre for Jewish Studies and Research at the University of Cape Town, and Haim Sheer of the Kaplan-Kushlick Foundation. Alexander Judelis, once the only living survivor of the Holocaust in Riteve and who died in 1996 in Lithuania, also contributed a very helpful testimony. Thanks also to the team, headed by Alter Levite, which edited the Hebrew book some 20 years ago, and probably wrote much of the unsigned material; and to Sheila Barkuski and Lilian Dubb, who faced a very difficult task indeed when translating the Hebrew edition in 1988. Thanks go as well to Roni Stauber, a dedicated assistant, to Marian Robertson. Mendel Kaplan's editorial assistant and researcher, who gave editorial help and produced the book, and to the copy editor and proof reader, Tessa Kennedy

May the book be a tribute to the exuberance and vibrancy of a Jewish world that exists no more.

Dr Dina Porat
Department of Jewish History,
Tel Aviv University
Hanukkah 5759 (December 1998)

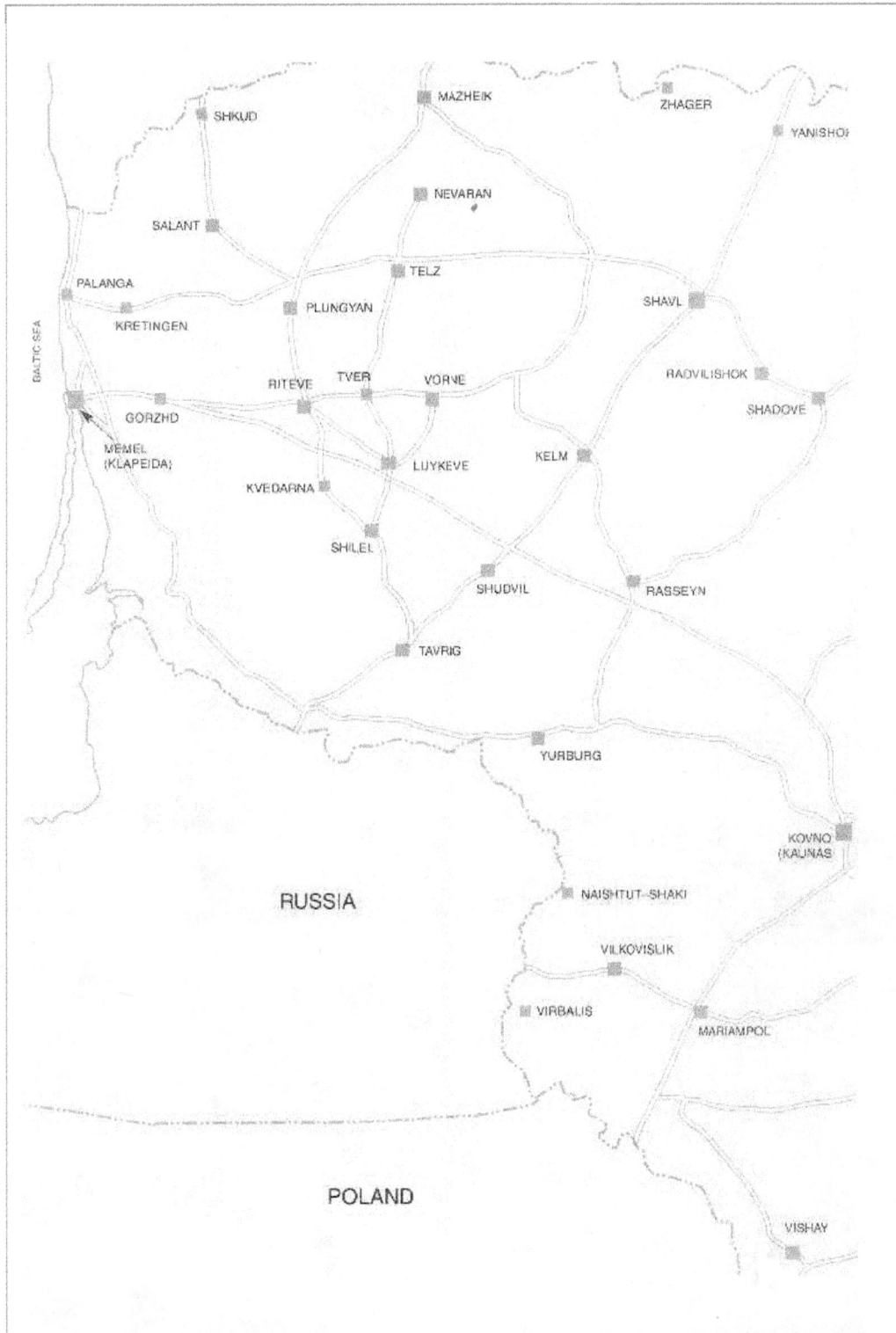

BALTIC SEA

SHKUD
MAZHEIK
ZHAGER
YANISHOI

NEVARAN

SALANT

PALANGA
TELZ
PLUNGYAN
SHAVL

KRETINGEN

RADVILISHOK
SHADOVE

RITEVE TVER VORNE

GORZHD

MEMEL
(KLAPEIDA)
LUYKEVE
KELM

KVEDARNA

SHILEL

SHUDVIL
RASSEYN

TAVRIG

YURBURG

KOVNO
(KAUNAS)

RUSSIA

NAISHTUT-SHAKI

VILKOVISLIK

VIRBALIS
MARIAMPOL

POLAND

VISHAY

LITHUANIA – (1999 borders)
Place names in Yiddish

KROK

BIRZH

PONEDEL

POSVOL

RAKISHOK

ABEL

LATVIA

PUMPIAN

KUPISHOK

KAMAI

DUSYAT

PONEVEZH

PANIMON

KRIAKINOVO

ROGORE

ANIKSHT

DAUGEL

SALOK

UTYAN

DUKSHT

KEIDAN

LINGMIAN

VILKOMIR

MALAT

SVENTZION

YANOVE

SHIRVINT

DUBINIK

KUSHIDAR

BELARUS

KATHSHOK

VILNA
(VILNIUS)

YEZNA

KENA

POON

AULAVA

ANISHOK

ALITE

DAUG

OLKENIK

GRAN

EISHYSHOK

[Page 12]

Chapter 1

A Background to the Story of Riteve

by Mendel Kaplan

Part One:
Lithuania and its Jewish Community

It appears ironic that the beginnings of Lithuania itself are tied into the Crusades and the ultimate ejection of the Crusaders from Jerusalem. While we were rebuilding Jerusalem after 1967, the mayor, Teddy Kollek, took me on a walking tour and pointed to a church that was being renovated to commemorate the site where the Teutonic Order of Knights was born. This Order of Knights fought their way to the Baltic Sea and eventually dominated the area known in the 13th century as Prussia. The pressure from this order together with the Livonian Order compelled fragmented Lithuania to form a governing body of some 20 dukes who are mentioned in the Wolhynia Chronicle and create a unified defense to maintain their independence.

From the 16th century onwards, the western part of Lithuania, in which Riteve is situated, that is to say the part bounded by the Nevesis River on the east, the Baltic Sea on the west, the Nemunas River on the south and the Latvian border on the north, was known as Samogitia, the name meaning 'lowland'. However, this name originated around the 14th century in various forms all starting with the syllable Sam ... 'Zem ...' or 'Zam ...'. Because its conquest would open up the way to the rest of Lithuania, Samogitia was right in the middle of the wars of Lithuania against the Teutonic Knights, starting at the beginning of the 13th century and continuing until 1422 when they were finally defeated. Samogitia's sufferings for over two hundred years isolated it from the rest of Lithuania and it developed differently Other areas were divided into palatinates according to the Polish system, but Samogitia had a nominal degree of autonomy as a separate administrative unit, being governed by a semunas (elder), approved by the Grand Prince. It had more private estates than royal ones and the peasants had more rights than their counterparts in Lithuania. They were not serfs and only paid a fee to the owners of the estates.

[Page 13]

The teacher Alter Leveite, left, editor of the original edition of this book, which was published in 1975, with a junior class at the Riteve Hebrew School in the 1920s or early 1930s

One duke, Mindaugas, is credited with having become the sole ruler king of Lithuania and the large district later known as Samogitia in 1236 and, in fact, was a Samogitian. He was assassinated in 1263 in an incident in which Treniota, the alleged son of Mindaugas's enemy, Prince Gykintas, who had died in battle in 1251, took part. Treniota succeeded Mindaugas for only a year until he, too, was murdered. No other Samogitians ascended the throne and, until 1672, Samogitia was ruled by the Vytenis–Gediminas dynasty.

The accession to the throne of King Gediminas in 1316 was the foundation of the empire of which Lithuania was about to become part and which ultimately stretched from the Baltic to the Black Sea. King Gediminas solicited foreign assistance to develop this empire and among those to whom he promised tax exemptions, freedom of worship and religious tolerance were

Jews, who then moved up either from southern Russia or the German river system. Lithuania was practically the last area of Europe to adopt Christianity; it embraced this only in the early 15th century. The Samogitians were the most resistant to this, although baptisms started in 1413. However, conversions happened slowly and even in the 16th century there were only 38 churches and some people still practised the pagan religion. So it was that the Jews who arrived from Western Europe did not suffer from Christian persecution as elsewhere, whether it was through the Crusades or for the Black Plagues of 1348–1350. Under Vytautaz the Great, who reigned from 1401 until his death in 1430, Jews settled in a large number of Lithuanian towns, including Vilnius. They were granted charters spelling out their legal rights and giving them opportunities for economic progress, exempting their synagogues and cemeteries from taxation as well as giving them personal religious security. These charters, their cancellation and re–establishment, were to dominate Jewish life in Lithuania and form the basis of their political, legal, economic and social structures until the 18th century.

[Page 14]

After Vytautaz's death, an argument over the union with Poland created a civil war which lasted nearly 15 years until the accession to the throne of Kazimier the Great. He allowed Jews to trade freely, hired them as financiers, permitted them to be tax farmers and appointed them as customs inspectors.

While the Jews remained under the Duchy of Lithuania, their conditions were reasonably stable; but once the Union of Lublin took place in 1569, merging Lithuania and Poland, their status altered. The increasing strength within this union of the Roman Catholic Church made the position of the Jews subject to the ruler of the day and his relationship with the church.

The 16th century saw the creation of an autonomous Jewish authority in the Council of the Four Lands. Under the Council, Jews were allowed the benefits of community organisation and responsibility. It ruled the Jewish communities which were part of the Ukraine. Belarussia, Lithuania and Poland, covering several million Jews. In 1590, the Jewish Regional Council, named Wad Lita, came into existence to speak for Lithuanian Jewry alone. Lithuania still belonged to the overall synod and sent members to its meetings, which were held during the great fairs of Lublin and in the five principal cities of the extended Four Lands: Brisk, Pinsk, Vilnius, Slutzk and Grodno, all of which had rabbinical courts. The establishment of the Councils in the middle of the 16th century was the implementation of the Polish authorities' decision to set up a centralised Jewish leadership. The venue and time of meetings of the Lithuanian Council were determined as circumstances required. The Council maintained a Pinkas (an official minute book) which recorded resolutions and the budget invested by the authorities. In 1763, the Councils both in Poland and Lithuania were dissolved in the wake of the decision of the Polish authorities to change the taxation system.[1]

[Page 15]

Although at times their rights were increased, as in the reconfirmed charter of 1644, the Jews were often restricted in terms of trade and residence. The latter restrictions marked the beginning of fie Jewish ghettos and the eventual establishment of the Pale of Settlement. The slaughter of the Jews in 1648 during the Ukrainian Cossack rebellion under Chmielnicki had its repercussion in Lithuania. However, more important was the invasion of Lithuania by the Russian army and Swedish forces during the Swedish expansion. This was best described by Moises Rifkus, who fled to Amsterdam at the time:

> The whole of Lithuania is suffering from bands of Russians and Cossacks, who destroy cities and kill the people. Thus fell Polock, Vitebsk, and Minsk. In Vilnius, Voivode Christopher Radziwill and his army, as well as many citizens, fled. The murderers looted the houses before burning them. Most of the Jews escaped, some by horse and cart. Others, carrying their children and Torah scrolls, walked for miles in search of shelter.

> I left my beautiful house, abandoned my inheritance, my books, my goods, and also my work on the Talmudic Tractates Zevalim and Menahot. We went into exile, not knowing where to go, accompanied by the cries of terrified refugees. We reached the German–Prussian border, where the Swedish army stripped us of the rest of our belongings. We boarded a ship and came to Amsterdam.

> There, the Sephardim and their scholars took pity on us and kindly gave us lodging food and clothing. Some ships with refugees were sent off at their expense to Frankfurt and other communities. Everywhere, the Jewish communities received the refugees with kindness. I was invited to stay by Chief Rabbis Saul Halevi Morteirc and Isaac Aboab, and their philanthropists provided me with a comfortable home where I might dwell.[2]

The commonwealth that had been formed by the Union of Lublin began to disintegrate in the 18th century and by 1767 Catherine of Russia had become the protectress of the commonwealth. Poland and Lithuania were finally partitioned in the last years of the 18th century and in 1795 Lithuania and Samogitia became a part of the growing Russian Empire. In 1843 Samogitia ceased to be a separate administrative unit and became part of the newly created province of Kaunas (Kovtio) in Lithuania and its original name is almost forgotten today.[3] Prom 1795. When Lithuania and Samogtia first came under the domination of the Russian Empire, the Jews began to experience maltreatment. By an edict of the tsar, they were restricted to an area described as the Pale of Settlement. This curved across the western border of Russia from the Black Sea to the Baltic. Educational and vocational opportunities were limited by quota and by law.[4]

In 1827, Tsar Nicolas I (1825–55) issued a decree that the exemption from military service that the Jews had formerly enjoyed would now cease. This was not because of military demands, but – and he made no secret of the fact – because he hoped that separation from their communities would result in converts for the Orthodox Church. The age for conscripts was usually 18, but the age for Jews was fixed from 12–25. Although other conscripts had to serve for 25 years, the time of service for a Jew was to count from the age of 18, thus some had to serve for over 30 years. There were some exemptions, including the only son of a family, and merchants. The Jewish communities, which were responsible for the filling of the quotas, employed kidnappers (chappers) to seize the youngsters. Not until 1874 was the age for military service made the same for Jews as for other members of the population. The time of service was also reduced from 25 to 6 years. Communal responsibility for finding the quota of recruits was abolished, but so were the exemptions, except for only sons. Jewish merchants objected strongly to their exemption being removed as it could ruin their businesses and affect their families' livelihood. Each potential recruit was personally liable to serve. In order to escape conscription, young men were known to change their names and move somewhere else or emigrate.[5]

[Page 16]

Conscription once more became a fear for the Jews when the war between Russia and Japan broke out in 1904. The bone of contention was the whole area of Manchuria and Korea. The Russian army was defeated and Japan gained large territories and became a world power in the Pacific. The total defeat of the Russian Empire had a very strong impact on the internal situation and precipitated the revolution of 1905 after, on the tsar's orders, there had been a brutal massacre of demonstrators against the war in

January of that year. The revolution was crushed by government reprisals against the peasants, sailors and soldiers who had mutinied and also against the workers. Some 15 000 people were killed and 70 000 were arrested.[6]

For a Jew, conscription meant being totally unable to follow his religion, including dietary laws. It was usual for a Jew to be posted to a far distant place in the Russian Empire: he had no chance of promotion and very often never saw his family again. The threat of conscription caused many Jews in Lithuania to emigrate.[7]

For more than a hundred years Russian influence reduced the economic stature of the Lithuanian province to a degree which led to mass migration to the West both of Jews and gentiles. The ability to migrate and to take with them their learning heritage, community organisation and economic abilities was developed by Jews during the period when Lithuanians to an extent controlled their own destiny.

Landownership should be mentioned as a factor influencing emigration, although discrimination here did not apply only to the Jew. Until the reform of 1861, when the serfdom system was abolished, the land in the Russian Empire was owned exclusively by the tsar and the aristocracy. In the instance of west Lithuania, in the districts of Telz and Tavrig, these were Polish aristocrats. Under the serfdom system, the serfs were in bondage to the landowner. They could be used by their owner for any kind of work and could even be bought and sold. When in 1861 (in 1836 in Riteve through the local landlord) the serfs were emancipated by an edict of Tsar Alexander II. This decree gave them legal freedom yet left them economically bankrupt. They had to pay a high sum of redemption money for the land, which they could not afford, and so they remained bound to the soil. In the beginning of the 20th century, about 48 per cent of the land was still in the hands of Polish and Russian landowners. During the first half of the 19th century, the landowning lords in Riteve were Mykolas Kleopas Oginski, who purchased the land in 1812, and his son, Irenaeus Oginski (1808–1863), who had two sons. As will be seen later in this volume, Irenaeus Oginski persecuted the Jewish community.[8]

In January 1863, a Polish revolt broke out when an attempt was made by the Russian tsar and his officials to conscript young Polish patriots into the army. The Lithuanians supported the Polish revolt but, by the end of the year, it had been crushed. Many Polish patriots, like Oginski of Riteve, were arrested before and after the outbreak of the revolt.[9]

The marketplace at Riteve, drawn from a photograph in the original book by Dean Simon. The photograph was probably taken in the mid-1920s.

[Page 17]

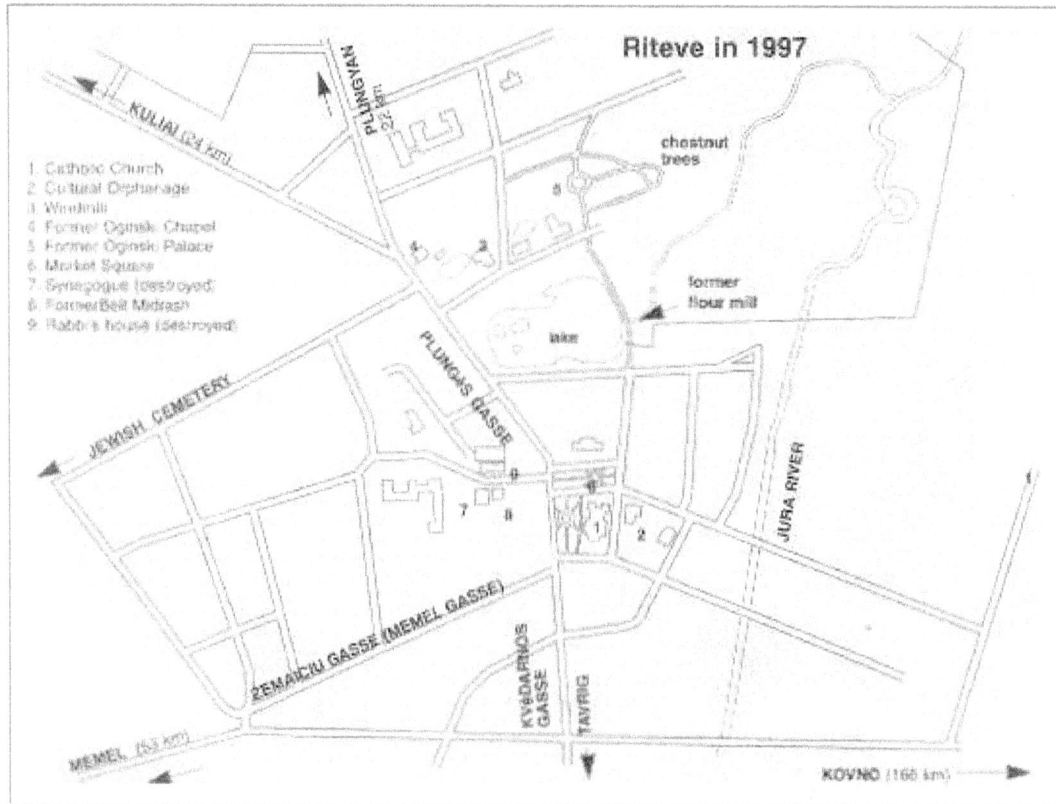

Riteve in 1997

1. Catholic Church
2. Cultural Orphanage
3. Windmill
4. Former Oginski Chapel
5. Former Oginski Palace
6. Market Square
7. Synagogue (destroyed)
8. Former Beit Midrash
9. Rabbi's house (destroyed)

Eighteen years later there was far more serious trouble. Pogroms began in the Ukraine and Poland and, although persecution of such severity did not occur in Lithuania, minor incidents were not unknown. Pogroms were riots against the Jews encouraged by the Russian government, which tried to find a scapegoat for the country's most difficult internal problems, especially the strengthening of the revolutionary movement. In 1881, pogroms broke out in a number of towns and villages in southern Russia. Similar pogroms were repeated in 1882, 1883 and 1884. Also, during the 1880s the previous policy of a liberal education available to all was countermanded. The number of Jews attending secondary school or university was limited to 10 per cent within the Pale of Settlement, even though the Jewish population there varied from 30–80 per cent; outside the Pale, limitations were worse – 5 per cent of students in St Petersburg, for example, and only 3 per cent in Moscow.[10]

[Page 18]

A postcard of Riteve, probably from the early 1930s, giving some idea of the countryside
Collection of the late Many Singer

Restrictions on Jews became more severe in May 1882 when the cabinet of Tsar Alexander III published the Temporary Laws. These restricted the limits of Jewish residence to small towns and villages, making farming impossible for the Jew in the country, for example, or industry in the city.[11]

The basis of South African Jewry was emigration from the Lithuanian shtetlakh. The final influences which determined this emigration were the conflicts that arose in the 19th century and the failure of the Enlightenment Movement to guarantee equality of treatment of Jews in the expanded Russian Empire. The Enlightenment had postulated the possibility that Jews could live a normal life as full citizens in a majority culture. The pogroms had questioned this and, consciously or subconsciously, the Jewish community of Lithuania developed four responses.

The first was the rise of Zionism, both in the rest of the Pale of Settlement and in Lithuania itself. This was welcomed as an answer to Jewish problems as it would normalise the Jew by giving him his own national state. In Lithuania, including Riteve, Zionist societies were established. Rabbis supported the Zionist movement – in fact, before Theodor Herzl began the Zionist movement, the Mizrachi religious movement was begun by Rabbi Jacob Reines at Lida. And he was only following the views of the Vilna Gaon – who sent some of his students to Eretz Israel – and other rabbis from Lithuania who established a colony in Jerusalem in the 19th century. This was one answer to the pogroms. Another

answer was provided by the development of the Bund, which stated that the Jews should be integrated into the local society, and the struggle for the liberation of the worker. Political development should be encouraged whereby the worker dominated and eventually overthrew the controlling authority.[12]

The third response was to return to the ghetto – spiritually if not physically – and concentrate on the world of the shtetl and the world of one's own people. Because of the restrictions in Lithuania on Jews owning agricultural land, and the fact that the majority of non–Jewish Lithuanians lived in the countryside, 50 per cent of the inhabitants of most villages and towns were Jewish. Therefore, to the outsider, and to the Jew who lived in the shtetl, the proportion of Jews in Lithuania seemed much greater than it really was. And it was comfortable to return to a life of homogeneity; even though it was one of great deprivation.

The final response of the Jews of Lithuania was to leave the country of their birth for the freedom of the West; to reach towards the 'Golden medina' of America who, in the words of Emma Lazarus on the Statue of Liberty, 'opened the golden door to all migrants', or to other places. And one of the places to which the Jews of Lithuania chose to go was South Africa – some 40,000 Litvaks chose this destination between 1880 and 1910. And that is how the world of Riteve came to the village of Parow, Cape Town, my birthplace.

[Page 19]

Part Two:
Riteve and Its Jewish Community

Year	Total population	Jewish population	Percentage
1859	964	–	–
1897	1,750	1,397	80
1923	1,720	868	50
1940	–	500	–
1959	2,882	1	0.03
Table from Pinkus Hakehillot (Dov Levin, Editor).			

Riteve is first mentioned in historical documents dating from 1253 and from 1527 belonged to the Grand Prince of Lithuania. It was granted permission to hold a weekly two–day market and an annual fair by King Zigmond Vaza in 1590 – from 1767 the number of fairs grew to four per year. Riteve was elevated to the status of a city in 1792 and, three years later, came under the rule of Russia (1795–1915). It was then first incorporated into the Vilna district and, from 1843, into the Kovno district. The aristocratic Polish Oginski family owned the town's lands and neighbouring estate from 1812–1909.

[Page 20]

While this family left many tyrannical stories within the Jewish community, especially that of the desecration of the Beit Midrash, they developed their estate and the town of Riteve in exemplary fashion. As was mentioned in Part One, it was under Mykolas Kleopas Oginski that the estate was purchased in 1812 and under his successor, Irenaeus Oginski, that it was developed. Irenacus Oginski abolished serfdom as early as 1835, well before it was abolished by the tsar in the rest of Russia, and between 1842 and 1850 initiated and encouraged the opening of six savings banks which were the first to be opened in Lithuania. In 1846, Uurynas Ivmskis, with the encouragement of Oginski, published the first calendar in Lithuania. On 1 January 1857, the first Lithuanian weekly, by the same man, was distributed, only to be prohibited shortly thereafter by the tsar. In 1859 the first agricultural school was established and Irenaeus's successor, his son, Bogdan Oginski, developed the first professional music school with a six- year curriculum and programme. By 1885 they had developed a 60-piece symphony orchestra.[13] The school building still exists. Today it has been reopened under the auspices of the Catholic Church with some arts and crafts featuring as part of its curriculum.[14]

In 1874, the major Catholic Church in the centre of the town, begun under the aegis of Irenacus Oginski, was completed by his son. In 1882, the first telephone line in Lithuania was opened between Riteve, Plunge, Krctinga and Palanga and in 1892 the first electrical lights in Lithuania were created in the town of Riteve.[15]

The first known census of Jews in Riteve was in 1662, when they numbered 421. As can be seen from the table heading Part Two. Riteve reached the zenith of us Jewish population around the end of the 19th century and then declined until the remaining inhabitants were wiped out during the Nazi period.[16]

The decline of the Jewish population in Riteve came about as a result of the conditions discussed in Part One and a large number of its Jewish population moved to South Africa between the end of the 19th century and the 1930s. The life of the Jewish population, as with the general population, was tied to the attitudes and progressive reforms of the Oginski family and even today remnants can be seen of the music school, the lake and the forests, as well as the tower windmill which created the first electrical power.

Of course, the synagogue and Beit Midrash stood at the centre of the town's religious life. The synagogue was used during summer and High Holidays, but the Beit Midrash served as a place of learning throughout the day where practically every Jew came to study Mishnah and Ein Yaacov or a page of Gemara. Many famous rabbis were born in Riteve, some mentioned in the text of this book including Aharon Shlomo (Solomon) Zalmonovitz, known as the Riteve Rov, to whom a South African rabbi. Rabbi Aloy, remembers giving a Shiur in his town before he left Dokshitz for Canada. One of the writers and translators. Rabbi Getzel Zelikovitz, was an Orientalist and researcher, a lecturer in Egyptology at the University of Pennsylvania. Among the rabbis who served in Riteve, the last rabbi was Rabbi Shmuel Fundiler, who, having suffered a martyr's death as described later, has since been reinterred in Jerusalem.

[Page 21]

**Harry Singer, standing right, and members of his family from South Africa, a photograph taken in Israel at meeting of the Fellow Townsmen Association of Ritevas in Israel and Abroad in the early 1970s.
Harry, who died in 1998, collaborated with the later Alter Levite in obtaining material for the original book and was one of the early members of the Fellow Townsmen Association.
As the Association is no longer active, he willingly gave permission for the new edition and took much interest in it.**

The world of the shletl revolved not only around the synagogue and Beit Nlidrash, but also the school system which had a cheder and Talmud Torah and later a Hebrew school which began in 1919 as part of the Yavneh School System. The most brilliant of students went on to study at the yeshiva or Jewish Gymnasium in Telz. My cousin, Alexarder Judelis, was a student at the Telz yeshiva and had chavrusa with the son of Rabbi Bloch.

As will be shown, a philanthropist born in Riteve, Kruskal from Frankfurt am Main, made possible the building of a school and residence for the rabbi during the 1930s. The religious life of the community demanded involvement in welfare institutions such as the Bikkur Cholim Society and Ma'ot Hittim and others described in detail.

Zionism came early to the Jews of Riteve where the Hibat Zion Movement had many members. By 1898 a B'noth Zion Association was founded. (Soon after, in far distant Cape Town, another B'noth Zion was founded in which my mother was happy to serve for over 50 years.) This association distributed the Zionist shekel and Jewish National Fund Stamps. Between 1898 and 1903 there is a record of three lists of contributors from Riteve to the Jewish population in Palestine. Among the canvassers was one Shmuel Sacks whose descendant, Archie Sacks, was a mentor of both my father and myself in the Zionist Movement of the Cape.

[Page 22]

Riteve Jewry participated in elections to the Zionist Congress that took place from 1925–1939. The largest number of votes was in 1935 when 142 votes were received by Labour Israel, 11 by General Zionists and 101 by the Mizrahi. The Zionist Youth Movements, especially Hashomer Hatzair and He–Chalutz, operated in town as well as an extensive Maccabi segment. As a result of the Zionist movement, many Jews migrated to Palestine in the 1930s.[17]

The Jews of Riteve dealt in trade and crafts and provided their labour as Jewish plasterers, carpenters and blacksmiths. The following is a survey done by the Lithuanian government in 1931:[18]

This book is partially dedicated to the memory of a Riteve Jew, Alexander Judelis, who was the only family survivor of the destruction of the town by the Nazis and Lithuanian collaborators who ended hundreds of years of development. It is for those descendants of Riteve Jewry whose forebears had the prescience to migrate and who I hope will learn more about their shtetl that I have undertaken this project.

Type of business	Total no.	Owned by Jews
Butcher shops and livestock	2	2
Restaurants and bars	2	2
Food products	1	0
Clothing, furs and textile goods	7	7
Medicines and cosmetics	1	0
Watches and jewelry	2	2
Radios, bicycles and sewing machines	1	1
Miscellaneous	2	1

Part Three:
What Makes a Litvak a Litvak

The development of the Litvak character was influenced by a number of processes through which the Jews lived during the centuries. Va'ad Lita, the break– away Council of Lithuania, met on a large number of occasions in different towns, one of which occasionally was Riteve. The Council was based on Kehillot of the various shtetlakh and a hierarchy with a 15–man standing committee who were composed of the two lay leaders and Av Beth Din of the five most important communities. The treasury was operated by a salaried trustee, or Ne'eman, and there was a shtadlan who represented the Jewish interests vis–a–vis the government. The ledger or minute book of the Council of Lithuania is intact for the years between 1623 and 1764, until it was ended by Catherine II, and was edited and published by Simon Dubnow in 1925.

[Page 23]

It is quite obvious that the structure of the community was taken by the Litvaks to the regions of the Diaspora to which they migrated. In such places they became part and parcel of the Diaspora Kehillot in which they lived. That is why South African Jewry is so well structured, with an understanding of the role reserved for religious and lay leaders heavily accentuated. It is also the reason why there is a clear differentiation between the Av Beth Din, the lay leadership and the government negotiator.

In 1652, the council ruled that any community which had its own rabbi should have a yeshiva both for adults and youths. This amplified what was already well known about the Litvak: his striving towards education.

Torah study was universal in Lithuania. With the abolition of the Council of Lithuania in 1764, the needs of yeshiva students and the respect of study for study's sake suffered a relapse. In 1803, Rabbi Chaim of Volozchin met this challenge head–on by overhauling the method of financial support for yeshivot and for the young students. Instead of students being responsible for their own financial existence, the yeshiva became the central arm for all its students and was responsible for their financial support. Rabbi Chaim also discarded the pilpul method and based recommended study on the methods of his mentor, the Gaon of Vilna, whose methodology became universal and led to the creation of great yeshivot throughout Lithuania. Among the most well known were those of Telz, Slabodka and Ponevezh. Ponevezh had a South African connection with Rabbi Kahaneman, who was a superb fundraiser, and, with the results of his successes in South Africa and his emigration to Palestine, he was able to continue with Ponevezh in Bnei Brak.

From the middle of the 19th century, the Haskalah (Enlightenment) Movement, which had originated in Germany and swept central Europe, became influential among Russian Jewry. The Maskilim, as its followers were called, sought to promote secular education and productivity among Jewish communities, believing that this would bring them into the more modern world. Although there were circles which supported complete assimilation, the majority of Maskilim sought a middle way which would preserve the national identity of the Jews.

The yeshiva movement felt, of course, the impact of the Haskalah. Should you study secular as well as religious knowledge? After all, did not the Vilna Gaon, the central sage of Lithuanian Jewry, have Euclid translated into Hebrew? But were not secular studies only the beginning of the movement away from Judaism and from the practice of Jewish life? Did not the Haskalah, in the end, mean an ultimate conversion to another form of religion – even if that were the religion of science? These thoughts battered on the doors of the yeshivot of Lithuania.

[Page 24]

To some extent, the conflict had a response in the development of the Musar movement: the need for adding moral instruction and ethical development to an individual trained strictly in the Halachah. This was a specifically Lithuanian phenomenon developed by Rav Israel Lipkin of Salant, known as the Salanta, in the 19th century. It was an attempt to meet the rising tide of secularist assimilation: to understand the reasons for anti–Semitism; to help the Jews overcome the poverty of their physical state, and to reinforce the yeshiva graduates as they moved into the outer world. The yeshiva world and the world of the Lithuanian Mitnaged continued their way of a dynamic Jewish life based on study and intellect. Rabbi Salanta brought the intellect into the living room of real life. Although the Musar movement split into many groups and divided many yeshivot it eventually became part of the curriculum of most Lithuanian yeshivot.

It is because the anti–Hassidic movement started in Lithuania with the strong stance of the Vilna Gaon on Hassidism that the Mitnagdim traced their origins to his doctrines and are known today as Litaim or Litvaks. The issue of the day was the Hassidic reaction against the control of the communities by the intellectual leaders of the Jewish religion. What of the Amcha (the general society) and the spiritual joys and mystical content of Judaism? What of song and dance? What of respect for the common people? This, then, was the outer clash between Hassidism and Mitnagdim; but inside was a striving for the control of the community and a basic attack on the structure of such control. The Hassidim soon developed a taste for the formation of courts around charismatic personalities and these rebbes became an intermediary between the Amcha and G–d. The question of Hassidism's support of the false Messiahs added fuel to the fire. All this and more was illustrated in 1780 by the Besht Book in which an Hassidic disciple, Jacob Joseph, criticised traditional Jewish leadership and its values. In 1781, the Gaon confirmed the ban on Hassidism and the excommunication of its followers. This strife continued for many years and only when the communities had to meet the common threat of increased anti–Semitism and poverty did it reduce in its intensity. However, South Africa as a Lithuanian community based itself on its Mitnaged origins and with very small Hassidic congregations. Even recently with the advent of the Lubavitch Movement in South Africa, there was strong opposition to the proposed appointment of a Chief Rabbi who was an adherent of Hassidism, to succeed Rabbi Casper. The South African Mitnagdim unified their efforts and were successful in the election of a Lithuanian Mitnaged born in Glasgow, Rabbi Cyril Harris.

The final aspect that gave Lithuanian Jewry and its South African satellite their specific character was the attitude towards Zionism. As stated earlier, the religious Zionist movement was begun in Lithuania. While, as is shown later, there was conflict in Riteve between those who wanted to say Kaddish for Herzl and those who felt it to be incorrect, there was little conflict within the Diaspora community where the Litvaks were a majority in their altitude to Zionism. In Riteve, the development of Zionist societies was mirrored by the involvement in South Africa of their kinsfolk in the creation of a strong Zionist movement, possibly the strongest in the Diaspora.

[Page 25]

Thus the Litvak character can be said to have been responsible for the disciplined institutional life; the drive towards Jewish education as evidenced in the extraordinary day school movement in South Africa; the non–Hassidic approach to Judaism, and the centrality of Zion in the life of the community.

Footnotes

1. Haim Hillel Ben-Sasson, Continuity and Variety (Hebrew) Tel Aviv, 1984, pp. 239-257

2. Waclow Nalkovsky, The Commonwealth of Poland and Lithuania. London, 1911 quoted on pp. 33-34 in Masha Greenbaum, The Jews of Lithuania, a History of a Remarkable Community 1316-1945. Gefen Publishing House. Jerusalem. 1995

3. Enc. Lithuanica EL. Boston, Massachusetts, Vol. V, p. 49

4. Mendel Kaplan, Solomon Kaplan and Marian Robertson, From Shtetl to Steelmaking Kaplan Kushlick Foundation, Cape Town. 1979

5. Israel Cohen. Vilna. Jewish Publications Society of America, Philadelphia, 1943 Facsimile reprint: Jewish Publications Society, Philadelphia and Jerusalem, 1992. pp 266-9, 276, 289

6. David Thompson. Europe since Napoleon. London, 1982, pp 337-338

7. Kaplan et al.

8. Enc. Lithuanica. Vol. V, pp. 109-110 and recollections in the text of the book

9. Greenbaum, op cit

10. Ibid

11. Ibid

12. Shmuel Ettinger. History of the Jewish People (Hebrew). Tel Aviv. 1969. Vol. 2. pp 193-197

13. Enc. Lithuanica, op cit. and document prepared for the 100th anniversary of electric lights in Riteve by its municipality. Translation given to Mendel Kaplan.

14. I have this personally.

15. Dov Levin, ed .Josef Rosin, asst ed.. Pinkus Hakehillot, Encyclopaedia of Jewish Communities from their foundation till after the Holocaust. Lithuania. Yad Vashem, The Holocaust Martyrs' and Heroes' Remembrance Authority, Jerusalem, 1996.

16. Ibid.

17. Information comes from the text of this book.

18. Levin, ed., op cit.

[Page 26]

Chapter 2

The Jewish Shtetl in Lithuania

by Dina Porat

All over Eastern Europe hundreds of small towns existed for centuries with Jews forming the majority of their populations. These little towns had so much in common that one may refer to them as to one phenomenon, although they were spread over a large area in many countries. Was the Lithuanian shtetl – there were about 200 of them – unique in any way? Let us first try and sketch a picture of a typical shtetl before the Holocaust came and wiped them all out.

One could define a shtetl as a place where the majority of the population was Jewish and could be identified as such because of the most common language – Yiddish; also the typical buildings such as the synagogues and the Mikveh, the Beit Midrash and the cheder. Moreover, despite the process of secularisation, at least some of the inhabitants, especially the older generation, still grew beards and side–locks and women as well as men wore their distinct clothing. Life in the shtetl progressed according to the Jewish calendar – the Sabbath, the Holidays, the daily prayers. The crowd in the streets moved and lived according to the ebb and flow of the Jewish Halachah and traditions.

Most of the homes in the shtetlakh were low wooden huts, enlarged according to the needs of the families. It is no wonder, therefore, that almost every Yizkor book includes a section entitled â€˜The Big Fire', and sometimes â€˜The Big Fires'. Since the shtetlakh were located in the countryside, sometimes near lakes and rivers, the local nobility built their palaces in the vicinity, thus enjoying the view as well as the services rendered to them by 'their Jews'. The services of a priest were also needed, and so a typical triangle was created – the shtetl, the priests' parish and the nobleman's palace.

According to the testimonies, Riteve numbered about 200 families in the 1930s, 1600 individuals at most, many of them children. No matter how small the town was, public life was amazingly intensive: the Kehillah had its departments and services, funded by the taxes collected from the population and by wealthier members of the community. Thus the Kehillah managed to maintain the religious, educational and welfare services, which operated alongside a variety of voluntary organisations. The best example mentioned in most of the memoirs on Riteve is the Linat Tzedek', the spending of the night at the bedside of the sick, a voluntarily organised and extremely efficient operation.

[Page 27]

An educational system was developed for all ages in Yiddish and in Hebrew, for the religious and the secular. The term 'People of the Book', relating to the Jews in their shtetlakh, was not an empty title: they were an island of literacy and constant study from a very early age, among illiterate and primitive peasants. A small place such as Riteve had a rich library and the leading newspapers reached it.

Another aspect of public life was the large number of political parties and organisations, which is perhaps characteristic of Jews: Socialists and Zionists, Communists and right–wingers, ultra–orthodox and atheists – the 20th century witnessed all these trends together, very often in the same family let alone in the same town. It seems that the most active, or at least the most conspicuous, were the many and varied youth movements, which enriched public life.

The economic life of a shtetl also had its unique character: the marketplace and the market days, when the gentiles would conic to exchange their agricultural products for other goods; the small shops, mostly kept by women; the artisans' booths and stalls, where they both produced and sold their products; the peddler making his rounds among the villages with small merchandise – all these gave the shtetl the positions of mediator between the towns and villages and provider of services to the local peasantry

It should be emphasised that, between the lines of nostalgia written in so many memorial books the poverty and the meagre means of many of the shtetl inhabitants may be clearly observed. Many needed the support of welfare organisations, both local and abroad. During the thirties, when the anti-Semitic economic policy of governments, such as that of Poland and Lithuania, made the Jews even more destitute, the emigration increased especially from the small towns. The young people, who felt that there was no future for them, left for the outside world. Many of them who started earning a living outside Europe sent their earnings home, thus supporting, sometimes actually saving, their families and the public facilities in their home town.

The Jewish shtetl led the autonomous life of a closed community headed by its leaders and guided by the Jewish codes of life. There were neither Jewish police nor a judicial authority or prison. And there was hardly any crime of any kind and almost no sins were committed. Heavy drinking, adultery, beating one's wife and children, all so common in the local society, were almost totally absent. It was the Jewish law, the Halachah, coupled with the intensive public pressure exercised inside a small group that kept the individual in line.

Even when the process of secularisation started changing the shtetl, it still retained many of its original features and religious leaders were respected by secular youth and vice versa. The best illustrations are the repeated descriptions, written by all survivors, of Rabbi Fundiler, the last rabbi of Riteve, being tortured to death by the Nazis. The grief as if for a common father, is shared by all. People born in shtetlakh felt, even long after leaving the place, a strong bond that tied them together, and the use of the Yiddish term 'shtot bruder' (town brother) is very common among then. Despite the poverty, the primitive physical conditions and the lack of constant communication with the outside world, these were places where a warm feeling of togetherness prevailed, and found its expression in a rich literature, memoirs and research.

[Page 28]

Returning to the question we started with, we see the Lithuanian shtetl as basically the same as all the shtetlakh. Yet, as much as it is possible to detect its characteristics, it gave birth to a special type of Jew – the Litvak, namely the Lithuanian Jew: rather more logical than emotional; a bit more suspicious of others; very independent in his thoughts and deeds; exceptionally sharp and intense in his study of the Torah; quite proud of his uniqueness, as compared with the type of Jew created in other countries. In short, a Mitnaged – an adamant opposer of Hassidism, not only as a trend in Jewish thought, but as the expression of a group practising together the over–emotional external ceremonies, giving less scope for forms of individualism. Such Jews, coupled with their world–famous yeshivot which attracted scholars from other countries, the intensive study of Hebrew, the development of the Zionist movement, and the strong public cohesiveness, made the Lithuanian shtetl in certain respects a unique phenomenon.

[Page 29]

Chapter 3

The Jews of Lithuania in the Inter–War Period

by Roni Stauber

The First World War brought about great changes in the history of Lithuania and its Jews. After being part of the Russian Empire from the close of the 18th century, the Lithuanians were determined to take advantage of the consequences of the war to create their own national state. The defeat of the Russian army and the occupation of Lithuania by the Germans enabled the Lithuanian National Council (Lietuvos Taryba) to proclaim Lithuania as an independent state on 16 February 1918.[1]

The Lithuanians had to fight for their independence, especially for the right to retain Vilna (Vilnius) as their capital. A serious challenge to the new state came from both Russia and Poland. At the end of 1918 the Red Army invaded Lithuania and occupied most of its territory. When Vilna fell to the Bolsheviks, the Lithuanian government moved to Kovno (Kaunas). The government in Kovno appealed to its inhabitants to join the Lithuanian army and help defend their country. As a result, the process of organising a new Lithuanian army began. There were many Jews among the volunteers in the Lithuanian resistance forces.[2]

By February and March 1919 the Lithuanian army, with the aid of the German army and Western equipment, had succeeded in checking the Russian advance and begun to drive the Russians from its territories. By July 1920, a peace treaty was signed in Moscow. However, the Lithuanians were now forced to repel another invader, the Polish army. The new Polish state, whose independence was also a direct outcome of the war, sought to restore its historic boundaries. The aim of the Polish government, under the leadership of Jozef Pilsudski, was to force unification upon Lithuania, or, failing that, at least to annex Vilna. In April 1919 the city was occupied by Polish troops. This act of aggression was the beginning of a bitter dispute

between Lithuania and Poland and between 1920 and 1923 the two countries
were in a state of war.[3]

[Page 30]

**Night classes were held in Riteve during the inter–war period
although, strangely, these were not referred to in the recollections.
This group of night classes I and II in Riteve was taken in 1919,
indicating that they were used mainly by young women.**

**Only the woman's names are provided in the original caption, but
24 instead of 25 are provided. No indication was given of
identification, but the family names are of interest to those with
Riteve connections:**

**Dvora Levite: Rachel Friedman; Chana Miller; Menucha Segal; Mita
Singer; Alte Gross; Esther Shapira; Malka Geniss; Penina Palukst;
Rachel Leah Feldman; Chaya Averbuch;**

**Feige Rosa Shapira; Sarah Gitel Rabanowitz; Chaya Singer; Zipora
Prisman; Miriam Levite; Hirshovtz; Tamar Sans: Gila Safes; Bila
Miller; Ziva Verkul; Zini Nigowitz; Shenka Goldberg; Feige Babush.**

The Western Powers, the Entente and later the League of Nations made many attempts to settle the Polish–Lithuanian dispute. They tried to establish an acceptable line of demarcation, but the two rivals could not reach an agreement about what constituted 'Lithuanian territory. The crux of the matter was the 'Vilna Question' – the possession of the city, and its environs. The Polish government claimed that the Poles constituted a majority in the city which was also Polish in culture. The Lithuanians claimed it as their historic capital. The aim of the foreign policy of both countries was to convince the League of Nations to accept their arguments and support them in the dispute. In this political struggle the Poles had an advantage over the Lithuanians. The rebirth of Poland was one of the goals of the Entente in the First World War. Poland was officially invited to the Paris Peace Conference and enjoyed the special protection of France. Lithuania, by contrast, was viewed with great suspicion by Western diplomats as a product of German intrigues.[4]

The Vilna Question was not the only object of Lithuanian foreign policy. An attempt was also made to convince the League to recognise its right to annex Memel (Klaipeda). The Treaty of Versailles had separated Memel from Germany on the grounds that the majority of its population was Lithuanian, and since France and Poland opposed the German position, Memel was turned over to independent Lithuania.[5]

[Page 31]

The Lithuanian political efforts to obtain international recognition and support for its claims concerning Vilna and Memel had important consequences for the status of the Jewish minority in Lithuania. The Lithuanian leadership sought to use Jewish influence in the West in order to break Lithuania's political isolation. The support of the Jews was also vital to the new state, which was fighting for its existence. The Jews were the largest national minority. According to the census held in 1923, the Jews numbered 153 743 (7.5 per cent of the total). Moreover, the Jews formed 40 per cent of the population of Vilna. Any state which sought to rule the city could not ignore this fact.[6]

The Lithuanian representatives to the Peace Conference at Versailles declared that the new republic had accepted the right of the Lithuanian Jews to national autonomy. The Lithuanian government ratified this obligation on its admission to the League of Nations. By that time a minister for Jewish affairs had already been appointed, the first being Dr Jacob Wygodsky who was one of three Jewish ministers in the first Lithuanian government. When the Lithuanian government moved to Kovno, Wygodsky remained in Vilna and was replaced by Mordecai (Max) Soloveichik, one of the leading communal and Zionist activists in Kovno. A Jewish National Council was appointed headed by Shimon Rosenbaum, and the Jewish community (Kehillah) was recognised as an authorised institution for religious and social affairs. The Kehillah was also empowered to impose taxes in order to finance its activities. Two communal conferences were held in Kovno in 1920 and in 1922, and delegates from all the Jewish communities in Lithuania participated.[7]

This policy of the Lithuanian government, which was based on political utilitarianism, did not last very long. When, on the one hand, the war against both the Russians and the Poles ended, and on the other the Lithuanian leadership realised that they had lost the political struggle over Vilna, the Jewish influence was no longer relevant. Contrary to the obligation made at the Peace Conference at Versailles, the Lithuanian Constituent Assembly decided not to include the clauses relating to Jewish national rights in the constitution. From the end of 1922 there was a permanent erosion of the Jewish autonomy, encouraged by the reactionary anti-Semitic circles in Lithuania. The cabinet formed in 1924 included no minister for Jewish affairs. At the end of that year the Jewish National Council was dispersed by the police, and the autonomous status of the Kehillah was abolished.[8]

[Page 32]

The anti-Semitic tendencies in Lithuania were strengthened at the end of the 1920s and during the 1930s. In 1926-1927 the democratic system in Lithuania was abolished and power fell into the hands of the Nationalists under the leadership of Antanas Smetona. The anti-Semitic policy during these years was directed especially against Jewish economic positions. The Jews, who formed about one-third of the total population of the larger towns, held many economic positions, mainly in small trade and crafts. The rapid process of urbanization after the war caused growing economic competition between the Jews and the newcomers. The anti-Semitic campaign in the 1930s was led mainly by the organization of Lithuanian traders and workers known as the Verslininkai. Its slogan was 'Lithuania for the Lithuanians'. The Lithuanian government encouraged the Lithuanians in this competition. Lithuanian traders, for example, enjoyed reductions in taxation, whereas the Jews were systematically dispossessed of their economic positions. As a result, many Jews were deprived of their livelihood and had to emigrate. Between

1928–1939, 13 898 Jews emigrated from Lithuania; 4 860 (35 per cent of them went to South Africa.[9]

The two brothers, Alter and Zahnan Lab Levite, closely resembling each other in appearance and both teachers in the Hebrew School in Riteve, were active leaders among the young people of the shtetl.
Alter Levite was to become the editor and main driving force behind the original edition of this book. Above: Zalman Levite teaching a class of older girls.
Below Alter poses with a class of eight older children.

Portraits of the two Levite brothers Zalman Leib Levite, left, and Alter Levite, showing their close resemblance to each other. They were both dedicated leaders

In October 1939, the Soviet Union took the first step to achieve control of Lithuania. These steps were carried out according to the secret agreement between Germany and the Soviet Union which divided Eastern Europe into their spheres of influence. Lithuania was compelled to admit Soviet garrisons and to grant air bases. The treaty between the Soviet Union and Lithuania also included the Soviet approval of the annexation of Vilna to Lithuania.[10]

Lithuania remained an independent state for the next seven months in spite of Soviet limitations. During these seven months 14 000–15 000 Jewish refugees, of all parties and professions, escaped from Poland to Lithuania. Most of them, 10 000 in number, went to Vilna. Many of them hoped to emigrate from Lithuania, if possible to Palestine. The Jewish communities made a great effort to assist the refugees. A special committee headed by Dr Jacob Robinson coordinated all the relief and legal activities.[11]

[Page 34]

On 15 June 1940, about 20 years after the National Council's proclamation of Lithuanian independence, Lithuania was occupied by the Soviet Army. Although many Jews were very seriously affected by the Communist economy which was principally against any private enterprise, they were considered by the Lithuanians as supporters of the Soviet regime. This popular opinion was based on the fact that Jews held important positions in the new regime.[12]

Soviet rule in Lithuania was terminated on 22 June 1941, when the Germans invaded the Soviet Union. This occupation opened a new and tragic era in the history of the Jews of Lithuania: during the war years most of the Jews of Lithuania were exterminated by the Germans and their Lithuanian collaborators.

Footnotes

1. A Gerutis. ed., Lithuania 700 years. New York, 1969, p. 154.

2. Don Levin, 'The Jewish participation in the Lithuanian War of Independence' (Hebrew), in: Kivanim, Vol. 13. 1981. p. 81.

3. Alfred E Senn. The Great Powers, Lithuania and the Vilna Question 1920–1928, Netherlands, 1966, pp.1–102.

4. Ibid., p 14

5. Gerutis, op cit.. pp. 203–213.

6. Ettinger. op cit., p. 236.

7. Leib Garfunkel. 'The Struggle of the Lithuanian Jevs for their National Rights' (Hebrew), in Yahadut Lita, Vol. 2. Tel Aviv, 1973. pp. 37–57.

8. Ettinger. op cit., p. 236.

9. J Leschtchinsky, The Economy and the Demography of the Lithuanian Jews' (Hebrew), in Yahadut Lita, Vol. 2. 1973, pp. 91–100.

10. David Thompson, op cit., pp. 756–766; Gerutis, op cit., pp 239–262.

11. Don Levin, 'Yerushalaim d'lita' as a temporary shelter for Jewish refugees in World War Two" (Hebrew), in: Nationa and Language (ed M Zohori et al.). 1985. pp 95–114.

12. Don Levin the relationship between the Lithuanians and the Jews during World War Two' (Hebrew), in Kivunim, Vol. 2. pp. 29–43.

The Beit Midrash in about the mid-1920s, drawn from an old photograph by Dean Simon.

[Page 35]

Chapter Four

History of Riteve

Townsfolk

This chapter relates the history of the Jewish community in Riteve as it was written by known and unknown landsleit of the town. It includes stories, engraved in the memory of the inhabitants, such as the great fire, the building of the new school by a donor, the suicide of the Polish tyrant who embittered their lives, etc. Although the name of the town and those of its rabbis are first mentioned in the 18th century, and the first Jews settled in Riteve probably a hundred years before that, most of the history related here dates from the middle of the 19th century – that is, more or less three or four generations before the Holocaust, the number of generations back generally retained in the collective memory of a family.

DP

———

The history of the Riteve community

Author unknown

Riteve was an ancient Jewish town in Zamut, Lithuania, with Memel to the west and Telz seven miles away to the east. Two hundred years ago, its name could already he found in the Pinkas (annals) of The Council of Four Lands. Riteve was situated in the province of Kaidan. The largest of the provinces in the northwest of Zamut. The annals mention a number of conferences of the Kaidan communities which were held in Riteve.

Riteve's place on the map was secured by the River Yureh which flowed into the Nieman, an important route for the transport of timber and ferries to Germany. Timber merchants and officials of the industry would visit Riteve fre– quently. The flax industry also flourished there. Since it was a town situated at the crossroads, the rabbinical courts dealt with many disputes between the merchants and the administration. Thus a wise and alert rabbi, knowledgeable in commercial matters, was required to decide in these complicated disagreements.

Above all else, Riteve was known for is scholarship. Even the shopkeepers and businessmen were experts in Mishnah studies. Feivel Udwin, for example, whose eyes had become weak in his old age, could recite the Mishnah by heart in particular the Tractate Chulin. Another scholar, Joseph Stras (known as Reb Yoshcik), had studied in the yeshivot of Volozhin and had such a penetrating mind that when he asked a question regading the Mishnah, it was very difficult for anyone to answer it. A qualified teacher, Mordechai Isaac Segal, was an expert in Agadah (stories and legends explaining the Halachic text in the Talmud) and when he taught on Saturday afternoons the synagogue was full. They were not the only scholars, but they were the most senior. There were others, for example a younger scholar, a chemist by profession, Eliezer Prisman, a graduate of the Telz and Slobodka yeshivot, who was outstanding in his scholastic achievement. Other outstanding young yeshiva graduates who lived in Riteve and earned on their studies after their graduation from Telz, Mir and Slobodka were the sons–in–law of businessmen in Riteve. Three such young men were responsible for maintaining tie Riteve yeshiva after the First World War and for its worthy name. Hundreds of students from the surrounding areas studied in the yeshiva in Riteve.

[Page 36]

The Hebrew school

Author unknown

The Hebrew school equipped its pupils with the skill to read and write Hebrew plus a knowledge of grammar, the Bible and Jewish history. It prepared the children spiritually for the new age which was dawning in our town. It became, with the passing of time, the source from which they drew inspiration for redemption and freedom. Indelibly engraved in our memories are the early stirrings of the National Movement and the rebirth of the Hebrew language which were, as yet. Ideals for the youth who graduated from the school.

And in our memories the festivals and celebrations and the many dramatic presentations which were offered at the school live on.

A list of the teachers follows:

Avraham (Alter) Goldberg
David and Moshe Kos
Alter Levite
Miriam Levite (Tsvik)
Frieda Levinson
Loyova Melamed
Rachel Friedman
Zvi Faktor
Miriam Rabinowitz
Izchak Zvi Paktor

[Page 37]

A posed group of a senior class of girls at the Hebrew (Jewish) School taken during the second half of the 1920s with teachers Moshe Kos, center left, and Alter Levite.

Alter Levite poses with 63 school pupils, all of whom he taught, in about the early 1920s.
This is the only photograph which gives some idea of the outside appearance of the first school building, made from wood and with shuttered windows, typical architecture of the shtetl.
It was replaced in 1924 by a brick building.

[Page 38]

Two teachers – the one on the left is Alter Levite– with a clas of 12 girls, probably aged between 12 and 14, taken in the late 1920s.

The third graduation class of the 'Yavneh' School (Hebrew School) taken in 1931.
The teachers seated front are, from left to right: Izchak Paktor, Miriam Levite; the examiner Dr Pirkin, and Miriam Rabinowitz

[Page 39]

A group photograph of the Hebrew School taken in about the
late 1920s with their two teachers in the middle.
The one or the left is Alter Levite.

The school with the teaching staff.
Rachel Friedman, Loyova Melamed and Alter Levite, taken when it had over a hundred pupils, probably in the mid–30s.

[Page 40]

Riteve – its history, character and essence
Alter Levite

Riteve is a little town in the lower part of Lithuania, an area with an abundance of lakes, swamps and a great deal of dust in the summer season.

Jews lived in this place since ancient limes, but no one investigated when the Jews first arrived there. Everyone was too busy making a living, so there was no interest in questions of this nature. The old cemetery, which was quite big, testified that many generations had lived in this town, that many had passed on to the next world and that their remains were buried in this ground.

The place is very far away from the main road, and if there were wars in this part of the world, the Jews could tell you stories about them, but they had never seen them with their own eyes.

The chapter which was of great interest to the Jews was the rule of the Oginskis, Oginski the First and Oginski the Second, the Pritzim of the place. The first Oginski, who lived in the middle of the 19th century, was a tyrant and ruled the place without any limitations, He had serfs and slaves who feared him, and the Jews were afraid of the tyrant and did not dare to disobey his orders. Evidence of the tyranny of this Poritz was the old Beit Midrash. This building served in the olden days as a place of worship and study for the congregation of Riteve. But once, the Jews 'sinned' against the Poritz and he sent a group of his henchmen, who took the holy articles out of the Beit Midrash and brought in pigs in their place. Afterwards they turned the place into a dwelling for his land tenants and his servants. For many years the Jews looked at the building and their hearts trembled with fear of those tyrants. This happened in the 1860s and only after the Great War in the year 1918 was this place returned to the Jewish community by Graf Zalutsky, the heir to the Oginskis.

The Jews saw the hand of G-d in the vengeance which was visited upon this Poritz. In 1859, Oginski was arrested by the Russian government for taking part in the preparations for the Polish rebellion which was about to break out. Oginski committed suicide on the eve of Purim that year. Many generations remembered that day and every year they celebrated a double Purim: the down- fall of Haman, and the downfall of Oginski.

Professor Zelikovitz, who was born in Riteve, tells more about the tyranny of Oginski the First. One Saturday, when the Jews were sitting in the Beit Midrash, as they were accustomed to, the door suddenly opened, and a Jew came in trembling as he told the congregation the news that the Poritz had sent his henchmen to the old cemetery, to plough it up. The Jews were terrified on hearing this news, but did not know what to do.

The professor also tells in his stories, Mein Shtetle Ritevas, about the beauty of the town and about the road that the Poritz had paved towards the Prussian border. It was apparently his intention to be connected to the city of Memel and the Baltic Sea, so that he could get arms for the rebellion which they were preparing against the Russian tsar. The Russian government suppressed the rebellion and they did not carry out this plan. The government wanted the swamps to serve as a protection for Russia and therefore did not worry about repairing the road. Slowly the line of communication with the west decreased and, at the beginning of the 20th century the roads to the west were so had that they were impassable on rainy days.

[Page 41]

The school in Riteve– probably taken when the new school building was opened in 1924. Five of the teachers and communal workers may be seen at the back, but six names are given.

They are Alter Levite; David and Moshe Kos, the communal workers of the school;

David Handler, Zalman Abelov and Shmuel Saks.

Oginski the Second also ruled the place with a strong arm, but he was not as bad as his father. He gave the Jews permission to build a new Beit Midrash and to add it as a wing to the synagogue which already existed. The synagogue was a place of worship and the Beit Midrash used to serve both as a place of worship and study. In the Beit Midrash, visitors could find a place to rest and even to sleep. This was permitted for respectable visitors who came to the village and could not pay for a room at the hotel.

Although there was no scribe to write the history of Riteve, the people related many events which took place during the 19th century. First of all they referred to the 'days of panic' when the Russian government published a law by which Jews were to serve in the army and only married men were tree of this duty. The Jews acted wisely and married off their sons and daughters at a very tender age. Then there is the story told about the young father who begat a son

[Page 42]

The 'Yahveh' school in 1929 or 1930 with teachers Miriam Levite and Izchak Zvi Paktor

and was too shy to take part in the B'rith Milah of his child. 'Kidnappers' came to the Jewish houses and snatched young children to serve in the Russian army. The poor children were sent to a faraway land to be brought up in the houses of the farmers and when they reached boyhood they were handed over to the military authorities to be trained as soldiers. At the beginning of the 20th century many of these soldiers of Nicholas I were still alive, and they could tell of their suffering and tribulations during the 23 years that they were absent from their homes.

From time to time plagues broke out in the village. The angel of death was active among babies and as a result there was no house where two or three babies had not died. The bereaved parents saw in this the act of G–d as punishment for a sin which someone had committed; they felt it was the duty of the people to find out who the sinner was and thus stop the plague. It so happened that a plague broke out among the babies and the sinner was discovered. It was said that he had been having an affair with a lady whose husband was overseas. The people gathered and wanted to lynch him, but the rabbi himself saved him. He hid him in his house for a few days until the anger had passed. One of the Jews went to the Pristav, the chief of police, and told him what was happening in the village. The Pristav himself went to the synagogue and warned the people that he would send all those who touched the sinner to Siberia. The words of the Pristav made an impression and the Jews were afraid to implement their decision.

On a similar occasion a plague broke out and, after investigating, they discovered that the reason for this was that it was being planned to cut down trees in the old cemetery and use the wood for building a new synagogue. The dead of Riteve were coming to avenge the living and that is why the plague had broken out.

[Page 43]

But as soon as they stopped cutting the trees, the plague passed. There were enlightened Jews who said the plague was a result of the poor sanitary conditions prevailing in the village. They were considered apikorsim (heathens), and those who had the fear of G–d in their hearts kept away from these 'wicked' people.

The people could also tell stories of days of famine in the land. The ground did not give forth its fruit and the lines of communication were very bad. It was impossible to bring grain from faraway lands. People were actually starving. If a man came into a bakery and wanted to buy a bagel, he was asked who was sick in his house.

In the 19th century, the houses in the village were all built to the same standard. Every house was divided into two or four apartments with a long corridor separating them. In the middle of the corridor there was a place for the people to cook and wash their linen. Smoke from the stoves would pass through a central chimney. No one could say which house was being warmed, or in which house the people were sitting and shivering. At a later stage every house was divided into four apartments. Special rooms were built to accommodate married sons and daughters. Riteve could not expand because of the order of the tsar, Alexander III, who had forbidden the Jews to live outside the village. In the middle of the shtetl there was the marketplace and around it were several structures of brick to distinguish them from the other houses, which were of wood. In these buildings, the Jews were trying to earn their living.

A very important event took place at the beginning ol the 20th century. The Poritz Oginski decided to install electric lights in his palace and in the streets of the little town. Thus Riteve was the first shtetl in Lithuania which had electric light, even before the city of Kovno. The Jews were surprised at the miraculous light, which was exploited by them for studying the Torah in the Beit Midrash. They no longer had to depend on the favours of the shammas (the synagogue's attendant), who distributed candles sparingly.

The Jews of Riteve studied the Torah diligently. Every morning, after the morning service, the people would sit and study a chapter of Mishnayot or Mishnah Brurah (regular Mishnah chapters and easier ones). In the evening after the Ma'ariv (the evening service) they would study a page of the Talmud.

Those who had not reached the standard of the Gemara would sit and listen to the chapter of the Sedra of the week. Especially important was the study in the Beit Midrash on Saturday, the day which belonged totally to G–d. The people enjoyed sleeping in the afternoon. Before Mincha (the afternoon service), they would gather in the Beit Midrash, some of them for a chapter in the Mishnah, or a page in the Gemara, and some for a chapter of Agadah. Between Mincha and Ma'ariv and the Tehilim (Psalms) Jews would take their place. The students of the Talmud were now quiet, because of the darkness which filled the house. There was a reader to read the chapters of the Tehilim, and the congregation responded after every sentence he recited. There was one Tehilim Jew who was called 'Baruch the Rebellious', for he would not listen to the order of the shammas and would continue reading the Tehilim even after the shammas had commanded him to stop because the time for Ma'ariv service had arrived. He would continue his reading until the congregants were all tired and their voices grew weaker, and he, the reader, remained the only one.

[Page 44]

It was very difficult to make a living. The town was full of small shops, and the shopkeepers waited for market day when the farmers would bring their produce into town to sell and, with the money they got from the sale of their merchandise, they would buy what they needed from the towns shops. The shopkeepers would stand in the doorways of their shops and call out to the farmers, 'Come to me, come to me, for a good bargain!'

There were also artisans to be found among the Jews: shoemakers and tailors who worked from first light until nightfall to support their families. Some Jews were peddlers who travelled to outlying villages and bought the farmers' produce, selling it in turn to the town's merchants. These peddlers would see their families only on Shabbat and Holidays, and during the week they would sleep in the farmers' village houses. It goes without saying that they would never have the opportunity to learn Torah during the week, and on Shabbat they would be too tired and fall asleep at the very table at which they would be studying Torah. Peddlers like these remained simple Jews, distanced from Torah learning and from the fear of G–d.

The Zionist movement, the beginning of which was Hibbat Zion, was also felt in this village. There were people who started to sell the Zionist shekel, and stamps of the Keren Kayemet. The congregation looked upon them as apikorsim who wanted to force the Schechina (Spirit of G–d) to come nearer. They believed, with all their hearts that the Messiah would come, although He was being delayed. It was forbidden, in their eyes, to change the ways of G–d, who had decided that the people of Israel must wait in the Galut (Diaspora) until He Himself with His glory would bring a complete redemption. When it became known in Riteve that Dr Herzl had died, the Zionists tried to say Kaddish for him in the synagogue, but their voices could not be heard over the noise made by their opposers.

The Russian war against Japan in 1904 shook the congregation from its tran– quillity. Some of the Jews were called to military service to fight an enemy whom they did not know and had not heard of. The war soon ended and the people returned peacefully to their families.

The rebellion in Russia against the tsar in 1905 found only a few people in this little town who dreamt about the general salvation that would come from it. There were no factories in the place and those who joined the movement of the rebels were primarily craftsmen who hoped that the rebellion would bring some changes to the community that they would not be discriminated against at the meetings of the congregation and at the synagogue.

[Page 45]

The Enlightenment Movement also found no response in this village. The Jews here knew that the boys had to learn in the cheder in the same way that they and their ancestors had learnt and they would not become goyim, G–d forbid. Some of the people, especially those who joined the Zionist movement, saw it as their duty to bring a teacher who would open a cheder meiukan (a modern cheder) but very few people agreed that their sons should he kept away from studying the Torah and give their precious time for secular study Some of the girls were sent to the Russian school for beginners. There they learnt the beginnings of reading and arithmetic, but the boys had to he satisfied with studying the religious subjects and twice a week they would go to a private teacher to learn to read Russian, without understanding a word of what they were reading, and to write an address in Russian or Latin characters.

The Jews were terrified when they heard about the pogroms which took place in the big cities of Russia. Even the Lithuanians, their neighbours, heard about the disturbances in which the property of Jews was taken from them. Their great wish to harm the Jews was not fulfilled. They only raised a fist when they saw a Jew walking in the street, but they did not do anything else, for the Pristav came to the assistance of the Jews after receiving a nice present from the Jewish leaders. He did not allow the crowd to touch the Jews.

Every village in Lithuania was devastated by a fire. Most of the houses were wooden structures covered with wooden shingles and, when the hot summer came, it was enough for one spark to touch one of the houses and the wind would do the rest. The wind caused the fire to spread, and the labour of many generations was destroyed in a day. But Riteve was an exception. The people of the village knew how to prevent such a tragedy. The Poritz established a fire brigade and when a day of reckoning came they would quickly gather and extinguish the blaze. But in 1911, Riteve, too, was destroyed by fire.

For many weeks there had been no rain and on the eve of Tisha Be'Av, a day which was always one of tragedies, a fire broke out in one of the forests of the Poritz. Naturally the whole fire brigade went to the forest to extinguish the blaze. In the meantime, a fire broke out in the village and there was no one to put it out. The fire spread very rapidly and most of the village went up in flames.

That night of Tisha Be'Av, the Jews of Riteve understood what churban (destruction) means. They were lying in the fields, on the bundles that they had saved from their houses, and saw with their own eyes the fire consuming every part of the village. There was nobody to save it. In the morning, when they walked through the smouldering ruins, they saw the churban of Jerusalem, for which they had mourned for so many years. Now another churban was added for the families who remained without a roof over their heads.

The Beilis trial had a depressing effect on the Jews of the town. Every Jew was named 'Beilis' and their enemies wanted to lake revenge on the Jews who allegedly drank the blood of Christians. By a miracle, Beilis was found innocent and the Jews could breathe easily again.

[Page 46]

The firemen of Riteve, photographed in the Shlomo Goldshmidt Center, which was named after the founder and chairman of the voluntary fire brigade.

During the years before the First World War, life was normal and the Jews had no desire to change their way of life. There were, however, some people who decided to depart for distant places in order to improve their economic situation. The Jews of Riteve found out that there were places where it was easy to make a good living and many citizens left. Many were especially attracted to South Africa where there were gold mines and the gold was there for anyone who could get there. Their intention was to save a few hundred pounds sterling and return home as the 'big shots'. These immigrants were quickly disappointed when they arrived in the land of gold. While they did have some savings, they actually starved themselves in order to collect enough pennies to make the few hundred they dreamed of, and then hurry back to their families in Riteve. When the First World War broke out many Jews found themselves in South Africa, unable to return home, while their families were left without a livelihood in Riteve.

During the first days of the war, news was slow and nothing was known about it except for the fact that some of the men had been drafted into the army No soldiers were seen in the town or its environs because it was quite a distance off the main road. It was only after a few months that a regiment of Cossacks came to guard the town from an attack by the enemy and to make preparations for the battle against the Germans. Those in the town who supported the Russians produced proof of their side's superiority, claiming that they would shortly reach Koenigsberg, and even Berlin, and that the war would soon come to an end. However, the German supporters knew for certain that the Russians would be disastrously defeated. The debates were quite heated, sometimes reaching abusive tones on both sides. The 'Germans' were overjoyed when the Russian attack on East Prussia failed. Some told stories of having seen with their own eyes how the Russians retreated, leaving their weapons. They saw G–ds work in the defeat of the Russians as retribution for the way they had treated the Jewish citizens of their country. It is true that the Germans did attack the Russians, expelling them from East Prussia and conquering all of the border towns, but they did not dare chase them through the great swamps and the unpaved roads.

[Page 47]

In the spring of 1915, the swamps dried up and the roads were reopened to transport. It was now that the Germans began their grand attack. Myriads of battle–tested soldiers were transported from the Western Front, and they roundly defeated the Russians. Within one or two days, all of Zamut was conquered by the Germans and when some of the Jews tried to escape to nearby towns they found, to their amazement, that the Germans had reached there first, leaving them no choice but to return home. In this way the Jews of Riteve found themselves transferred from Russian to German rule within one day. The decree to transfer Jews from the border towns to the inland cities of

Russia was late in coming and the Jews of Riteve remained in their homes – unlike the Jews of neighbouring towns – ignorant of what it meant to be refugees.

The change in ruler brought with it drastic changes in the lives of the Jews in the town. At first things were easier because the Germans treated the citizens more liberally, permitting them to travel to the coastal city of Memel and to trade throughout the country. Yet the Jews slowly began to feel the burden of the conquerors when the Gentians set up a military regime that meant to milk the country of its produce and send it to the German cities that had begun to suffer from lack of food. Those responsible for supervising this task set about their work with German order and method, setting quotas for each and every farmer, who was to bring his yield to the storerooms in their cities. The farmers were left with nothing to sell in the marketplace and there was a great lack of bread. The conquerors came to the aid of the townsmen and instituted a rationing system: bread was sold by ration, and families without the ability to buy bread on the black market began to feel a hunger that kept growing. The Germans tried to case the shortage of bread by replacing rye flour with oatmeal flour, but this caused terrible stomach illness.

The Germans were secure in their triumph and began opening schools to teach the local children the language of the conquerors. For some reason the Jews agreed to send their children to these schools. During the Russian rule only a handful of girls had frequented the Russian language schools, while the new German schools were full of Jewish students. Study was obligatory. The Russians had not cared about the education of the Jewish children. Apparently the fact that the Jews of Riteve had had mercantile ties with the city of Memel, a German town on the Baltic coast, even during the Russian regime, made the German school popular. The Jews saw attendance at this school as a practical step lor their sons to learn the language in which their German neighbours traded. Locals who knew a little German were appointed as teachers, though they had no pedagogical training.

[Page 48]

A Group photograph of the Jewish school after German rule during the First World War. This was apparently the school begun by the Germans for Jewish children and not the Hebrew School.

As the conquest lengthened, and the war continued, the Germans began to fear the indigenous younger generation. They found a way to subdue the youth. They would kidnap them and send them to forced labour camps, where they gave them hard labour, embittering them. Some managed to escape to the villages in the area, with awful consequences for anyone who was caught. They were tortured terribly and taught the lesson that it was not worthwhile to run away. Torah studies declined during the German regime. A curfew was instituted and it was forbidden to go out at night. The Jews had no choice but to hurry home after the evening prayers, hut continued, however, to study Torah in their homes, although the Beit Midrash was silenced throughout the long winter nights. The attitude of the conquerors toward the locals took a turn for the worse as the war continued. The Germans became anxious because the awful war seemed to have no end and they began taking out their anger on the communities' leaders. Only a lucky few who had contacts with the Germans lived a comforable life, while the majority of the townspeople felt the conquerors' increasingly heavy hand and were confused about what to do.

Not even the intermediaries were of help and the suffering grew from day to day.

[Page 49]

The German School in Rieteve in 1918

In early 1917, the Russian Revolution broke out and the Germans were encouraged. The hope was that the new government in Russia would make peace with them and then the entire German army would be free to make war on the Western Front. But their hopes were soon dashed. The Kerensky government declared that the war would continue and the Germans became embittered, taking out their wrath on the people living in the conquered territories. The year 1917 was a very difficult one for the Jews. The Germans forgot how the Jews had willingly received their rule and they were now treated like prisoners of war.

Neither did the revolution in October8 of that year bring any salvation to the Jews. The Germans were forced to fight on the Western Front and their attitude to the people did not improve and by the end of 1918 there were days of confusion. The Germans surrendered on the Western Front and the conquerors in Russia were ordered to clear the land which the Germans had held.

New states arose in agreement with the Germans and with the united nations of the Western Front. Thus it was decided to establish a new Government of Lithuania and Riteve went over from German rule to the rule of the new government. The Jews assisted their neighbours in organising the newly established government. There was an agreement between the Lithuanian National Council and the Jewish leaders that the Jews would he given certain rights as a minority in the new government. A special minister for Jewish affairs was appointed who was to organise the Jewish communities. The post was given to Dr M Soloveichik, one of the honourable people of Kovno, and he started his work with great energy. His task was very difficult, for most of the cities and villages were empty of Jews, who had been driven away to the far districts of Russia. But Riteve was one of the little towns that were saved from the exile of 1915. A council was appointed to supervise all the institutions of the town.

[Page 50]

In spite of the opposition of some ol the Gabayim (here meaning local religious officials), it was decided to open a new Hebrew school and in February 1919 the first class of this school was opened with Hebrew as the language of instruction. Riteve had lived to see something of which it had never dreamt, a school where all subjects were taught in Hebrew. This institution attracted the girls, but the boys were still sent to the cheder to continue their studies as in the old days. This school in Riteve was the only Hebrew one in the town while in the other villages and small towns of Lithuania the people were divided into camps, the Hebrew camp and the Yiddishistim. In Riteve there were no labourers and in the town there was no one who would bring the Bund's ideology to the inhabitants. This new institution, the Hebrew school, was founded by a group of young Zionists and they devoted themselves to its development. They were not just satisfied with the classes that were opened, but the committee also established a library for the youth and lectures on various subjects were held every Saturday.

In those days the Jews of Riteve ran a flourishing trade. But suddenly they became wholesalers. Whoever brought a parcel of goods would find immediate buyers who would snatch the metziah (the good bargain) from his hands. The Jews did not know that all the riches they were making from trade were just imaginary because the money they had received for the goods would be devalued in one night. People filled their pockets with German money which was devalued from day to day One day a rumour spread that the German mark with the red seal would not lose its value and the Jews believed it and started to fill their bags with these bills. Suddenly they became millionaires. The end of it was that the poor people did not know what to do with these bills which were not even good for papering the walls of their houses. This tzarah (disaster) was felt by all of them. Even the Germans were hit by this misfortune, years of saving being lost in one night. This money would not even be enough to buy one meal. The people opened their eyes and suddenly saw that with the millions they had saved they could not even buy a pair of shoes. They also learnt that the labour of many years was now worthless and there was nothing they could do about it. This madness ended when the Lithuanian government decided to introduce their own money system to be covered by dollars.

[Page 51]

Then the inhabitants of the town reminded themselves that there were counties where immigrants would be accepted and many of them started to leave Lithuania. The majority went to South Africa where many inhabitants of other towns and villages had settled. There were also many lucky people who received visas to enter the United States, but the majority of the people remained in Riteve and the sources of their income became less and less every day. There were some relatives in South Africa and America who came to the assistance of their brethren in need. Every week, on the day when the post arrived, the poor people of the town gathered at the postman's house waiting for a letter from overseas. Those who were lucky came home with their present in their hands – a letter with a cheque inside – but there were also many who returned home empty–handed.

After the First World War, with the establishment of Jewish communities in the Lithuanian cities, a benefactor was found who came to the assistance of the Jews of Riteve. He was Mr Kruskal of Frankfurt am Main, who had been born in Riteve. He discovered that the Jews of Riteve were in great need. They wished to establish various communal organisations but did not possess the means to do so. He made a generous contribution to the town, instructing the townsfolk to decide for themselves how to spend the money. A public meeting was called and it was decided that the first priority was a Talmud Torah, as the children had for quite some time been learning in shabby rooms that did not conform with the required hygienic standards of a school. A suitable house for the rabbi was also needed. In no time at all, an appropriate place was found for the construction of both these buildings – it was the spot on which the old Beit Midrash had stood. The Riteve community had the pleasure of seeing an area, which had been like a thorn in their side, dedicated to new buildings which was a joy to all.

When the buildings were completed, Kruskal sent two representatives to take part in the dedication ceremony. The parents thanked their generous benefactor for enabling their children to study Torah and Mitzvot in such pleasant surroundings.

These things I remember and am troubled

Miriam Brik

Riteve – an ancient and beautiful town – a renowned Jewish habitation. Only– two mass graves remain as a memorial for all time. They are the sole remnants of the thousands of faithful Jews who were massacred in those black days. For this destruction there is no comfort.

Riteve with its vital Jewish community nestled on the road to Shavli and Plungyan–Memel. The town's communal life was quite well organised with its Hebrew school and a library, with many volumes in Yiddish, Russian, Hebrew and Lithuanian, run by the Zionist youth Its scholars and great men were well known beyond its borders. The majority of its inhabitants were Jewish and they made their mark in the town. They were responsible for its growth and develop– ment and because of them its commerce flourished. Riteve was a Zionist town as the contributions to the National Funds and the Aliyah of its youth to Israel proved. The Aliyah movement began 40 years earlier and increased up to the period of the Holocaust. Many yearned for Zion, and most of the youth attended Hachsharah (preparation programmes) to prepare themselves lor lile in Israel. Prior to Aliyah, the youth would organise lectures, debates and many other activities which stimulated the cultural life of all circles in the town and an interest in Zionism.

[Page 52]

The Kruskal family from Frankfurt am Main made a generous donation to the building of a new school building and for the building of a house for the rabbi. This group of adults and some children was taken when the new school building was dedicated in 1924

Dedication of the school in the name of Kruskal on 23 Sivan 5684 (1924). This photograph, taken through a window from inside the school, shows a section of what must have been a large crowd.

[Page 53]

The Jewish quarter was poor and its inhabitants made do with very little. The youth, however, longed for change and a better life. They no longer bore the exile with the tolerance of their forefathers. In the marketplace, the Jews were to be found everywhere, discussing their fate at the hands of oppressors and dreaming of the advent of the Messiah and the wonders that He would bring. When the hour of prayer approached, they would make for the synagogue where they would immerse themselves in prayer and study and sometimes shed tears over the misfortunes that befell the Jews both there and in Palestine.

The Zionist activities were led by local committees. Speakers from the central organisation would also be brought out, and they gave encouragement to contributors and participants in the Zionist endeavour. The youth were divided into He–Chalutz, Hashomer Hatzair, Hitahudat and later also Betar. They would hold meetings at their clubhouses, sing and dance and also collect the money from the Blue Boxes ol the National Funds. An artisans' organisation also helped in the Zionist work.

There was no shortage of shops in Riteve. Customers came from afar to shop there. Tailors, blacksmiths, carpenters and seamstresses, all had bread to eat and clothes to wear. All the Jews of Riteve knew the secret of living frugally. The problem was especially acute before the Sabbath for, as much as one saved, there was always a lack of flour, yeast, candles, fish, meat and the ingredients for the tshulnt (the special Jewish Sabbath food that would cook slowly all night). If you chanced upon a Jewish home on the Sabbath, you might think that you were in a rich man's house. The table would be beautifully laid, the candles were lit and reflected the delicacies made in honour of the Sabbath Queen.

Once a week the market was held. Jews and gentiles bought and sold from one another in the process of making a living. The Jews bought mushrooms and pigs' hair from the peasants. The peasants frequented the bars. They would often arrive with a cartload of wood, which they sold, and would then drink up all the proceeds.

[Page 54]

The children of Riieve were serious and not given to pranks like the impudent peasant lads. They took their studies in the cheder, the Talmud Torah and the yeshiva seriously. They spent their playtime out of doors in the fields and yards. Never in their lives did they know pampering.

The synagogue was big, spacious and beautifully built, with hand–carved decorations. The shammas would sweep and dust meticulously and provide clean towels for the washing of hands. He would also bang on the bima (the podium) and announce the prayers, or extend an invitation to the congregation to join in the celebration of a B'rith (circumcision). The rabbi would preach every now and then on a point of rabbinic law or a topical subject. Frequently emissaries would come from the yeshivot or from the Zionist institutions and they would deliver speeches which left an indelible impression on their audience.

There were a few Communists in our town who held that the world of money and labour was not the only reality. They explained that the present order would collapse and a new and better world would take its place. To bring this about workers would have to mount the barricades. This led to stormy discussions among us. However, the ongoing suffering of the Jews strengthened growing national sentiment, while the spirit of the new Land of Israel inspired them. It is not surprising, therefore, that Riieve contributed both quantitatively and qualitatively to the pioneering efforts with excellent human material.

A strong national consciousness had taken hold of the Jews of Riteve. They did not put their trust in the Galut–inspired policies of the Bundists and the Folkists, nor were they led astray by new ideas of assimilation. Rather they believed that the apparent calm that reigned was merely a transient episode before the storms which only trust in the national and Zionist ideals could weather.

Study of Torah and a G–d–fearing way of life were characteristic of Riteve. Was Riteve a city of Torah scholars? It can be said that Riteve was characterised by the 'golden mean'. There were no very wealthy or very poor people, but rather all its inhabitants made a moderately good living. Likewise there were no extremely pious folk nor apostates. So in the matter of scholarship – there were a number of great scholars, but there were no ignoramuses. The majority of people were versed in Torah and Rashi and they studied their daily page of Mishnah and Gemara. There were the groups who studied Ein Yaacov and, from time to time, they celebrated the completion of a tractate – a celebration called Siyvum (end) – with a glass of spirits and cake. Most of Riteve's population was observant and very few were free–thinking. The pervading atmosphere was one of faithfulness to Jewish tradition. On the Sabbath all the shops were closed, and the synagogue was filled with worshippers. Even the younger generation remained, in the main, close to tradition. Out of respect for their parents (Kibbud Av) they attended the synagogue and observed the dietary and other laws and customs.

[Page 55]

In the matter of personalities and devoted workers for the community, Riieve had nothing of which to be ashamed. Riteve was beloved for itself, its parochialism. its little houses and businesses. What could one not find in Riteve? Rabbis and learned scholars on the one hand and followers of the Enlightenment, who yearned to understand everything, on the other. There were also young people who read Mapu's The love of Zion and the articles of Lilienblum. The Hebrew school had a profound influence not only on the young but on the adults as well. The singing of the school children could be heard throughout the town. The young had been captured by the spirit of the Zionist movement and from a small group there grew a large movement: He–Chalutz, Hashomer Hatzair, Betar, and Hitahadut. The Hebrew language could be heard in Riteve's streets. Emigration to the Land of Israel followed and Riteve folk can be found today in the towns and villages of Israel.

[Page 56]

Guests leaving the synagogue after a wedding in riteve in about 1927– the synagogue is on the left and the Beit Midrash on the right. This was drawn by Dean Simon from a photograph in the original book.

[Page 57]

Chapter Five

Memoirs From Riteve

Townsfolk

This chapter describes life in the shtetl, as remembered decades later, with love a warmth and nostalgia. We retained the characteristics of the material although some details are mentioned repeatedly, and the style is loose and personal. Some of those who contributed their memoirs were very young at the time they lived in Riteve, before leaving it for other countries. Their anger and pain over the killing of their families by the Germans and the Lithuanians during the Holocaust made them all the more regard the Jews of Riteve as martyrs of a holy, exemplary community.

DP

Our town that is no more

Miriam (born Levite) Tsvik

Our town, which was destroyed by the oppressor, was noted not only for its rabbinical scholars, but also for its ordinary folk: its righteous ones, its shoemakers, tailors, butchers, bakers and peddlers.

Riteve did not have the resources to develop industry and commerce, which would have provided employment for its inhabitants. There were various shops in the town, but most of the shopkeepers made a meagre living. The shopkeepers would sit in their shops for hours awaiting customers. In the winter they would be wrapped up in warm coats and on the counter would be a pot of burning coals. When their hands and feet froze from the cold, they would walk around in their shops to keep warm. Only on market days was there great activity.

A number of Jews lived from peddling. All week they would travel around the villages with haberdashery, coloured yarns, kerchiefs and cloth. Frequently they were not paid in cash, but would receive eggs, chickens, mushrooms, skins and pigs' hair from the farmers in exchange. The craftsmen were mostly shoemakers and tailors, some of whom, being skilled in their craft, made only new garments. Others took care of the needs of farmers in the district, working less meticulously. There were also carpenters and plasterers, blacksmiths who took care of the horseshoes, cart wrights, and even one photographer.[1] On market days, the farmers brought their products and their craft work to town, the market being the main source of income for the Jews.[2]

[Page 58]

A wedding group from Riteve taken in the early 1930s. Harry Singer Collection

Miriam Tsvik and Sarah Yavoski (see recollections on pages 57 et seq. and 72 respectively) were sisters of Zalman Leib and Alter Levite and both made Aliyah to Israel.
This photograph was taken with the pupils Miriam taught, on a cold winter's day some months before she left in April 1933, together with another teacher, Frieda Levinson.
No indication of their placing was provided in the original book and it has proved impossible to identify them with certainty.

[Page 59]

The Jews of Riteve, especially members of the older generation, were mainly graduates of the cheder and the Beit Midrash, and led their lives according to the teachings of the Torah. This gave content to their lives, and moulded the image of a whole Jewish generation which lived its daily life according to the Mitzvot. Every Jew knew that upon rising in the morning, his first duty was to go to the synagogue to pray with a minyan and then to read some chapters of the Psalms. Later he would eat and only then turn to his business. As evening fell, he would again go to the synagogue to take part in the Mincha and Maariv prayers. After the evening prayers, he would study chapters of the Mishnah and Ein Yaacov (Agadah) and peruse a page of Talmud. Even where the religious hold was somewhat weakened[3] community life still retained a strong sense of traditional observance. This feature of their lives was especially marked on the Sabbath and festivals.

The qualities of mercy and care for the needy, so deeply rooted in our people's tradition, found expression in the establishment of various charitable and communal organisations. I remember from my youth that young girls were sent to spend the night in the homes of the sick so as to give members of the family some respite. This service was performed by pairs of girls, or two women or men, as the need dictated. If the family of a sick woman needed help with the children during the day, this service was also arranged. This organisation was called Linat Tzedek – a righteous overnight stay – and it was a social welfare group whose help was very practical and valuable.

Parallel to the Linat Tzedek was the Bikkur Cholim – visits to the sick – which saw to material assistance for those who were ill. It provided medical care, both in the form of paying the doctors' bills or for medical appliances. It is impossible to evaluate the services of these groups. They deserve to be remembered for their outstanding devotion to the care o' the less fortunate. There were no hospitals or nurses. A sick person lay in hi; bed at home and his overworked wife had to shoulder the burden of caring for the children, the household and the patient. Or, if the wife was ill, the father was burdened with the domestic responsibilities as well as the demands of his work. The members of these social welfare groups would volunteer their services wholeheartedly. Dr. Pikin frequently gave his services free of charge. If a family was in need he would leave an anonymous gilt of money to provide for their needs. He did this even for non- Jews and was known to be a generous and compassionate man. His only daughter lives in South Africa. The chairman of Linat Tzedek was Meir Hon. "Meir the Meirer". Miriam Zaltsman chaired the women's group and Reb Moshe Aharon Heyman the Bikkur Cholim.

Torah students formed the Chevra Gemara group. In the mornings their sweet voices could be heard from afar. In the synagogue the Riteve Jew found peace of mind and it was here that he gathered the strength to enable him to overcome life's difficulties. Here he would pour out his grief before his Creator and here he would rejoice in his moments of pleasure and cry in his agony. Among those who zealously attended the synagogue and the Beit Midrash was my late father, Reb Dov Ber Joseph, and his co–student of Torah – Reb Feivel Udwin. Both of them were blind. They had learnt pages of the Gemara and Mishnah by heart, as if they had foreseen their fate.

[Page 60]

In the Riteve cemetery, many righteous and G–d–fearing people found their eternal rest. The Chevra Kadisha (burial society) was well organised. It was headed by the beadle, the late Aharon Ben Dov Zaacks, assisted by Moshe Galaun and Mordecai Isaac Segal. The women's society was headed by Ida Yanke Dovar and Feige Rachel Hirshowitz, assisted by Sheva Katz Mcyerowitz who was a true 'woman of valour'. She looked after the Mikveh (ritual bath) and introduced modern improvements to the bath house. These women also supervised the sewing of shrouds. Shmucl Zvi Zaltsman, one of the prominent men in the town, a timber merchant, provided firewood to heat the houses of the poor. The synagogue manager was Nachum Saks.

Our town throbbed with life and creativity. On Sabbaths, we would gather at the synagogue to listen to lectures and readings by Ema Orbach. Emigrants from Riteve who had settled abroad did not forget their kin at home and some, like the family of Amula Todres who settled in the USA, used to send gifts of money twice a year towards the Matzot Fund for Pesach for helping the poor to heat their homes.[4]

Can one ever forget a wedding day in Riteve? It was a holiday for the whole town. Everyone, invited or not, knew the hour of the ceremony and all came to watch. The ceremony took place in an area between the 'Di–Shul' synagogue, a very attractive wooden structure, and the Beit Midrash. The couple would be accompanied on the route by fcfeizmcrim (folk musicians). I remember the conductor whose name was 'Liba the Musician' – he also played the violin. The weddings were usually held on Fridays. On the Sabbath the meals took place at the bride's home, and at the conclusion of the Sabbath, the celebrations were resumed. All the young folk came to juin in the wedding festivities with dancing. Everyone there paid towards the musicians' fee. Wealthy people provided free music'. After the ceremony, the happy couple would return to their house and Mina, nicknamed 'the Kitkah', would lead a welcoming dance with a kiikah (a sweet, plaited challah for Sabbath) held high in her hand.

I remember the wedding of the eldest daughter of Zlatta and Monash. The Sabbath meal was in our house. We weic the hosts to all the out–of–town guests, who spent the night in our house. My dear late mother was a pious lady. Before the meal, she asked the guests to permit my father to say the Kiddush over the wine, since, she said, no one had ever said the Kiddush in our home except our father. This was a gesture on the part of my mother not to embarrass the in–laws. So my lather performed the Kiddush in place of the father of the bride.

[Page 61]

'Scrolls are burnt and letters burst forth'
The beautiful town of Riteve on the occasion of the funeral of the Shemot (damaged religious texts which contain the Holy Name) in 5695 (1934 or 1935)

[Page 62]

I remember, too, the day of the Balfour Declaration.[5] How great was the joy in the town. Everyone went to great trouble to have a Hebrew flag of cloth or paper flying from his house. All morning we were busy rehearsing national songs, which we had learnt by heart. One of the songs was 'Carry a Flag to Zion' and another, 'Let all of us rejoice together'. We, the schoolchildren, were all dressed in festive clothes and we wore blue and white sashes from our shoulders to our hips. We all assembled at the appointed time on the corner of Plungyan Street and, under Lasovsky's direction, we marched to Memel Street. We halted at the house of Rabbi Avraham Shimon Geffen and his wife Lyova. Their veranda was festooned with flowers and a carpet. Here the towns leadership gathered, the late Dr Pikin, Mr Prisman, who was the representative of the Keren Kayemet (the Jewish National Fund lor buying land), Joseph Udwin, Samuel Saks, Mr Ehlin, the bank manager, Shima Verkul and Alter Levite. We began the assembly with Hatikvah. Then there were speeches. The chief speaker was Rabbi Geffen who lives at present with his family in Israel. The enthusiasm was very great – quite indescribable!

In the original book, the caption read: 'Members (gaba'im) of Chevra Kadisha (Burial Society) after the burial of the Torah strolls and the Shemot.'

In recounting a small part of my recollections of Riteve, I would not be wrong in saying that it was like all the other small towns in Jewish Lithuania. Yet the special combination of its inhabitants was outstanding One might have imagined that a talented director had placed each one in his particular place and allotted him his special role. The town, its landscape, its alleyways, its streets are closely linked with its personalities – with its vibrant Zionist youth, thirsty for knowledge and enlightenment. In the Hebrew school,[6] where I had the honour to serve as a teacher and supervisor, singing was frequent and important cultural work was abundant. Thus the pupils absorbed basic values regarding the heritage and the spirit of the Jewish people.

The school conducted various Zionist activities. There were parent/teacher meetings and public demonstrations of a Zionist nature on Lag BaOmer and other festivals. An atmosphere of love and respect was cultivated for the Hebrew society and the pioneering achievements in Eretz Israel. The pupils showed great interest in their studies, and both teachers and pupils worked in an atmosphere of pleasure and devotion to duty. The community library was exceptional. The students were keen readers of the thousands of volumes.

All these memories indicate that our youth in Riteve was not one of oppression. On the contrary, a golden light illuminated all our activities. However, at the edge of the town, among the dwellings of the gentiles, hatred seethed. This led us to cling together in order to protect ourselves. However, a frightful storm finally broke and knew no bounds.

How beautiful were those days! How great was my love for my town! I was bound to you with every fibre of my being and. to this day, your memory is very dear. May this tribute be a garland on the graves of our innocent martyrs.

———

[Page 63]

Riteve, my birthplace

Chana Goldberg Chinitz

If one looks at Riteve and wishes to measure it by the criteria of today, it might seem as if it were in the process of decline. In Israel today every remote village has attained a much higher cultural standard when compared with small Lithuanian towns like Riteve. But we shall be doing an injustice by comparing. Before the Second World War most of the countries of Eastern Europe were in a backward state and Lithuania in particular. The large cities did boast cultural institutions, but the villages were stuck in a state of decline. There was no state assistance to help them culturally and economically. In Riteve many young people without means of livelihood depended on their father's charity when often he himself was badly off.

I often wonder whence came the wealth of spirit in backward Riteve which sustained the youth of those days. Perhaps they were more vibrant then, alert and involved in everything going on around them. Or perhaps it was the material poverty which awakened our spiritual resources and our dedication to values of simplicity. The youth drew their spiritual values from the Hebrew school nurtured by the labour of a devoted group of teachers.[7] There were no financial means, the teachers were not qualified and premises were also lacking. I remember the landlady whose house accommodated the school on the second floor. She made the children's lives a misery because of the noise of their activities. It required much faith and willpower to maintain the school on a regular basis. I remember that we, the pupils, used to go and collect weekly contributions from the townsfolk for a new school building. Eventually a school building was built with the help of the pennies they had contributed. The school contained a few classrooms and only two of them were finally completed. The school and its teachers imparted to the pupils the values which we have preserved to this very day and for this we are very grateful.

———

Days of old

Hadassah Katz Landsman

Memories of light and shade come to mind when I recall Riteve and its personalities. I shall never forget this period of my life. Generally one remembers one's youth with recollections of innocence and beauty. One remembers the most sublime moments of one's life and these memories are never erased. Now that I have brought up my sons, I see myself once again as I was at their age. I tell my children at every possible opportunity of our life then, which had so much meaning for us because of our aspirations to build a national home for our oppressed people. With what seriousness and dedication we devoted ourselves to this hallowed aim. It expressed itself in limitless devotion and hard work on many fronts. This is a story in its own right – the story of the Chalutzim– the pioneers who came from Riteve.

[Page 64]

I wish to describe only one of the humane efforts of the ordinary folk of the town. I was only able to understand it in all its complexity 25 years later. This was the spirit of mutual aid which nourished among the people. For example, poor families with many children were helped by their better–off neighbours so as to avoid the shame of poverty. The help was given anonymously, in order, once again, to avoid pain and humiliation. Which home did not extend hospitality to a yeshiva student for one day a week, or sometimes more, on a full board basis?[8] Hosting a guest on Shabbat was a common practice. Donations to the Jewish National Fund were also the rule. Even the poor contributed to those donations. How sad it is that all these wonderful people and the special ambience of Riteve were destroyed forever. I am one of those who will remember Riteve for as long as I live.

The dream and the reality

Shimon Friedman

Riteve is before my eyes, Riteve which was destroyed so cruelly by the Nazi murderers. Riteve and all those people so dear to me pass through my mind and are deeply rooted in my heart. Parents, brothers, sisters, still live in my innermost being forever. The young and the old – I remember you all and feel your presence.

I remember, too, the streets and their lovely houses and the vitality which surged through them. The adult members of the community would spend their leisure time at the Beit Midrash where they found spiritual relief from their burdens. They would immerse themselves in the Book of Psalms with great enthusiasm and be refreshed from the days toil.

In another corner, groups would be studying a page of the Gemara with all us Halachic and Agadic polemic. In so doing they would rise above and divert themselves from the pressures of a hostile environment. The youth who had rebelled against the Beit Midrash and the exilic outlook were preparing themselves for a new life in Eretz Israel. In order to achieve this purpose they organised themselves in various societies. They also aspired to improve the life of the local townsfolk while encouraging them to emigrate to Eretz Israel. How tragic it was that young and old, mothers and babies, were all murdered by the Nazi hordes in the woods near Riteve.

We who were so greatly privileged to be rescued and to reach a safe refuge will retain your memory in our hearts and souls forever. We will not forget!

[Page 65]

The only information about the Dramatic Circle in Riteve in the orginal book consists of a bare mention in the text with the names of some of the members and this photograph, probably taken in the early 1930s

**Shimon Friedman, who
died on 18th February 1975
before the original book was
pubiished**

[Page 66]

My town, how I loved you

Tzila Beirak (Linde)

My town was a locked and enchanted garden. Here (in Israel in Kibbutz Kfar Masarik) I wander through the paths of my green village. All around flowers blossom and sun–tanned children frolic on the green grass where sprinklers dance. The children's houses are alive with joy.

Each morning, while the dew is still on the ground, the tall trees seem to announce jubilantly: 'See how we have sprouted and grown.' I stand amazed at nature's wonders and a prayer wells up in my heart. How beautiful and exalted is this tranquillity and this home which we have built. How wonderful that it fell to our fate to live here.

More than any other memories of my youth, memories of the landscape are imprinted on my mind. From my first day here (in Israel) I strove to create around me something of the landscape of my beloved youth. We would come from a distance on a wagon. Mother would point out to us the spire of the church, rising high in the pink evening sky. In my mind, the beloved scenes, both good and bad, are deeply embedded and remain vivid in my memory to this day.

Here is our house – a wooden house. It was surrounded on all aides by fruit trees and flowerbeds, which we cultivated with care. Mother would watch for every leaf and bud and she drew strength from them. At Pesach time, the signs of spring would be felt – a new moon, and a bright night light; the snow and ice melt and disappear. Mother goes out into the garden, removing pieces of ice from the trees, and behold, delicate buds sprout forth hesitantly, emerging into the world. In the evenings and in the mornings, I hear apples falling to the ground with a thump, and we go out to collect them. We also had vegetable beds and from all this we gained much pleasure and joy.

A little distance away flowed the River Yureh with its clear waters. We would skip through the fields and run barefoot through the colourful undergrowth, hiding among the tall and sweet–smelling young shoots. We were dizzy from the light of the sun and the perfumes all around us. We swam and paddled endlessly. We could not have our fill. Summer draws to a close, clouds gather and light rain falls intermittently, but we do not give up. We would run and dip in the water again and again.

The park was the pearl of the town. Many memories of its beautiful hiding places remain with me. One went through an iron gate above which two big lions with open mouths kept watch. On the right there was a well–loved windmill; on the left, the lake, tranquil and surrounded by thick growth, where could be found the secret places of many living creatures. Each bird had its unique call and the croaking of frogs could be heard from afar.

I found for myself a secret place among the tall dense trees where, with my book on my lap. I could forget reality and dream. How easy it was then to dream of a beautiful, good world, since all you had to do was to stretch out your hand and it was yours for the taking. I here was a Lovers' Lane too, where the buds of first love flourished.

[Page 67]

At the narrow stream's edge, blue and white flowers called 'Remember me' grew. We would bnng them home damp and fresh in honour of Shavuot. We would arrange them around a smooth stone in a white vase and at night the buds would open and light up like a blue flame. There were many wonderful and unforgettable paths to which we would constantly return. We strolled among fruit trees, but only picked the fruit that fell to the ground. The red raspberry bushes dropped wine and we enjoyed its sweet juice.

The great dark forest was enveloped in mystery. Where did it begin and where did it end? The forest was dense with tress and plants intertwined. Bright stones and great rocks were scattered among the rich growth. When one tramped through the undergrowth in the forest, it was as if one had penetrated another world, a world of fantasy, where one was hypnotised and far removed from reality. All the legends and tales of wonder, of good and bad spints, appeared before one's eyes and one lelt as if they had been created because of this forest alone. We would listen to the secret sounds of the forest while enthusiastically picking blueberries.

The centre of the town had a round area paved with smooth stones. Here the village gentiles would gather to sell their produce – butter of various sorts wrapped in fresh, green leaves, all kinds of fruit and sweetmeats. The villagers would get drunk while their horses and carts were tethered to poles. Drunken yells would pierce the air so that it was frightening to be out of doors.

I would pass the open door of the church with all its religious objects and experience great fear. It seemed as if a long arm would stretch out towards you and ...! We would walk beside the little lake alongside the church, which was surrounded by an ornamental iron fence. Every now and then we would take courage and peep through the iron fence to see what was taking place inside. How mysterious did their faith seem, whereas ours was so close and accessible. All I had to do was to enter the synagogue and I was at one with the congregation and could imbibe the atmosphere of a festival. I believed that everything I prayed for would be granted speedily. It was all so simple and good for the soul.

Although I was aware of the many shadows when I became a young adult and although there was seriousness and even a measure of sadness in the atmosphere at home, yet this did not cloud the good and beautiful things and the wonderful experiences of those years. How deeply engraved in my heart and how enchanted will they remain till the end of my days. The words of a poem have captured my heart:

Only about myself I knew to tell.

My world is narrow like that of an ant.[9]

Footnotes

1. After the First World War most of the Lithuanian Jews were engaged in small trade or in small factories and workshops. During the inter-war period many of them were ousted from their positions by Lithuanians. This was the calculated policy of the Lithuanian government, carried out very aggressively by members of the Verslininka, the association of Lithianian traders and craftsmen. The Jewish community in Riteve was also affected by this anti-Semetic policy and many Jewish traders were deprived of their livelihood.

2. The small trade in trie market was the main source of income for the many Jews in villages and small towns in Lithuania. During the inter-war penod the traditional role of Jews in the trade of agricultural products was rapidly reduced. The government initiated the formation of huge co-operatives which attained systematic control over this economic field.

3. The ideas of the Haskalah (Enlightenment) had already begun to spread among Jews in Lithuania by the beginning of the 19th century. Towards the end of that century and the beginning of the 20th century new secular ideologies penetrated the Jewish communities: Socialist ideas, advocated mainly by the Bund on the one hard and the Zionist views on the other.

4. Between 1928 and 1938 about 14 000 Jews emigrated from Lithuania. Most of them went to South Africa. Only 10.8 percent settled in the United States.

5. The 'Balfour Declaration' was issued by Lord AJ Balfour the British Foreign Minister, to Lord Rothschild and the Zionist federation on 2 November 1917. The British government declared its readiness to View with favour the establishment in Palestine of a national home for the Jewish people.

6. The Hebrew school for girls in Riteve was part of the Yavneh school system. There were three Jewish school systems in Lithuania during the inter–war period:

    i.   Tarbut which was Zionist–orientated;

    ii. Yidishist schools for the Socialist trend;

    iii. Yavneh, the religious traditional schools.

In the Tarbur and the Yavneh schools, the language of instruction was Hebrew The Yavneh educational system was established through the initiative of bothe 'Mizrachi' – the religious – Zionist party and 'Agudat– Israel' the non–Zionist religious movement Thepedagogical concept of the Yavneh system was based on integration between Jewish religious education and general knowledge.

7. Every Jewish school in Lithuania was connected to one of the Jewish school systems, yet they were established as a result of the initiative and effort of the local community.

8. 'To eat days' – a very common custom in Jewish communities. Yeshiva students were given free and full board in various houses during the week, generally every day in a different home.

9. Quoted from one of the best known poems of the poetess Rachel. Rachel Blauslein was among the first of the modern Hebrew poets in Eretz Israel. She was born in Saratov in northern Russia in 1831. In 1909, during the second Aliyalt, she emmigrated to Palestine. She become a pioneer and settled in Kinneret. During the First World War she contracted tuberculosis and spent the rest of her lile in hospitals. This poem, which begins with the words 'Only about myself I knew to tell', was written by Rachel in 1913, a year before her death and became a symbol of personal modesty, which is here akin to the modesty of Riteve.

[Page 68]

'How solitary does the city dwell'

Rabbi Aharon Ben–Zion Shurin

Pleasant and melancholy memories of youth float into my consciousness. My heart burns with pain when i think of all our loved ones from Riteve, a town which like all the Jewish habitations of Europe went up in flames.

I well remember my early youth, when my friends and I studied in the cheder and, later, in the yeshiva where my late father was headmaster.[1] I remember, too, the girls school, which was an excellent school and an example to all, run by my dear respected friend Alter Levite. My dear sisters, who are in America now, also studied there. When we meet, and we are no longer young, we recall fondly the days of our youth.

Yes, there was indeed a wonderful town called Riteve, and now one's heart constricts with pain and anguish when one recollects its fate.

I remember the hot summers when we strolled around the city and bathed in the River Yureh. In the cold winter we would slide in sleds through the streets and on the icy lake, which was situated opposite the church. On wintry days, when there was ice and snow outside, we, the children of Riteve, would gather in the Beit Midrash by the warm oven, and sitting crowded on the long benches would listen avidly to the stories cold to us by the elders of the town. I remember the wonderful walks in which young and old joined on Sabbaths and festivals. We would stroll through the town and in the woods, or in the Oginski Park with its antiquities.

I shall never forget Sabbaths at the Beit Midrash, where the learned as well as the dignitaries and the ordinary folk of the town gathered together. The Beit Midrash rang with their learning and their prayers. Where are all these dear folk now? The sounds of joyous children are no more. Only shadows of bereavement and mourning fill the deserted town. I wonder – does the sun still rise in our town? And does the moon, pale and pure, still shine down on it?

A cry tears at the heart: How solitary is she now, our town!

———

A lament

Ita B Karmom–Kemil

How securely Jews dwelt on the banks of the rivers Yureh and Nieman, and how was it that they were blotted out from under the heavens on one swift and bitter day!

On 22 June 1941 the terrible conflagration was kindled by the barbaric and so–called 'enlightened' Germans.[2] Fathers and mothers, how will we ever forget you? You were uprooted from your homes which had been your haven and left without hope of salvation. How shall we forget the cry of Jewish children, of handsome sons and daughters who had dreamt bright dreams of the future? How can we comprehend the desperate feelings of fathers and mothers who were unable to save their loved ones? Merely to embrace their children and to he permitted to die together was not always granted by the Nazis. Mothers, weakened and sickly, became as strong as lions, and dared to steal out of the ghetto by night to seek refuge for their children with the peasants. They would leave them with a peasant for any amount of money they could scrape together in the hope of saving their lives.[3]

[Page 69]

The Scout Group in Riteve–not to be confused with the organization founded in England by Lord Baden Powell. The top photograph is a group not wearing uniform- possibly taken in its early days- and the one on the next page shows the troop in a far larger group, all except a few in uniform, in a forest setting.

[Page 70]

It is difficult to write about a town of which not a trace is left. One has to draw on one's memory of 40 years ago. Memories ... A horse harnessed to a cart treading slowly from Gorzad⁴ – to Riteve, a stretch of 40 kilometres. The journey was fraught with difficulties: dust and mud, and having to lie in the open cart unprotected from the elements. Both in summer and winter there was heavy rain and we started our journeys mainly at night. The monotonous movements of the cart and the sound of the raindrops on the covering created a pleasant lilt which, with the fragrant smell of the hay on which we lay, put us to sleep. By morning we arrived at a little inn standing desolate on the main road and owned by Jews. My father would wake me to have a hot glass of tea and a fresh bun. This was a wonderful experience. We continued on our way with our destination drawing nearer. I would watch the horizon to see if I could spot the white church spire standing in all its glory in the midst of the town, opposite the entrance to the town, in Memel Street (named for the German city Memel on the Lithuanian border). We arrived at Gorzad, the town from where my father's large family had originated many generations earlier. Suddenly the church spire appeared on the horizon, and my heart would jump with pleasure and expectation at the prospect of meeting my beloved grandfather, who would come smiling happily to greet us.

My grandfather's life was filled with tribulation. His only daughter, who was our mother, had died in his home aged 32 years, leaving behind four young children aged from 6 years to 3 months. My grandmother, Sheina, fell into a deep depression as a result of this tragedy ard she too passed away not long after. My grandfather was very lonely and his only comfort was his grandchildren and letters from his son in America. My grandfather was an upright, naive man. He loved nature and was firmly rooted in his surroundings. He got on well with the gentile Lithuanians with whom he did business. He was modest in his needs and divided his time between communal activities like the Beit Midrash and the Chevra Kadisha and earning his living. I remember how he would have his breakfast of black bread and porridge and then would take his stick in his hand and set out for the surrounding villages with his wares. He dealt in colourful kerchiefs and small fancy goods which were required by the farmers. He would buy his merchandise in Memel and for his journeys there he would always dress in his best clothes.

[Page 71]

The Jews lived securely in Riteve. The Lithuanians were mainly illiterate farmers who lived in the nearby villages. They would sell their produce in the market square where little shops, workshops and saloons were situated. The Jews earned most of their living on market days, and there were jokes about how they got the better of the peasants. The Jewish shopkeeper would speak to his wife in Hebrew, so that the uncircumcised ones could not understand.

There was no entertainment in the town except for a silent film show once a fortnight. The audience had to guess the plot of the film as the figures moved across the screen, and each one did so according to his own understanding. The musical accompaniment was a single violinist who apparently knew only one tune. This tune accompanied me for many years.

Although we did not have much enteriainment in our town, we were never bored. The schoolchildren put on plays, usually on historical themes like Jephthah's daughter, played most successfully by Rachelle Linde of blessed memory, who eventually made her home in Kibbutz Amir in Israel. There were beautiful natural sites in Riteve like the park with its winter garden covered in glass, which has been described in books. Another spot which enchanted me in my youth and which was only a few minutes' walk from the study house was alongside a stream, where a white, round building with a circular roof and coloured windows stood. I imagined it to be an enchanted castle. I never enquired about it or its functions.

Three generations dwelt together in the houses of Riteve: the elderly, the middle–aged and the youngsters. Of course, the older people observed tradition and religious practices as of old. Our parents were more progressive and there were some who had learnt a foreign language like German. The young generation was mainly educated in Hebrew and belonged to Zionist youth movements.

Many jokes were told at the expense of the rather funny characters of the town. The Posel sisters, Leika and Esther, were the chief entertainers. We loved to gather on long winter nights in their spacious kitchen and listen with much enjoyment to their sketches and humorous presentations. Leika died in Haifa of a malignant disease at the age of only 28, but she continued to entertain and amuse others till the end. The very talented Esther died at an advanced age in South Africa.

In Riteve, as in the other towns of Lithuania, Jewish life was vigorous and the Jews were very proud. The youth was well educated and strong. There were links with the outside world because a number of the little town's sons and daughters had emigrated to America and South Africa to seek their fortunes. We, the last generation before the Holocaust, yearned to find happiness in the Land of Israel.

[Page 72]

To Riteve with longing

Sara Yarovski (bom Levite)

My soul is greatly cast down by the catastrophe which overlook Riteve like a thief in the night, as it overtook other dwelling places of Israel. Riteve, you are desolate and forlorn with no living creature in your midst, but you live in my heart. I remember your joys and sorrows, your learned men and your simple folk, your while winters and your fragrant springs, your scented summers and your sad autumns, the green hills arojnd your abundant gardens, your vigorous youth who yearned for knowledge and new horizons and all your inhabitants who were burdened by the yoke of earning their living in a spirit of silent forbearance.

How can one tell of the suffering which you bore with silent humility? My dear father, you sat night after night with the Mishnah Tractates Chulin and Sabbath, and with the holy Zohar.[5] You would take only a brief respite. You would be strong as a lion, rising early lor morning prayers. You sang in a voice full of longing in which we would hear the echo of the Levites in the ancient Temple. And you, my dear mother, always absorbed in the care of the household and the children. This town of ours succeeded in enveloping itself in a mantle of ancient sanctity, by candles that radiated holiness from every home and by the sounds of the shofar in the month of Elul.

We, the young ones, drank to the full from the age–old cellar in which the ancient 'wine' of Torah was stored. But we also rejected the old conventions and went our own rebellious way. We were perceived as having overthrown all authority when we were drawn to the Zionist ideal taught in the Hebrew school. We were seen as having breached the age–old fortress built of hewn stone over many generations to prevent the decline of Judaism. If you had not nurtured in us the love of Zion, would we today be in this land of hope? How did the cruel reaper pass among you, the innocents?

We had among us a troupe that staged plays from time to time. Amateur groups would visit and they would transform the day into a festival of youth. A group of young men, among them Dr Bendet Saks, Hillel Zaks, David Fundiler, Nathan Ploksht and my brother Alter at the head, brought the Hebrew school into existence. There was much opposition from orthodox circles who argued that there was no need for a Hebrew school; the children should study in the cheder, and as for the girls, there was no need to teach them since their role was to keep house until their marriage. But time changed all that. The school was established as well as a kindergarten. A start was made to collect books for a library, which pleased the youth. The opening of the Hebrew school raised the problem of providing more books and study material, but for this, too, a solution was found. Shimon Varkul who returned from German captivity was an expert in the 'hectograph and the spirograph'. The hectograph was set up in our house and my brothers Alter and Zalman Leib Levite used to prepare the material for printing geography, history and nature study books as there was a lack of textbooks. The townsfolk were very impressed with this printing activity, and soon publicity for Zionism and Israel was added to the printing of books and study material.

[Page 73]

In this photograph, the Scout Group is larger still and includes some younger children. It was taken in the shtetl, possibly in front of the Hebrew School, which was replaced by a brick building in 1934.

The publishing of the books spurred on the youth and they, too, wished to make a contribution. Under the leadership of my brother Alter, who was the moving spirit in the town, they began to organise the youth into an organisation known as Tsofim (Scouts). We used to meet a number of times each week and we held lectures and discussions. We also went on outings in the forest in an attempt to draw the Riteve youth to us. We became quite a large and well–organised movement, establishing contact with the central organisation in Kovno which sent us their representatives. I remember one of these representatives, Tsvi Brik by name, who arrived in Riteve on Shabbat Nachamu (the Sabbath following the Ninth of Av). He was a strong young man who joined us in our outings and talks in the forest. The adults of our community were not pleased with him and his influence on us. He was accommodated in our house. When my late lather arrived at the synagogue, he was surrounded by worshippers who said: "Welcome to your important guest." And when he asked whom they meant they answered: 'The young man in your house, who collected our sons and daughters, particularly on the special Sabbath Nachamu, and went with them into the forest!' My brother gave his all to the movement. He took great care in locating the sites of our camps where we could commune with nature. In the winter we would go out together to the lake, where we would clear away the snow and pour water on the ice and then skate on it with great enjoyment. He was our leader and the guide who directed all our activities.

[Page 74]

I remember a national camp which took place at Tsitibian.[6] There were an enormous number of tents. Singing anc dancing did not cease. The campfires rose higher and we thought that the meals we ate there were the tastiest of all. We bought the ingredients from the friendly neighbouring farmers. We established contact with the Hashomer Hatzair movement[7] and all who had given their loyalty to the movement publicly were now sworn in and became bound by its decisions and demands.

The youth was well aware of the happenings in our town and its surroundings. We felt that anti–Semitism was on the increase, and that the position of the Jews was deteriorating. Commerce was being taken away from us and our lives were becoming greyer and more depressed. A large business had been opened in the centre of the town and the priest used to preach continuously that the gentiles should not buy from the Jews whom, he said, cheated in prices and weight. This endless preaching found fertile soil in the minds of the gentiles and hatred of the Jews increased. A number of Jews lost their sourer of income.

The idea of Hachsharah (preparation for life in Israel) inspired me when I was still young. Happily for me there was a joint camp with the Blue–White movement[8] near Memel and I joined this camp. I had to battle with the central organisation to permit me to join the Hachsharah. My family was thunder-struck by my joining this group and leaving home. This took much courage on my part. My parents could not bear to think of my leaving home. My mother became ill from aggravation and all the letters from home constantly harped on the subject of my homecoming, for only this could make my mother well again. My brother Alter wrote to me that while he agreed with my action he had to leave the decision to me, while my sister Miriam continued to urge me to return home. As for me, I was more than ever determined to go to the Land of Israel but my conscience bothered me for many years. In our group, because of which I had caused such a cloud in my home, we worked very hard. The preparation activities lasted for four months and, when I had to return home, it was difficult for me. It was a Friday and my father was still in the synagogue. People there had already informed him that I was home. He entered the house in tears and stood at the door opposite me. I asked: 'Father, will you take me back?' He stretched out his arms and embraced me and we both wept with happiness.

I remained in contact with the movement and, after a few months, I was informed that I must do another stint of Hachsharah, this lime for a longer period. I made up my mind that this time, too, if I did not obtain my parents' consent. I would go ahead without it. I spent nine full months at Hachsharah and on my return home, I started preparing for Aliyah. For, indeed, the hour had come for me to realise all my yearnings to emigrate to the Land of Israel.

[Page 75]

In the original book, this photograph was entitled "Youth in Riteve." The clothing suggests the late 1920s or early 1930s. As the background is a typical painted scene used by photographers of the period, possibly five friends went together to have their picture taken.
Right to left, top, David Salzman, Leib Katz, Eliezer Lande; below, Gutman Shmole and Asher Erman.

My father suffered greatly on this account. The whisperings and the gossip in the synagogue continued, since all knew that I was about to join a kibbutz and, for them, kibbutz life was considered to be wanton and lawless. His pain knew no limits and he used to say: 'I am no longer able to show my face.'

Although I endured very great hardships in the Land of Israel, I was happy with my lot. But I retained the memory of Riteve in my heart. Our home there served as the youth centre of the town. My brother Alter was talented, knowledgeable and untiring. He was busy on all fronts and any emissary who came from the central office or from Israel would obviously be accommodated in our home. My brother would draw the young people of the town into the circle of activities. Alter was the secretary of 'Ze'irei Zion'[9] and its main driving force until he moved to Tverige.[10] Then my sister Miriam filled his place. She taught in the Hebrew school and was responsible for all the cultural activities and Zionist endeavours.

[Page 76]

It was customary in Riteve that when the mail arrived in the afternoon all would gather to read newspapers like Yiddishe Shtimme Hapoel–Hatzair Juedische Rundsriau, the Davar[11] from Israel and many other youth and general publica tions. Then our house would become one large reading room. All were interested to know what was taking place outside of Riteve and especially in the Land of Israel. When they completed their reading, they would play chess. In summer there would be outings to the fields and forest until late into the night. We had an orchestra in which my brother played the violin and the mandolin. There was a guitar player, too. Every minute was planned and well used.

My mother was young in spirit, despite the fact that she was observant. Every Sabbath she would go to synagogue and in the afternoons she would read aloud to the ladies from the popular women's Bible, the Tze'enah Urenah. There were many women who were illiterate but Feiga Basha Velves knew it all by heart. The prayers my mother read left a strong impression on the women, specially the Yizkor prayer. My mother was very busy on Holidays when she would cook and bake and don her special wig. The youngsters would gather around her table and the gossips in the synagogue would complain to my father: "Why do you permit those idle ones to eat and drink in your house and also the boys and girls who dance together?"

I remember a Hannukah celebration at which Alter, my brother, delivered an emotional address about the Maccabees. He and Dr Bendet praised the courage of the Maccabees who endangered their lives for the national cause. My father overheard him from the next room and then spoke his mind to the older folks saying: I do not understand the opposition to our young people. They are involved with our history and they succeed in inspiring our children to appreciate the heroism of our 'people Israel.'

The fact that emigrants from Riteve, whether in America, South Africa or the Land of Israel, retained their connection with their home town proves the degree of cohesiveness which Riteve engendered. It led to mutual concern and great willingness to assist their brethren in times of need. It seems to me that Riteve can be compared to a magnet, and that the values which it inspired became a source of longing for its inhabitants. Even after the Holocaust, the sorrow and bereavement, the Riteve of the world to come, the ideal Riteve of our memories, remained alive. It forever embodied all the good and positive qualities which to this day unite all its dispersed children.

From the distant past – my parents' home

Rivka Zaltsman

My family was not born in Riteve. My father, Shmuel Tzvi, was born in Loknik.[12] My late mother, Sara Frida, was born in the village of Tans near Pyora.[13] My father, even before his bar mitzvah, studied in yeshivot in various towns and ate days (i.e. was given free board in different houses during the week), as was the custom then. Later he studied at Kelm[14] — at the famous Talmud Torah. We lived in a village near Riteve and, just before the First World War, we moved to Riteve. My father was employed by various timber firms and supported his family well. There were numerous forests in the area, where the trees served the paper indus– try in Germany. When the firms changed hands, there were periods of unem– ployment, but we did not feel the consequences at home. Father often said that we children had much more than he had had.

[Page 77]

The sons studied in the yeshiva and Father supported them generously. Despite his business preoccupations, he found time to participate in communal activities with the help and encouragement of my mother. My father was well liked by all, excelling in wisdom, integrity and sincerity and was often chosen as an arbitrator in disputes. He was a committee member of both the girls' schools and the boys' Talmud Torah and he took care of the yeshiva students in the town. He would use wood that he received from his firm to distribute among the needy for heating in winter. He built a modern mikveh (ritual bath) from contributions which had been given anonymously by Feige Rachel Hirshowitz who was a generous and active communal worker. Before the outbreak of the Second World War he managed to complete the wooden roof of the summer synagogue, also with anonymous contributions.

When my mother died in 1933 1 remember that, on our return from the funeral, my father, weeping bitter tears, said: 'You, my children (there were eight of us), have accompanied your mother to her eternal rest – who will accompany me?'

Indeed, he was buried with his sons – the eldest Shlomo Yaacov and his youngest Israel Ezekiel – in a mass grave in Telz.

———

Once there was a town

Gilat Saks and Yehuda Chazan

My town Riteve, in which I was born and which is clearly etched in my childhood memories, lay among forests. The roads to the large cities, Memel, Tverige and Telz, which were 40 kilometres or more away were dust tracks and transport between the cities was by horse and cart. Often the drivers were compelled to pull the cart out of the mud. In the winter, covered toboggans slid through the snow which covered the ground. The town belonged to a Polish aristocrat who did as he pleased with its inhabitants. Many stories are told of the suffering which the Jewish inhabitants endured on account of their ruler's whims and fancies. On the other hand, he also took care of the needs of the town, supplying it with electricity before any of the other towns. Riteve's streets and the marketplace were paved with river stones. There was a summer garden with well-established hothouses where the temperature was kept under control so that tropical and subtropical plants could be cultivated.

Trees and beautiful flowers surrounded the aristocrat's palace and the whole town. With the establishment of the Lithuanian state after the First World War, the garden became an agricultural college.

[Page 78]

The Jews of Riteve made a living from the small trade which they conducted with the farmers of the district, who flocked to the market held twice a week and on Sundays and festival days. The peasants would come to sell their produce and also to pray in the church which stood in the centre of the town. The proceeds of this trade were meagre and, in the absence of hope for the future, the young people emigrated to faraway lands overseas, especially to South Africa. These emigrants were an important source of help to their families who remained behind since they sent them money from their savings. The centres of commerce were Memel, Lithuania's only seaport. Telz and Kovno, the latter being the temporary capital of Lithuania. These vibrant centres of Lithuanian Jewry exerted a strong influence on the life of the community.

Riteve, being small and poverty stricken, could only afford to maintain primary educational institutions, and, in the main, the youth obtained their higher education outside of its boundaries. Memel was a source of Western cultural influence. Kovno a Zionist national influence, and Telz a moral and religious influence. The Zionist activities, for example, were many and varied. The National Funds (Keren Kayemet and Keren Hayesod) were not merely fundraising instruments, but also played a vital educational role for the national ideal. This led to the Aliyah (emigration to Israel) of large numbers of pioneering youth of all persuasions, who today are spread throughout Israel and constitute the saving remnant of Riteve.

During the Holocaust I lost all the members of my large family, except for my brother Gabriel, who had emigrated to South Africa in his youth. My parents had come from learned stock. My father, Nachman Zaks, was a scholar and was possessed of outstanding qualities. His sincere counselling was much respected and often he was the arbitrator in differences of opinion. He also served as the treasurer of the synagogue. By trade he was an experienced dealer in flax. My mother was also of a generous nature and a good-hearted lady. She helped the needy and was devoted to her family and to her friends. She was concerned with educating us in the virtues of sincerity, honesty and caring for others. My brother, Yoel Dov, studied at the Telz yeshiva and was ordained as a rabbi. He was the editor of the paper Agudat Israel and was also a gifted orator and knowledgeable in areas other than the Torah. My brother, Bendet, also studied at the Telz yeshiva and then went on to higher university education, becoming a successful medical doctor. He was an active Zionist and headed the student association in his time. My sisters. Sheina, Rachel, Feiga, Rozelle and Masha, received religious and Zionist education. But the hand of the wicked murderers put an end to these young, innocent and vibrant lives.

The town, Riteve, our beloved town, suffered total annihilation.

———

[Page 79]

Fragmented memories

Rachel Karniel (Groll)

The remnants of the Jews of Riteve, who are no more, were destined to serve as a living memorial.

Although our parents were not steeped in Jewish history and Zionist ideology, they nevertheless followed intently all that was happening in the Land of Israel. They also spoke of it longingly, yet the gip between dreams and reality was wide. The impression was formed that life there was difficult from the economic point of view and this served to deter emigration. Even among the many Zionist parties this view held sway. Communal activity and donations, yes – but to realise one's dreams and to emigrate, no. The reports that reached us from the Land of Israel about bloodshed and unemployment cast doubt on possibilities of a future there. However, real efforts were made to put the ideal into practice. The Hebrew school encouraged a lively interest in everything connected with the Land of Israel. In our home hung a large pictuie of Dr Herzl. I keenly absorbed everything told to me by my late brother and sister, who were active in the youth movements.

In the Scout movement, we were taught to serve others and to love our home– land. The Linat Tzedek, which helped the sick, was a particularly important feature of our lives. I remember how we would volunteer to sit up at night in the homes of the ill so as to give the members of the family some relief. In the Hashomer Hatzair movement, we were taught to love the Land of

Israel. In this connection, I cannot fail to mention the name of Abraham Linde of blessed memory. It was his nobility of character and dedication to the national ideal that inspired many of us to go on Aliyah to the Land of Israel. He and Sarah Levite were the founders and devoted leaders of a large movement. It is the greatest tragedy that the parents and families of these emigrants did not foresee the tragic end in store for them and thus did not leave Lithuania.

Our lives in general were led in a spirit of tranquillity and we loved our town in all its beauty. In the front of our houses fruit trees grew and it was great fun when the children in our street helped us to shake the fruit from the trees and gather apples. The plum tree in the yard was very beautiful in spring when it was full of white blossoms. At the edge of the yard, where a fence separated us from our neighbour, Mrs H Galaun, there was a large expanse of lawn. We spent the days of our childhood amidst natural beiuty and we loved our town very much. We would look at the ruins of the palace with great admiration. It held great magic and enchantment for us, with its winter garden and its walls of glass, and the steps leading to the nursery surrounded by lawns and shrubs, where we spent happy and tranquil childhood days.

[Page 80]

We were not aware of anti–Semitism. Unfortunately, we had no contact at all with the lives of the Lithuanians. We were indifferent to them and this later added to our downfall. When the Holocaust came, the Lithuanians were unrestrained and unsurpassed in their cruelty.

Riteve, a vital and culturally rich town, possessed a well–stocked library which was far in excess of the requirements of its population. This cultural activity is today carried on by its sons in Israel.

May this book published by Riteve survivors serve to keep alive forever the values that the martyrs stood for, so that our children will cherish the memory of their forebears.

———

Riteve – a childhood landscape

Chaya Saks–Noy

Forty years after leaving Riteve thoughts of my childhood there still pass through my mind. It was a small but beautiful lawn, surrounded by forests, in which we spent Sabbaths and festivals. We would collect blackberries there. The girls of Riteve were renowned for their beauty.

The youth strove to rise above the problems of life in the Diaspora. One could hear Hebrew spoken in the streets. Some of the young people went to Memcl to study and to work. The Hashomer Hatzair movement prepared its members for life in Israel.

We went on outings to the garden which belonged to Count Oginski and enjoyed the fruit of the trees. I can picture the River Yureh which flowed by before my eyes. I would sit on the river bank, reading a book or watching the women washing their clothes. Near our house there stood a long bench, where in the mornings those who came from morning prayers would sit and chat, and in the evenings loving couples would meet there. The village watchman would drop off to sleep there and we would hear his snoring.

My parents were simple, good–hearted people. My father would rise early for prayers; most of the week he would travel around selling flax. My mother bore the responsibility of the care of the children.

One of my brothers completed the teachers' seminar in Kovno and served as a teacher in Yurburg[15], Sarhai, Meretsh, Mariompol and Shavli. He assisted the family with his earnings, and my sister, Miriam, joined him in Yurburg. My brother was very good–hearted and on an occasion when he was travelling by train he found a man freezing from cold since he had no coat. My brother gave him his own newly acquired coat, although he did not even know the man. This was characteristic of him. He was the pride and joy of the family. He was also active in the Ze'irei Zion youth movement, but fortune did not shine on him. He was put to death at Bergen Belsen.

[Page 81]

Sons of Riteve– students of the Telz yeshiva. It's of interest that two groups of these young men, at different periods, went together to have their photograph taken for friends and family at home, indicating their closeness while away studying.

Above, right to left: Shalom Saks, Shmuel Peskin, Zvi Gillon, Moshe Ballin, Shlomo Babush, Shlomo Jakov Salzman. Taken Nisan 5688 (1925).

From the clothing, this was probably taken some years later, maybe even in the early 1930s.

**Sons of Riteve– students of the Telz yeshiva. It's of interest that two
groups of these young men, at different periods, went together to have
their photograph taken for friends and family at home, indicating their
closeness while away studying.
Above right to left: standing: Chone Babush, Shimon Friedman, Jehiel
Tollman; Peskin; Baruch Strass;
seated: Chaim Itzkowicz; Ze'ev Heiman and Izchak Wolf.
From the clothing, this was probably taken some years later, maybe even
in the early 1930s.**

[Page 82]

My brother, Shalom, completed the yeshiva at Telz at an early age and both
he and my father were ordained rabbis. Shalom became head of a yeshiva. He
had also studied mathematics and languages. He was much respected for the
advice he gave to all who approached him. My brother, Aaron, left home at 15.
He emigrated to South Africa where, after initial difficulties, he became
successful. My sister, Esther, being the eldest, shouldered the responsibility of
caring for the family. She, too, died in the Holocaust. My sister, Yocheved, had
wanted to go to Israel, but was persuaded to join our brother in South Africa
where she died in Cape Town. I left home for Hachsharah training and then

went to Israel. My parents were not happy with my leaving home, since they seemed to sense that they would not see me again.

The Holidays left a deep impression on me, especially the preparations for Passover. After the hard winter, all the household goods were taken outside and thoroughly cleaned. The children took part in the preparations and then enjoyed the wonderful ritual of the Seder. The melodies of the traditional Passover Seder could be heard all around, and our hearts were uplifted with the joys of the festival. The Sabbath, too, with its rituals, the challah and the tsimes (a dish made of sweet carrots), all left an indelible impression on me.

Our house was full of children and friends, and a spirit of love and concern for each other prevailed. But the joy did not last long.

My heart is with our dear ones in their eternity.

Memories of Riteve

Rachel Arman–Piyorski

Zionists and pioneering Jews of Riteve, where are you?

From my earliest youth I was taught to care for my fellow human beings. The Hashomer Hatzair youth movement, the Linat Tzedek (overnight stay with the sick) and the atmosphere at school also strengthened this feeling. From my house I could easily observe the pulsating life of the school. My teacher was Alter Levite who invested much energy and talent in the education of the children. I remember how he carefully demonstrated to the class a pencil box which had arrived from America and was regarded by all as a wonder.

Riteve: I remember its clean streets, its green fields, its beautiful flowers and its sparkling lake; its population was mainly Jewish. The River Yureh divided the Jewish population from the gentiles. I remember its market days with the Lithuanian peasants bringing their produce for sale and its Sunday cinema shows with the kleizmerim playing their eternal melodies nearby.

[Page 83]

What more can I say? My heart is broken at the thought of these dear innocents who met their death at the hands of those beasts of prey in the shape of humans, who murdered without mercy, young and old, fathers and mothers, young scholars and students. And there was no one left to mourn for them.

My father, my brothers and sisters and my whole extended family never dreamt that they would fall prey to those murderous hands.

Jews of Riteve, martyrs to G–d's holy name – farewell to your ashes.

———

Flickerings of memory

Ya'akov Weiner

A community lived there, died in flames and lives only in our memory. We shall not forget them. We will not allow them to be forgotten. Dear G–d, gather them from their graves in Giroli[16] unto Yourself. Bring them near to us in the Land of Israel and keep their memory bright among all the martyrs of our people.

This book is neither an autobiography nor even a biography, but a book of personal memories. We ask ourselves why we have raked up the past. What has motivated men and women in the autumn of their years to write their memoirs? The answer lies in the subconscious. We wished to save memories from the flames, memories which were hidden in the depths of our hearts. They were personal memories, but are no longer private ones. They are memories of a reconstructed past. Memories are not history; nostalgia casts a spell over the past. But perhaps, being dredged up from the heart and the head, they are indeed the very stuff of history.

I tremble when I recall that all my friends, colleagues in communal and Zionist causes, and townsfolk, young and old, were led to the slaughter. The little dark, deserted houses to which their inhabitants did not return, the blue and white boxes which hung on the walls alongside pictures of the Rambam, the Gaon of Vilna and Dr Herzl are all abandoned and now spiders spin their webs undisturbed. Our good neighbours inherited a windfall in the houses which remained ownerless.

What was the fate of the Beit Midrcsh which absorbed years of devoted prayers, and what of the Holy Ark beautifully engraved and of the Eternal Light in the south wall, by whose light Jewish scholars sat devouring the pages of the Gemara, which they regarded as Holy Writ? There too we had listened attentively to many orators, religious or Zionist. It is impossible to believe that all this is no more.

In the Beit Midrash all sections of the community met, be they working Jews of tradesfolk. All were partners in the study of Torah. Riteves beauty derived from an inner wealth. Life was conditioned by customs that had passed from generation to generation. Its joys were mixed with sadness. Even bridal music was bitter–sweet, since under the bridal canopy the sobbing of the Jewish mother and grandmother was heard. Even good news would elicit tears. Music was ever present be it the chanting of the yeshiva student, or the tailor over his cloth, the shoemaker at his last, or the rabbi humming before his lesson to the congregation.

[Page 84]

However, life was not limited to religious ceremonial alone. Not only Sabbaths and Holidays had their rituals. The special dishes that were prepared for certain days, or how one put on and took off one's shoes – each activity had its appropriate wording, its own melody.

Troubles and misfortunes were many. Although bars were to be found in the town, Jewish drinkers of alcohol were practically non–existent. They did not look for solace in drink, but in study. After a hard day's toil, a Jew found comfort in his Gemara and its commentaries. The popular lullaby ran: 'Torah is the best merchandise.'

The new–born baby was welcomed with the words of the Shema (Shema Israel). When the child was brought to cheder he was wrapped in a talit (prayer shawl). The prayer book was the common man's way to the Divine. It was holy, every word a precious stone. There was pleasure in observing the commandments.

Who in Ritevc spoke of faith? Who could not sec that G–ds glory filled the earth? It was superfluous to ask these Jews to keep the commandments. To live by the tenets of the Shulchan Aruch (Code of Jewish Law) was a natural thing to do. Life without Torah and commandnents was a life of emptiness.

———

'I was young and now I am old'

Anonymous

I remember my first meeting with my grandfather. I was confronted by large eyes whose brilliance almost blinded me. I was a young boy, greatly awed by a bearded presence. 'How ae your studies?' he asked me gently Shyly I smiled and replied, 'Fine'. 'And do you love the Holy Torah?' he asked. 'Yes, Grandpa. I do.' I replied. I wanted to stroke the snowy beard and come close to the wonderful tenderness that surrounded him. He took my hand in his and then blessed me.

I grew up and was about to emigrate to Eretz Israel. I went to Grandpa to receive his blessing. The tears welled up and overflowed. He was not embarrassed. 'Go in peace to the Holy Land, and build it with pride,' be said.

My heart is overwhelmed by sorrow at the thought that all those innocent people, family and friends, went to their graves unshrouded. No memorial prayer (Kaddish) was said in their honour, no period of mourning was observed, no garments were rent. And like those precious souls, so the holy books were defiled and lost. I am comforted by the thought that Riteve folk in Israel have not forgotten and that this book will serve as a living memorial (Yad VaShem) to our community.

[Page 85]

Whoever peruses this book will find in it faithful descriptions of life in Riteve – a life in which hard work and study of Torah were inextricably bound, a town which raised its sons to Torah excellence; a town materially poor but rich in spirit, a town whose inhabitants worked hard all week and found spiritual upliftment on Sabbaths and festivals.

The book in all its various sections sheds a great light which serves not only as an emotional release, but enlightens in depth and with great skill. In reading this book, forgotten memories of many generations are awakened, the sounds and sights of childhood are brought to life and they cause a shudder of delight. In the book are to be found the Jewish archetypes of the town who were nurtured by their ancient Jewish sources: the Jewish mother in her devotion to her family, the home of a Jewish father, where the Divine Presence dwelt, and family life that remained pure. Friendship and love, generosity and an aristocratic bearing, love of nature, love of all living creatures, were the values which were cherished. The heart weeps for all that is no more. Although the pain is not assuaged, the purity which shines forth from this hook will last forever. It is important for the sons and daughters of Riteve who knew the reality. It is important for the young generation who will find in it the very soul of its people. The book is a sad one; it is a prayer book; a hook of lamentation. It is a perpetual light in memory of the martyrs of Riteve; it is a testament and an eternal resting place for the spirits of the departed.

———

My unforgettable shtetl

Author unknown

I remember, as in a dream. Riteve's quiet narrow streets, even though 35 years have gone by and all has vanished.

Riteve has been destroyed, its life obliterated. Thorns and weeds have over–grown its once lively streets. I am overcome with emotion when I remember the old days; the streets appear before my eyes. The broad marketplace, the small shops, the shul (the synagogue) with its carved wooden Holy Ark. Images float before me of Shabbat and Yom–Tov, Mother and Father, attired in their Sabbath clothes, walking slowly and gravely to shul.

Riteve, the Jewish shtetl, has disappeared in a flame, leaving only derelict ruins of houses, through which the cruel winds blow. From these ruins, a spirit of holiness had once emanated: hymns of the Sabbath and Havdalah (the ceremony of transition from Sabbath back to working days) – the 'G–d of Abraham' prayer, which was tearfully offered by our mothers and grandmothers – all this was extinguished after the final 'Shema Israel!' of our unforgettable martyrs.

[Page 86]

Who will visit the graves of our fathers? In winter they are covered with snow and in summer overgrown with weeds. The rain alone will shed tears over the graves. Our tears cannot reach them any more.

How can we forget our talented children? I remember the eminent scholars, the various political groups, the school with its high educational standard, the library, the shops, the bank and the welfare institutions.

Marriage celebrations were shared with all the townsfolk. I remember the wedding processions: the musicians accompanying the dancing: 'machetinistres' (mothers–in–law) dancing. I remember the funerals: mourners with their sad laments, the cries of 'Charity saves lives.' of the beggars, the weeping women and men with bent heads, like a black forest.

I remember the families of Riteve, their joys and sorrows, their hopes for better days. I remember Riteve, steeped for so many generations in its Jewish ethos, a town whose great–grandfathers, like ancient trees, were rooted in their Jewishness. Today the silent streets resound with the haunting echoes of the Jews of Riteve.

Let us remember the people of Riteve at their work and at their Mincha and Ma'ariv prayers and at study. Among them were many great Talmud scholars.

Accompany me on a journey, my brothers and townsfolk from Riteve, through the empty streets, past broken windows, which used to be lit up by the Sabbath candles. Let us together remember Riteve's great past. Generations of our brethren toiled and strove with great energy and diligence to make of Riteve a truly Jewish town, whose people had great pride and much love for their Jewish heritage.

Riteve is no more; all its vital forces have been destroyed. No longer do we hear the sounds of joyful children, nor the hustle and bustle of the town, nor even the peaceful silence of the Sabbath.

The earth can no more absorb our tears
Nor can the heavens still our pain
No longer is there any trace nor remnant.

Our book is presented with pain and sorrow, as a memoir of the Riteve of the past. Let us not forget them!

———

My town Ritevc

Getzel Zelikovitz

I have been away from Riteve for many years. This little town in which my forebears lived and died remains vividly in my memory. I remember the streets leading to the baths: Schiler. Memel and Plungyan streets – especially the main street leading to the square of the two brothers, the Dukes Oginski. For many years they held the Jews in subjection like Oriental tyrants. The very name Oginski was enough to throw Riteve into a state of alarm. Not only the 200 Jewish families, but also the peasants in the region, lived in fear of the Oginskis.

[Page 87]

Yeronim [Irenaeus] Oginski, the father, was a well–known Jew–hater. Any Riteve person still alive today remembers clearly the church bells announcing the good tidings that Oginski had passed away in 1859. The tyrant had taken his own life minutes before the Cossacks arrived to arrest him as a Polish traitor. This caused a double celebration on Purim – the downfall of Haman was completely overshadowed by the downfall of this Polish duke, who had oppressed the Jews more severely than Pharaoh of Egypt.

I do not have first–hand knowledge of the despot Oginski, but I have heard much of his autocratic actions, and that he ruled with an iron fist. I did how– ever meet his two sons who inherited their father's authority. I will never forget what happened one Sabbath after lunch. The congregation had gathered in shul as usual, some were praying, others were reading from the Psalms while others were listening to reading of legends, some were nodding over the Gemara. Old Reb Mischel sat in a corner with the 'Alfas' (commentary). Someone else was perusing a secular book and Leibchik, the astute one, and Getzka, the young genius, were studying a collection of commentaries. Suddenly into this peaceful Sabbath quiet broke Wolfe the shammas (the synagogue attendant) at a run. Breathlessly and with a half stifled cry he announced, 'Oginski has sent in his men to dig up our cemetery!' So it was. The brothers Oginski had indeed sent their men to dig up the graves while they themselves were supervising and enjoying this act of mindless vandalism!

In spite of all the adversity, Riteve produced many internationally renowned Jews, among them great rabbis, famous musicians and eminent writers of Yiddish and Hebrew as well as great specialists in medicine and mathematics.

Riteve was one of the most beautiful towns in Lithuania and it is possible that living surrounded by so much natural beauty its inhabitants developed a fine aesthetic sense. The high spires of the church could be seen at a distance of three miles, enveloped in clouds. Beautiful flowerbeds were planted on either side of the bridge. A large rectangular–shaped pond separated the town from the Oginski residence. On all sides of the pond were beds of flowers and lawns. On the far side of the pond there stood a beautiful palace which could take its place on the Champs Elysees, Piccadilly or 5th Avenue, New York.

The houses of the town were tastefully laid out with flowerbeds in the front gardens and fruit trees at the hack. The trees were full of nests and towards evening the birds filled our ears with song.

Here I spent my childhood and here I was known as the Riteve prodigy, although I did not deserve this honour.

The Oginskis had spent great sums of money to make Riteve into their family seat, to turn this town into a little Paris, a gem. Here all could enjoy the beauty of nature.

[Page 88]

Thoughts on the destruction of my home

S. Halkin

It is difficult lo write about the destruction of one's home, about the annihilation of one's family, friends and relatives of whom nothing remains – only scattered ash and grassy mounds over their graves. In those dark years of terror and humiliation, when the Angel of Death had spread his black wings over most of Eastern Europe, we were made aware of the fate of our former beloved homes. They had been destroyed and our dear ones were wiped out. As the appalling news reached us, our spirits were filled with sorrow and woe.

Come, my townsman, and let us stroll through Riteves' streets on a Friday afternoon. Let us see the townsfolk, who all week long are wrapped up in the struggle for existence, and in what princely fashion they welcome the Sabbath. Women with their baskets and bags filled with Sabbath provisions rush home-wards. Sounds of fish being chopped, shoes and boots being polished; girls are shining up the brass candlesticks and children are having themselves scrubbed and cleaned while protesting loudly. There is a coming and going from the ritual baths. The men arrive with clean clothing carried under the arms; they emerge scrubbed and cleansed in honour of the Holy Sabbath.

At home, mothers kindle the Sabbath lights with reverence, together with their daughters in their Sabbath clothing and with their hair neatly plaited.

The young men accompany their fathers, festively attired, on the way to shul. When the eyes of the young girls and boys meet, the girls blush modestly.

After the shul service, the Sabbath meal with us white challah and the participation of all the family in the Sabbath songs linger on in the memory. The 'Shabbes Goy' lights the oven, his wife milks the cow; the household prepares hurriedly to go to shul carrying their prayer books and talitim. Young men and women hurry around to take home their cholents from the baker's oven; the mingling of the delicious smells emerging from the cholents enriches the Sabbath atmosphere.

After the Sabbath meal, the whole village drops into a deep slumber. The enjoyment of the Sabbath afternoon sleep is in itself a great Mitzvah. The young, however, stroll in the woods. They read the works of Sholem Aleichem and Peretz in discussion groups and end up singing together joyously. Towards evening they take a Sabbath stroll, enjoying the fresh air. When the first stars appear, the men return home from shul and all participate in the Havdalah service.

Oh, my hometown Riteve, where my childhood memories linger as in an unfinished symphony! I remember ihe sun–bathed days, the town sunk in a sea of green, and at a glance I can see fields of corn, orchards with fruit, gardens with flowers and the shimmering lake.

[Page 89]

It was a small, modest town, hut full of life and intense vitality. It had Jewish merchants and artisans, all leading decent lives and carrying out their communal and moral obligations. It had its study houses and schools. It celebrated its Sabbaths and festivals. The people lived to the full, celebrating their joys and sharing their sorrows. It had exceptional young people who were keen on learning, education, building and creativity.

This was a community of studious Jews, both rich and poor. I remember their celebrations; their Shalosh Se'udot (the three meals on the Sabbath, especially the third one); their taking farewell of the Sabbath with sorrowful melodies. I remember the Passover Seders and the joyous procession around the bima with the Torah on Simchat Torah nights; I remember our gentle and tender mothers – all the mothers and the bobbas (the grandmothers) – their sincere devotion to Jewish traditions: their gladness as they welcomed the Sabbath, their sadness as it ended. I remember, too, the daily struggles for existence – for a livelihood. I remember the Linai Tzedek which helped the poor and healed the sick; the Hachnasat Kalah which provided dowries for poor brides; the Gemilut Chesed which gave loans to those in need; Maos Chitim, the organisation which provided matzot for the poor at Pesach.

In Riteve every type of communal organisation nourished – from the Folksbank, to the learned study groups in which men, after a hard day's work, could find spintual uplift in the pages of the Gemara. I remember Riteve from the most orthodox circles to the most lively political parties.

————

Footnotes

1. On Rabbi Moshe Shurin see Chapter Six.

2. On 22 June 1941, the German army invaded the Soviet Union. Shortly afterwards the Germans began to carry out the extermination of Lithuanian Jewry.

3. See Chapter Nine.

4. Gorzad (Gargzfai) was a small town on the border with Germany where about 700 Jews lived prior to the Holocaust.

5. Zohar (the Book of Splendour) – the central work in the literature of Kabbalah (Jewish mysticism). The book is a collection of several sections which include short midrashic statements (rabbinical commentary on the biblical text), homilies and discussion. It was probably composed by Spanish Kubbalists at the end of the 13th century.

6. Forests near the small town of Tsitibian, in the Raseinai district, central Lithuania.

7. On Hashomer Hatzair see Chapter Seven.

8. Blau–Weiss was a Zionist youth movement established in Germany in 1912 and was the first Jewish youth movement. It followed the pattern of the German youth movement Wandevogel. The Zionist ideas of the movement penetrated into circles of Jewish youth of assimilated and semi–assimilated families, and helped them find their way to the Jewish, people and to Zionism.

9. Ze'irei Zion was a Zionist Socialist movement formed n Russia at the beginning of the 20th century by young Zionists. They emphasised

the necessity of redirecting the Jewish masses to productive employment and the establishment of a Jewish labor commonwealth in Palestine. They were organised in East and Central European countries and later also in the USA, Argentine and South Africa.

10. A district in west Lithuania, on the banks of the River Yureh, near the Lithuanian–German boarder.

11. Yiddishe Shtmme was the acknowledged organ of the Lithuanian Jewry in the inter–war period. Since 1919 it had been published in Kovno by the General Zionist Organisation of Lithuania. Hapoel–Hatzair ('The Young Worker') was the first newspaper of the labour movement in Palestine, 1907, as the organ of the Ha–Poel Hatzair movement, a labour party founded by the first pioneers of the Second Aliyah. Juedische Rundshau was the organ of the Zionist Federation in Germany. Founded in 1896, it had a profound influence on Zionist activists in Germany. During the Nazi period its editor Robert Weltzsh helped to strengthen the Jewish morale. In 1938 the newspaper was banned by the Nazis and ceased publication. Davar was the organ of the Hitsadrut Ha–Oyedim (General Federation of Labour in Israel). Founded in Tel Aviv in 1923. Its first editor was Berl Katznelson, one of the most outstanding leaders of the Jewish Labour Movement in Palestine.

12. Luakeve Lithuania. Located in northwest Lithuania, in the Telz district.

13. Located in west Lithuania, in the Tverige district.

14. One of the most famous small towns in the Jewish world, known as the centre of the Musar movement in Lithuania. Located in central Lithuania, in the Raseiniai district.

15. Yurburg – a district city in western Lithuania; Sarhai (Sierijai) a town in southern Lithuania, where 200 Jewish families were living before the Holocaust; Meretsh – a small town in southern Lithuania, 10 kilometres Irom Alytus.

16. Giroli– a village near Telz. On 29 August 1941 all the women over the age of 50 and the boys of Kiteve were killed there by the Germans.

[Page 90]

Chapter Six

Personalities in Riteve

Townsfolk

In the original memorial book on Riteve, a chapter was devoted to personalities, most of the the writers being anonymous. Comparatively few of the recollections were personal. Some related stories passed down by older members of the community, now dead, and were vague about dates, which had to be gleaned from internal evidence; others seem to have done some research in books of reference. The chapter was overlong and sometimes repetitive. It has been fairly heavily edited and an attempt has been made to arrange the personalities into their periods. It is hoped that this will give a better picture of the shtetl at different times in its history and point to personalities who were living in Riteve contemporaneously.

Lithuania was famous for its Jewish scholarship and, up to the time of the Holocaust, many notable scholars who had been born or lived in Riteve were proudly remembered and comprise by far the majority of the personalities. Rabbis, heads of rabbinical courts and of various institutes of religious studies had yiches, an untranslatable Yiddish word (the closest one can come in English is 'status'). Values may have changed today, but a wealth of scholarship – not wealth in terms of worldly possessions – was what was most honoured by the Jews of Lithuania. The survivors of Riteve thus recalled not only scholars who lived and worked among them, but those born there who had moved out to any one of many other places in Lithuania, including the most important centres of rabbinical study, people about whom stories had been told up to the time of the Holocaust. They also noted marriages to scholars of the Torah – for family genealogies are important for yiches – and the publication of original commentaries on holy scripts.

Lithuania before the Holocaust was one of the most important centres in the world for Jewish scholarship. Through the stories of scholars associated in some way with Riteve, the very intensive study in the realm of

Jewish thought may be perceived. Riteve was not unique in this respect. In every small town, no matter how small, there was a strong need for Jewish institutes and leaders, for studies and ordained teachers. Although some learned men made Aliyah to Israel, few emigrated to other parts of the world because it was hard to live as an observant Jew in the Diaspora. Only when we realise the enormity of the human treasures produced in one little town, do we begin to understand the scope of the losses caused by the Holocaust.

DP and MR

[Page 91]

Gavriel (Gabriel) Ben–Ze'ev Grod, born in Riteve in 1890, who was to become a famous composer, was the great–grandson of the noted early rabbi of Riteve, Baruch Bendet, whose original name was Grod.

Gabriel Grod's father, however, was Reb Z'eve Zvi, a rich merchant, which suggests that he took his mother's surname for professional reasons, possibly because of the alliteration of the name.

Gabriel Grod emigrated to Palestine in 1924

The earliest rabbis remembered

A street scene in Rietve in the 1930s, drawn from photographs by Dean Simon.

It is known that from very early times there was an important community in Riteve in the province of Kaidan, the largest province in Lithuania. The meetings of the Kaidan province sometimes took place in Riteve. The earliest rabbi recalled who served in the town was Rabbi Mordechai Yaffe who died in about 1775 – many other rabbis ministered there before him, details of whom have not survived. Typically, what is recalled of Rabbi Yaffe is his descent from another Rabbi Mordechai Yaffe, author of Hale'vish (the attire), who lived in Plungyan, located near Telz in west Lithuania, and of his own distinguished descendant, his great–great–grandson Rabbi Benjamin Rabinowitch, rabbi of Wilkomir in 1905.1 To the Jews of Lithuania, these family connections were all important.

In 1910, when the book Nachlat Avot (Heritage of the Fathers) was published in Vilna, 'the great Rabbi Herz' of Riteve was mentioned. Rabbi Naftali Herz was the head of the rabbinical court in Riteve and took a great interest in mystics and Kabbalah. It was observed that he was a 'pious and modest scholar' and four of his works were mentioned, one of which was on the Kabbalist ways of interpreting the Torah. But nothing further is known of him – not even his dates of birth and death. However, by 1842, Baruch Bendet was the rabbi in Riteve and head of the Rabbinic Court.2 His original name was Grod, and his great–grandson, Gavriel (Gabriel) Grod, was a famous composer, born in Riteve in 1890 and son of Reb Z'eve Zvi, a rich merchant and charitable Maskil. Gabriel Grod emigrated to Palestine in 1924.3

At the time the original book was written, Miriam Tsvik was able to recall the story of her great–grandfather, who was a rabbi in Riteve in the mid–19th century, at the time of the notorious lord, Irenaeus Oginski, and a contemporary of Rabbi Bendet.

Rabbi Itzchak Aharonowitz

Miriam Tsvik

My great–grandfather, Rabbi Itzchak, son of Menachem Aharonowitz, was an outstanding, aristocratic personality. He was an excellent Torah scholar, pure– hearted and G–d–fearing, yet very modest. He was known as 'Itcha the Judge'.

My mother would talk about him with great admiration. He served as rabbinic judge for 75 years in Riteve. Even Oginski, the elder feudal lord, who was a cruel tyrant towards the Jews in our town, respected him and had his picture hanging above his bed, as a kind of talisman against evil!

[Page 92]

Rabbi Itzchak Ben–Nachum Menachem Ahronowitz was called 'Reb Itcha the Judge' and was a 19th century rabbi. No further information was provided about him in the orginal book, except that he was 'of Riteve' and, several pages beyond his portrait, the title page of his book was given, seen right

In his youth. Itzchak would travel every week to visit the rabbi and greet him with a Sabbath blessing. The rabbi then blessed him and wished him honour and length of days. Both these blessings were realised, for he lived until the age of 95, leaving three daughters, one of whom was my grandmother, and a son who followed in his father's footsteps. Another son was a well–known merchant in Amsterdam.

One of Rabbi Aharonowitz's grandsons, Nachman Lipman Chananya, was head of the yeshiva at Varna, located in the district of Telz in west Lithuania. Among Rabbi Aharonowitz's works was a book of commentary known as Sefer Kesher Torah, which was published posthumously in 1904 by his family.

Rabbi Abraham Licht – first to go on Aliyah

The first Riteve–born Jew to go on Aliyah to the Land of Israel took this step during the time of rabbis Aharonowitz and Bendet. He was Rabbi Abraham Licht, son of Aharon Licht, and a great Torah scholar as well as being involved in communal affairs. He settled in Jerusalem probably just after the mid–19th century. Rabbi Abraham Licht made two missions abroad, one in 1863 and the other in 1869, and in Pressburg published the well–known religious, philosophical work, Akeidat Yizchak (the sacrifice of Isaac), written by Rabbi Isaac Ben Arama (1420–1494). Rabbi Ben Arama, who lived in Spain but died in Naples, used Aristotelian philosophy in order to establish the superiority of the Torah. The publication of this book included an original commentary by famous scholars. While he was engaged on his missions abroad, Rabbi Licht joined the newly formed Hibbat–Zion movement under Rabbi Zvi Hirsch Kalisher. Rabbi Kalisher (1795–1874) was actually an ideological predecessor of the Hibbat–Zion movement and is considered, together with the Sephardi Rabbi Alkalaim, a harbinger of modern Zionism.

[Page 93]

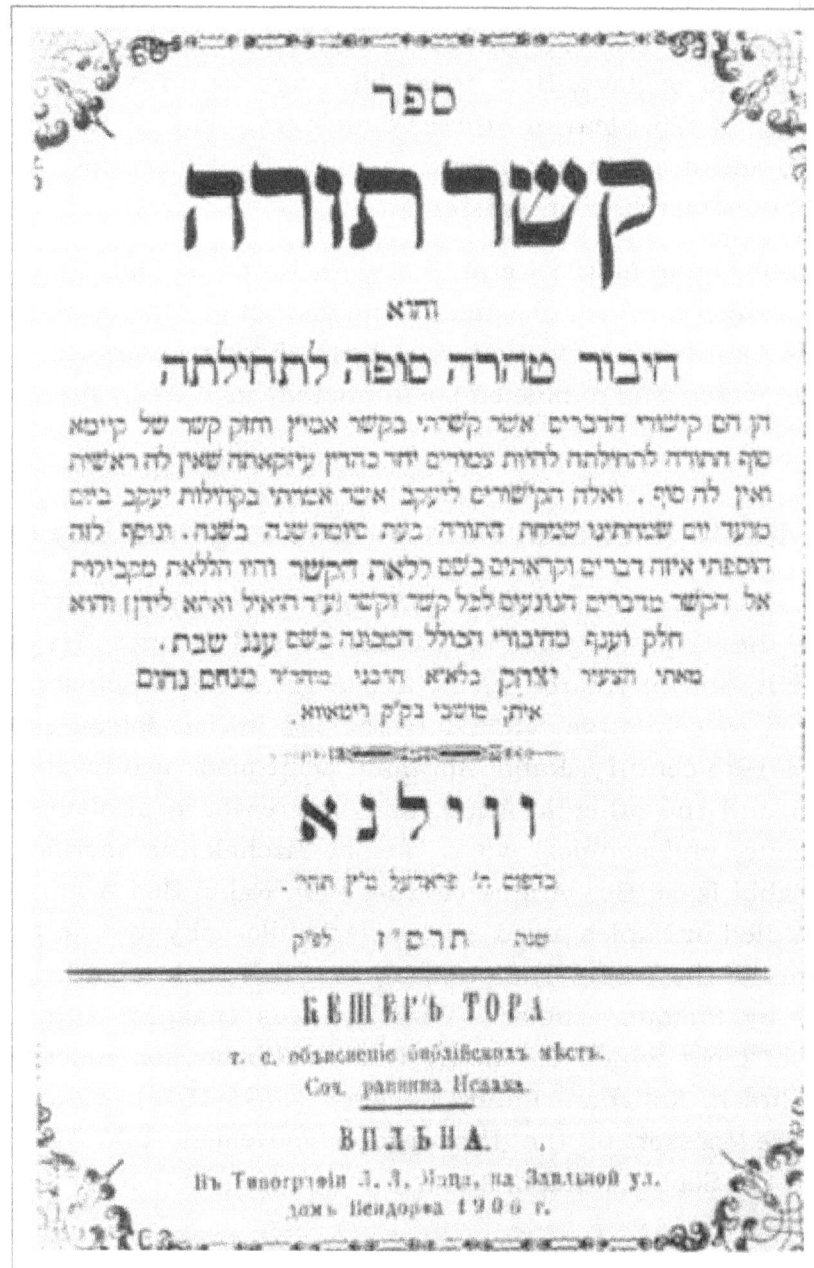

ספר
קשר תורה
והוא
חיבור טהרה סופה לתחילתה

הן הם קישורי הדברים אשר קשרתי בקשר אמיץ וחזק קשר של קיימא
סֵקֶה התורה לתחילתה לחיות צמודים יחד כהדרין עזוקאתה שאין לה ראשית
ואין לה סוף . ואלה הקישורים ליעקב אשר אמרתי בקהילות יעקב ביום
מועד יום שמחתנו שמחת התורה בעת סומה שנה בשנה . תיופא לזה
הוספתי איזה דברים וקראתים בשם כלאת הקשר והיו הללאת מקבילות
אל הקשר טדברים הנוגעים לכל קשר וקשר ועד האיל ואהא לידן והוא
חלק וענף מחיבורי וכולל המבונה בשם עֶנֶג שבת .

מאתי הצעיר יצחק כלאא חובני מהדיר מנחם נחום
איתן מושבי בק'ק ריטאווא.

ווילנא
בדפוס ה' פיראדעל בנ'ק תהר .
שנה תרס'ז לפ'ק

КЕШЕРЪ ТОРА
т. с. объяснение библейскихъ мѣстъ.
Соч. раввина Исаака.

ВИЛЬНА .
Въ Типографіи Л. Л. Мацъ, на Завальной ул.
домъ Вейдорфа 1906 г.

**Sefer Kesher Torah– title page from a book by
Itzchak Ben–Nachum Menachem Aharonowitz of
Riteve, published in Vilna 5667 (1906)**

[Page 94]

Rabbi Aron Zalmanowicz

Rabbi Avraham Aron
Burstein

Rabbi Chaim Zalman Ben–
Eliyahu Leib Karon

Rabbi Joseph Ze'ev Lipovitz

Of these rabbis, only their photographs were provided in the original book. They appear to be from the period between the wars, which suggests that they were well known in Riteve at the time and that the first readers would have required no further information about them.

[Page 95]

The two doctors

Growing up during the years of rabbis Bendet and Aharonowitz were two boys born in Riteve who were both to become doctors. This must have been recalled with pride, partly because it was so difficult for a Lithuanian Jew to qualify in such a profession, but also because of their distinguished careers. The first was Mendel Yehuda Leib Shera, born in Riteve in 1849, the son of Rabbi Vol Shlomo Shera, who received a true Torah education from his father. He studied at Telz and was graduated as a teacher at the age of 17 by the rabbis of the yeshiva with whom he participated in settling rabbinic disputes in the vicinity.

After the death of his father at the age of 45, Mendel Leib Shera decided to become a doctor of medicine. For this purpose, and with a great deal of application, he obtained a matriculation certificate and went to Berlin to study medicine. He obtained help from Rabbi Dr Azriel Hildesheimer and, at the age of about 29, succeeded in obtaining the degree of a doctor of medicine in 1878. He returned to Petersburg where he worked in a clinic and obtained permission to practise as a doctor, happy in the realisation of his dream. He moved to Riga and became well known in his profession. He earned the respect of his colleagues and of his patients, many of whom streamed to him for specialised attention.

With all his great professional success, he still continued his scholarly pursuits and regularly devoted time to Torah study. He corresponded with rabbis and heads of yeshivot and his home was a meeting place for scholars. With the establishment of the world body of Agudat Israel, he was invited by the leaders of the German Orthodox Movement to be a member of their council and he became one of their advisers. 'This man of Riteve, a synthesis of scientific and traditional learning,' wrote the anonymous writer in the original book, 'gained the honour and respect of the intellectual of Russia of that time.'

The second doctor was Elikum Yehuda Goldberg who was born in Kelm at a date unknown, but studied in Riteve during the mid–19th century and was most probably a contemporary of Dr Mendel Shera. It is not known where Dr Goldberg studied, but it was probably in Germany. He became a doctor in Zichron Ya'akov in the Land of Israel but, due to differences of opinion with officials of Baron Rothschild, he left there in 1885 for America. He settled in New York where he contributed greatly to Jewish learning. He wrote Talmudic commentary in which his vast learning was evident.

Getzel Zelikovitz – linguist and journalist

In 1865, about 25 years later than these two doctors, another boy was born in Riteve who was to follow a professional career, in this case the most unusual one of a specialist in Egyptian hieroglyphics – he was a notable linguist – and later as a writer. His name was Getzel Zelikovitz. In February 1913, on his fiftieth birthday, a tribute was paid to him and his efforts to maintain the Hebrew language by three professors, two rabbis, three judges, six publishers, nine fellow authors, the owners of the publishing company Yehuda Katzenelenbogen, two other individuals and no fewer than 30 Jewish and Hebrew organisations. This was commented on in an article on his life published in Hatzfira on 20 February 1913. Hatzfira wrote:'G. Selikovitch was born in Riteve in 1863 where he received a traditional education in the Cheder and Yeshiva. His father Reb David wished his son to be a Rabbi and by the age of 13 he was already known as the "Riteve genius'. Under the influence of his well–educated mother, Rachel, he learned Russian, German and Hebrew. An inheritance from his grandfather enabled him to go to Paris where, with his talent for languages, he studied Semitic languages at the Sorbonne under Ernest Renan, Joseph Durenberg, Josef Halevi, Julius Aport and others.

[Page 96]

In 1883 he went to Egypt as an interpreter of Arabic and English to the British Army. On his return to Paris in 1886 he continued his language studies and added hieroglyphics to his knowledge. At this time he started submitting articles and poetry to Ha–Melitz and Ha–Magid, both Hebrew newspapers. His travel memoirs were well known for their content and style. Later they appeared in a book published by the Tushiya Press.

In 1887, he travelled extensively in the Middle East and then to the United States. He was appointed faculty member of the University of Pennsylvania as lecturer in hieroglyphics. But he soon moved to New York where he became a journalist on the daily Yiddish paper Tagblat. He published profusely, both articles and humorous verse, under the pseudonym of 'The Lithuanian Philosopher'. The need to please the news– paper's management was not to Zelikovitz's liking. He stated frankly that his popular articles in Yiddish were specifically written to please the publisher and not according to his own taste. He wrote, too, that his real love was Hebrew, and he found himself longing to be able to write in that language. But this was not possible in the prevailing conditions of the time.

Rabbi Mordechai Izchak Segal who, from his appearance, ministered to Riteve between the wars. No Information was provided about him so he was probably well known to the first readers.

[Page 97]

The philanthropist Feige Rachel Hirshowitz (in the white scarf) and her family. This photograph appears to have been taken in the late 1920s. She was a leader of the Women's Society and provided funds for the modern mikveh (see pages 60 and 77)

Rabbi Berl Ritover

Memories of Riteve move now to later in the 19th century. Rabbi Bendet's son- in-law was Rabbi Berl Ritover, one of the leaders of the community and a scholar who, like Rabbi Bendet's son, Yoel, gave scholarly Talmudic lessons in Riteve to the Shas (Mishnah) group, among whom were the most learned men of Riteve. Rabbi Ritover had yiches through his descent from the great genius of Vilna, Rabbi Eliyahu. Rabbi Ritover's daughter married Rabbi Isaac Gershon Berman of Riteve who was a Maskil of the traditional type and a writer.

Rabbi Isaac Gershon Berman

In Rabbi Berman we see some of the stirrings against the Musar movement, which had a strong following in Riteve. This was a movement of the individual towards strict ethical behaviour in the spirit of the Halachah, as against the dangers of the modern era. It arose in the 19th century, continuing into the 20th. In the Jewish culture of the Mitnagdim (opposers to Hassidism) in Lithuania. The attempt of the Musarniks to introduce this trend into the yeshivot of Lithuania gave rise to sharp criticism from their opponents, who feared that the study of Musar would result in a neglect of Torah study. Rabbi Berman published a critical article in Ha–Melitz against the Musar Rabbi Jozel Hurwitz, author of Hachorim (the holes), which created a great stir among the readers of the Hebrew press.

[Page 98]

Rabbi Yitzchak Eliyahu Geffen, rabbi in Riteve contemporaneously with Rabbi Berman, remained'uninvolved during the days of the famous controversy between the Musar followers and us opponents, and did not openly come out in support of either side, nor did he make known his personal opinion on the matter'. Yet, wrote an anonymous author in the original book,'he privately upheld the inclusion of Musar teaching in the yeshivot for the purpose of strengthening and crystallising the spirituality of the students as a shield against the objectionable Haskalah movement which had begun to penetrate even the yeshiva circles'.

Rabbi Yitzchak Eliyahu Geffen

Rabbi Geffen was a most distinguished scholar. He was born in Vabolnik, where his father, Rabbi Daven Ben Zion Geffen, was the rabbi, and was taught by his father. Even as a young boy, he stood out among his peers and later studied for some time in the small town of Eishyshok. He married the daughter of Rabbi Shlomo Zalman Simcha Troyv, head of the rabbinical court of the prestigious community of Kaidan. For a number of years Rabbi Geffen sat in the house of learning in Kaidan, provided by his father–in–law, where he specialised in the theory and practice of teaching. Because of the greatness of his talents and expertise, he was made acting Moreh Tzedek. This appointment meant that he substituted for his father–in–law when the latter was absent from the city.

He later served for a time as the head of the yeshiva in Slobodka, Kovno which, founded in 1882, had become a large institution which attracted gifted young students from near and far. At this time, Rabbi Geffen lived in a lodging in Slobodka together with the spiritual leader of the yeshiva, the esteemed Rabbi Natan Zvi Finkel who was later to become known as 'the Grandfather from Slobodka'. From here, Rabbi Geffen moved on to become rabbi of Yosvein, a young community near Kaidan. When Rabbi Avraham Hacohen moved from Riteve to Aniksht, Rabbi Geffen was appointed to Riteve, which was an important community.

While he was at Riteve, Rabbi Geffen's reputation as a brilliant scholar grew. His father–in–law, the rabbi of Kaidan, frequently used to invite him to sit with him and deliberate over difficult Halachic laws or give his opinion in complicated matters concerning prohibition and authorisation. Rabbi Geffen would find solutions to these complicated problems, displaying knowledge and sensitivity.

His fame reached the prodigy, the renowned Rabbi Joseph Rosin, head of the rabbinical court of Dvinsk, Latvia. From the beginning, Rabbi Rosin realized Rabbi Geffen's potential and held him in the highest esteem. He recommended to the community of Freil, located near Dvinsk, that they hire Rabbi Geffen as chief head of the rabbinical court. However, Rabbi Yitzchak Elliyahu Geffen preferred to take up a position in the quiet, traditional town of Riteve, blessed with learned scholars. He remained in Riteve with these fellow scholars even after he began to receive propositions for better paying positions in more prestigious communities. He remained loyal to Riteve to his dying day.

[Page 99]

As the rabbi of the town, his brother–in– law's son, the exceptional Rabbi Avraham Eliyahu Kaplan, was under his direction for quite a time. The father of this prodigy, who died in the prime of life, had the same first names and was also an exceptional scholar. Rabbi Geffen directed his nephew's' studies from the very beginning, from the yeshiva boy of Telz and Slobodka to the head of the yeshiva in the Orthodox Rabbinical Seminary founded by Rabbi Dr Azriel Hildesheimer in Berlin. Dr Hildesheimer was a well–known 19th – century leader of German orthodox Jewry who led the struggle against the reform movement. The academy he founded was the most important of its kind in Western Europe.

**Rabbi Yitzchak Eliyahu
Geffen, rabbi of the town
before the ministry of Rabbi
Fundiler**

During the First World War when the Jews of Riteve were expelled to the cities of central Russia, Rabbi Yitzchak Eliyahu Geffen lived at Homel, where he gained the respect and esteem of the Jewish citizens, both Hassidim and Mitnagdim, of this large city. There he befriended Rabbi Dr Chaim Heller, who was also an emigre in Homel. From that time on, they kept up their friendship and correspondence, even when Rabbi Heller moved to Berlin, where he founded the'Academy for Advanced Study of the Torah and Jewish Wisdom' for outstanding Torah scholars.

Rabbi Geffen returned to Riteve. However, the negative effects of what he had experienced during the war depressed him greatly. He went to Koenigsberg together with his son, Rabbi Avraham Shimon Geffen, where he died in 1920.

Rabbi Avraham Shimon Geffen

Rabbi Avraham Shimon Geffen was born in Kaidan. For seven years he had an outstanding career at the famous Telz yeshiva where he was the pupil of the Illustrious scholar, Rabbi Eliezer Gordon. Rabbi Avraham Geffen was a member of the prominent Talmudic circle headed by Rabbi Chaim Ozer Grudzenski, one of Lithuania's greatest rabbis, head of the'Knesset Israel' yeshiva in Slobodka, Kovno – an admired teacher who died in July 1944 during the liquidation of the ghetto of Kovno. This Talmudic circle brought together all the best students of the Lithuanian yeshivot. Rabbi Avraham Geffen married into a well–known Riteve family but did not exploit his Talmudic knowledge as a source of livelihood. Instead, he became a merchant and owner of a respectable household in Riteve. He ran the Mishnah (Shas) circle in his local community and gave lessons regularly. He was an active Zionist and head of the leaders of the Keren Hayesod in the whole of Lithuania. With the economic crisis of 1922–26, his affairs declined and he and his family emigrated to America. He became a rabbi in New York and made a great contribution to education in Torah and Mitzvot. He latter settled in Bnei Brak, Israel, and he and his wife were privileged to see the establishment of the State, an ideal which was very close to his heart.

[Page 100]

Two boys born in Riteve in 1870 were to become distinguished rabbis, although the careers of both were to take them far from Lithuania: Rabbi Baruch Marcus and Rabbi Solomon Zalmonowitz.

Baruch Marcus was the son of Rabbi Meir Falk Marcus. He became a graduate of both Slobodka yeshiva and the Talmud Torah of Kelm. In 1891, he went to the Land of Israel on a mission inspired by his teacher, Rabbi Simcha Zissel, to found a Musar institution in Jerusalem and was, in fact, the pioneer of the Musar movement there. He founded, and for 14 years directed, Yeshiva 'Or Chadash' (new light) in Jerusalem, but in 1906 was persuaded to accept the post of rabbi of the Ashkenazi community of Haifa, which then numbered about 50 families. After a distinguished career, which included being one of the founders of the Chief Rabbinate of Israel and a member of its council, becoming instrumental in its legal deliberations, he died in Haifa in 1961

**Rabbi Avraham Shimon
Geffen, one of the dynasty of
rabbis, weaver of the golden
threads of the spirit of Israel
in the United States. At the
time of the publication of
the original book, he was
living in New York**

Rabbis Baruch Marcus and Solomon Zalmonowitz

[Page 101]

About Rabbi Baruch Marcus's contemporary, Rabbi Solomon Zalmonowitz, there is a tradition that he was the model for Chaim Nachman Bialik's famous poem, 'The faithful Yeshiva student'. This poem became the symbol of generations of yeshiva students, absorbed in their studies, cut off from the surrounding world. Rabbi Zalmonowitz gained prominence as an exemplary and diligent student at the Telz and Volozchin yeshivot. Bialik was a student at Volozchin from 1890–91, at the same time as the Riteve scholar.

Rabbi Zalmonowitz served as rabbi and head of the Beit–Din in Safizishuk in the province of Kovno and, after this, in Dokshitz, which was a border town between the wars. In 1924, round about the same time as Rabbi Avraham Geffen went to the United States, he emigrated to Canada and served as rabbi in Montreal until the day of his death in 1941. He was chairman of the Rabbinical Committee of Montreal and an honorary member of the Association of Orthodox Rabbis of America and Canada. Although works of his appeared in HaPardess, a monthly journal on Torah subjects produced in Chicago, he left many manuscripts on learned Torah subjects which were never published.

The Musar movement

The Musar movement aimed for the education of the individual towards strict ethical behaviour in the spirit of the Halachah, as against the dangers of the modern era. It arose in the 19th century, continuing into the 20th century, in the Jewish culture of the Mitnagdim (opposers of Hassidism) in Lithuania, becoming a trend in its yeshivot. The attempt of the Musarniks to introduce this trend into the yeshivot in Lithuania gave rise to sharp criticism from their opponents who feared that the study of Musar would result in a neglect of Torah study.

As memories of personalities of Riteve turn towards the 20th century, we see the childhood memories of survivors of the Holocaust and shtetl'characters' and teachers are remembered.

Ya'acov Leviatan

Alter Levite

Ya'acov Leviatan was a marvel to all. He was known in Yiddish as Yankel der Lerer, namely Jacob the teacher. It was wonderful to see his meticulously clean appearance, when all the townsfolk found it difficult to keep their clothing from being soiled by the muddy streets. He, on the other hand, always sported polished shoes, which was regarded as a wonder.

[Page 102]

Ya'acov Leviatan

He came to Riteve as a Hebrew teacher and not as a 'Melamed', that familiar cheder teacher. He had accepted an invitation from the Zionists, followers of Herzl, to take up the post. The Zionists were regarded as dangerous rebels by the traditionalists, who feared their influence. Yankel spoke gently to the children and he did not use the cane, which was commonplace in the cheder. He introduced the use of spoken Hebrew. He sold the Keren Kayemet stamps and the shekels for Zionist funds, which were earmarked for buying land in Palestine from the Arabs for the settlers who would come from all over the world.

His opponents accused him of capturing souls, or wanting to convert Jewish children. Leviatan gave his own children unconventional names like Theodor Herzl, and he had the courage to say Kaddish in the synagogue when this 'strange' man died. The orthodox element was so shocked to hear Herzl's name in a holy place that they made a terrible noise to disturb the prayer.

How did this man come to Riteve? He had been a teacher in Sweden, where he was one of the founders of the Zionist movement. He taught the children songs which contained a Zionist message, that is that the Jews should leave the wasteland of the Diaspora and go to Palestine. He brought with him books written in a style suitable for children, which his opponents regarded as dangerous, 'extraneous' books.

He had difficulty in finding suitable premises for the new type of cheder which, by a play on the Hebrew words, was made to mean 'the dangerous' cheder. The only accommodation was in a widow's house where she also had the candle factory, which gave off a stench. But the children were so enchanted by him and his new teaching methods that they did not notice the smell. They enjoyed the stories of the Bible presented in a realistic way. The Lag Ba'Omer outing into the forest with songs taught by the teacher expressed the Jewish yearning for freedom.

Unfortunately, Ya'acov Leviatan did not remain in Riteve. His wife's family in Copenhagen heard of him and his great abilities and he was offered a post there as secretary of the community in the big city, where he spent many years. This was a great loss to the enlightened members of the Riteve community for it was not easy to find another teacher who would be a friend and pedagogue to their children.

[Page 103]

Riteve 'characters' – Elka Ittes and others

Mirian Zvik

Elka Ittes was a saintly lady whose concern it was that the poor should not lack food on the Sabbath. On Wednesdays and Thursdays she would go around to the housewives to collect donations of bread, meat and so on for the needs of the poor she knew so well.

She would teach the women to read from the prayer book and also from the popular women's Bible Tze'enah Urenah. We would come to hear the words of the Torah from her lips. She lived modestly in one room that served as a living room, a bedroom and a kitchen. She had two sleeping benches, one at the window and one at the table. We, her students, sat around the table waiting to be examined by Elka, who sat there with her pointer in her hand.

Sometimes she would rope us in to help her prepare her husband's meal, which always consisted of yellow peas. While we sorted the peas, we would sing Yiddish songs like 'A Brivelle der Mame' (a letter from Mama) or one of her favourites called 'Menshele' (a small person). Between songs, she would be busy with the preparation for the meal and would shed a tear of happiness and contentment. She was blessed with two sons who were Torah scholars.

There were other lovable personalities in town like Sore the 'Drei Kop' (chatterbox, a nag, a nudnik) and Meir Yanke 'The Hare' who would call people to the synagogue with the cry 'To Shul! To Shul! ' When there was a funeral, he would knock on the doors, calling out 'Kum zu die Levaya!' (come to the funeral).

Riteve 'characters' – Leib der Satnik

Rivka Zaltsman

Leib der Satnik was the courier of the bank and postman to the Jewish community. He was a wise and lovable man, loyal and honest. Even though he did not know foreign languages, he never made a mistake delivering invitations or letters.

I used to be very fond of him. He would tell me stories of the early days of the Oginskis since his family had been in Riteve for many generations. For his loyal service, he received a medal for excellence from the president of Lithuania, Antanas Smetona.[4] He was survived by many descendants spread throughout the world.

Two rabbis of the early 20th century: Rabbi Avraham Aaron Borstein and Rabbi Moshc Aharon Davidowitz

The Jews of Riteve followed with pride the careers of those associated with their town, whether they were born there or served there. One who was a rabbi there for a comparatively short time, probably around the turn of the century, was Rabbi Avraham Aaron Borstein, born in about 1867, a celebrated scholar who was considered third in the hierarchy of great rabbinic teachers, coming after Rabbi Chaim Halevi Soloveichik ard Rabbi Itzchak Yaacov Rabinowitz of Ponevezh. Being an individualist, however. Rabbi Borstein resigned as head of the yeshiva at Slobodka, Kovno,[5] and became rabbi first at Zamut, then in turn at five other towns, Tsitovian, Riteve, Anikst, Shadove and Tavrig. Former students wanted him to return to teaching and so he founded a small centre of Talmudic study at Tabruk. He was finally to emigrate to Eretz Israel in the 1920s, but was a sick man as a result of his sufferings in the Ukraine where he was a refugee during the First World War. He died in 1926 aged only 59.

[Page 104]

Another Riteve rabbi of the early years of the 20th century was Rabbi Moshe Aharon Davidowiiz, son of Rabhi Avli Movson, author of Ahavat Eitan on the Mishnah and its scholars. Rabbi Mosie Davidowitz's daughter, Ruth, married Rabbi Moshe Shurin (Mishuris) who, through this marriage, was eventually to live in Riteve.

Rabbi Moshe Shurin (Mishuris)

Rabbi Shurin was born in 1890 in Turtsin in the province of Volliymia, Russia.6 He studied under Rabbi Chaim Soloveichik in Brisk, and at the famous Mir yeshiva in northwest Byelorussia, founded by Rabbi Samuel Tiktinski in 1815. This yeshiva played a central role in the spiritual life of the community and became known among Jews in Eastern Europe. (Fortunately, before the German invasion during the Second World War, its students and rabbis all managed to escape and reach Shanghai, where they stayed in the local ghetto until the end of the war.) Moshe Shurin studied at Mir for two years and then spent a further two at the yeshiva at Novogrudok, also in northwest Byelorussia and one of the main yeshivot of the Musar movement. He was only 21 when he married and, after this, he continued improving his knowledge of Mishnah and Law at the Kollel of Kovno and was ordained as a rabbi by the great rabbis of Kovno and Slobodka. Rabbi Shapira, Rabbi Epstein and Rabbi Leibowitz. Rabbi Shurin then accepted a post as rabbi in the small town of Navran, 14 kilometres from Telz, where, before the Holocaust, there lived only about 100 Jews. Soon after he took up this position, however, the First World War broke out and he moved to Riteve where his father–in–law still lived. It is not recorded whether or not the family had to leave during the war but, in 1916, Rabbi Shurin founded a yeshiva at Riteve which he ran for 12 years.

In 1928, he received a call to Cambridge, Massachusetts in the United States and, in his seven years of ministry in this place, he took advantage of the famous institutions of learning there to pass his matriculation and to complete two years of study at Harvard. During this time, he gave weekly lectures in Judaic subjects to the Jewish students. He then became a rabbi in the Bronx, New York. Throughout this period his family remained in Riteve.

[Page 105]

In 1935, he emigrated to Israel, taking his family with him. He lived first in Jerusalem and then became an administrative organiser of the yeshiva of Petach Tikvah. Two years later, he returned to America without his family, who joined him in 1939 after the outbreak of the Second World War. Here he became a rabbi in the synagogue of the people of Slutsk (Landsleit) in New York, dying there in 1941.

Rabbi Moshe Shurin had six children, four daughters, Chaviva, Chasida, Ella and Dana, who all married rabbis and heads of yeshivot in America, and two sons, both rabbis, Aharon Ben–Zion, who was also an author, and Israel, who became a rabbi in Brooklyn, New York.

Rabbi Moshe Shurin
(Mishuris)

Rabbi Aharon Ben–Zion Shurin

Rabbi Aharon Ben–Zion Shurin[7] was born in Riteve in 1913, probably at his grandparents' home as this was before the family's move. He studied at the cheder at Riteve and in the local yeshiva headed by his father, and later in Telz and Ponevezh. He went to Israel with his parents in 1935. He studied in the yeshivot of Hebron and Petach Tikvah and also at a night school. While in Petach Tikvah, he played a part in its defence during the riots of the Arab Revolt from 1936–39 that broke out two weeks after his arrival. During this three–year period of disorder and violence, Arabs in Palestine revolted against both the Jews and the British administration.

In 1939, he was ordained by the great rabbis, Chief Rabbi Herzog, Rabbi Melzer and Rabbi Katz of Petach Tikvah. Rabbi Shurin went with his family to America in 1939 where he studied science for four years at Yeshiva University and also at Columbia. He also lectured on Hebrew language and literature at Yeshiva University. He edited the Hebrew section of a memorial book which was brought out in honour of the head of the institution, Rabbi Dr Dov Devel.

In 1942, Rabbi Shurin was appointed rabbi of the congregation of Slutsk in New York, his late father's post, and two years later married Aliza, daughter of Rabbi Moshe Rivkin, head of Brooklyn Yeshiva Torah Va'Daat (Torah and knowledge). In 1945, he was appointed to the synagogue 'Torah Moshe' in Brooklyn and was also head of the new Talmud Torah. He was a member of the Assembly of Rabbis of America and a member of the Jewish writers' and journalists' club of New York, named for YL Peretz. Also in 1945, he helped to found the organisation of workers, Agudat Israel, in America and was its first vice– president. Later he cut himself off from political activity.

[Page 106]

His literary work had started in Lithuania with articles in the journal of Telz, and later in Kol Israel, a weekly newspaper of Agudat Israel in Jerusalem. In America, he wrote literary articles in Hebrew in two rabbinical monthlies and also in the Yiddish press, contributing to the orthodox press of the youth movement and editing its journal. Two of his articles were published in a special publication, one being a biography of Rabbi Fundiler for the original volume of this work (see below). From 1944 onwards, he wrote regularly for the daily Yiddish paper Forward about the love of Eretz Israel and the hallowed values to be found in Jewish thought and history. Many of his articles were signed by the author and others made use of his pseudonyms, either AB Roztan or YYD, the initials of his sons, Yaacov, Yosef and David.

Rabbi Aharon Ben–Zion Shurin, living in New York at the time of the publication of the original book

Two famous Riteve rabbis, who built up the Riteve yeshiva and developed it into a well–respected institution of learning, were Rabbi Joseph Ze'ev Lipowitz and Rabbi Shmuel Fundiler. who worked together from 1912–1924. Rabbi Fundiler, however, who was Riteve's last rabbi, appears to have arrived before Rabbi Lipowitz and died with his people in the Holocaust.

Rabbi Shmuel Fundiler

Rabbi Ben–Zion Shurin

Rabbi Shmuel Fundiler was one of the greatest rabbinic personalities in the years before the Holocaust. He was among the leaders of the fourth generation of the Musar movement and exerted a great moral influence on his own generation. He was known as Rabbi Shmuel Brezner by his yeshiva associates because of the name of his birthplace, Brezin (Berezin).

[Page 107]

He received his initial Musar instruction from his mentor, Rabbi Natan Zvi Finkel (the 'Grandfather of Slobodka'), and was also a pupil of the great teacher Rabbi Simcha Zissel Ziv at the Talmud Torah of Kelm. At Slobodka, he acquired the practical knowledge of Musar and its application in everyday life, whereas at Kelm he acquired its theoretical potential. Here he delved deeply into the study of the potential basis of man's soul. These two elements created a wonderful harmony in his personality.

Rabbi Shmuel Fundiler was born in Berezin in the province of Minsk in 1875. His father was Rabbi Isaac Fundiler, son of Rabbi Reuben Fundiler, and his mother's name was Hilda. While only an infant, he was brought before Rabbi Israel Salanter (of Salent) Lipkin, the leading rabbi of the Musar movement, and the great rabbi blessed him. His talents were recognised early and his parents spared no effort in acquiring the very best teachers for their son. He was sent to Slobodka to the yeshiva bearing the name of Rabbi Israel Salanter, namely, 'Knesset Israel'. Here he came under the influence of Rabbi Isaac Jacob Rabinowitz, known as Rabbi Itzel of Ponevezh, who was head of the yeshiva. Rabbi Finkel encouraged Rabbi Fundiler in his studies and he became his close associate. Rabbi Fundiler later supported Rabbi Finkel in the great dispute which raged at Slobodka on the issue of the inclusion of Musar studies in the curriculum of the famous yeshivot of White Russia and Lithuania, namely Slutzsk, Mir, Telz and Slobodka itself.

(Rabbi Ben–Zion Shurin did not state where Rafchi Fundiler came to Riteve. Editors) He had a strong influence on Riteve and its institutions as he was respected by the business community as well as all other sections of the town. When, for example, the butchers came to him for a legal decision, he would delve into Halachic sources and deal leniently with them, so as to prevent pecuniary losses.

**Rabbi Shmuel Fundiler,
the last rabbi of Riteve**

The yeshiva students enjoyed his classes in Gemara and also in Ethics. He gave outstanding sermons to the general community. On Yom Kippur, he would lead the prayers for 'Ne'ila' (the concluding service). He also read the Torah portions on Rosh Hashanah and, in particular, the portion from the Prophets which, on this particular day, deals with Hannah who was childless. This was a very poignant occasion since he and his wife were themselves childless.

[Page 108]

Rabbi Fundiler devoted time and energy to the education of youth. He had a great understanding of the young, even though he had no children of his own, and when he recruited teachers for the boys' and girls' schools in Riteve, he looked for people who would teach with love and not with intimidation. He also opposed excessive party politicking, opposing the founding of parties, even religious parlies. He would say that strife was not a Jewish quality since strife leads to blind hatred which was the cause of the destruction of

Jerusalem. Although he yearned to emigrate to the Land of Israel, he did not attain his ideal.

Rabbi Joseph Ze'ev Lipowitz

Rabbi Joseph Ze'ev Lipowitz was the son of Rabbi Baruch Lipowitz of Treshner. in the district of Bialystok, who was a learned scholar and educated his son to follow in his footsteps. The young man studied at the Bialystok yeshiva, where he excelled. A turning point in his life was when, at the age of 16. he went to study at Slobodka with 'the Grandfather' at Knesset Israel, where he came under the influence of the Musar movement. Under the tutelage of Rabbi Mordecai Epstein, he was appointed to give the daily lesson to the townsfolk of Slobodka at the Chevra Shas, where there were ten minyanim (prayer quorums).

In 1912, he married the daughter of a well–to–do family in Riteve, where he settled, establishing a junior yeshiva and giving a daily lesson without any remuneration. Many of his pupils later went on to yeshivot in other towns and were very successful. He and Rabbi Fundiler built up the Riteve yeshiva and developed it into a well–respected institution of learning. On the High Holidays, Rabbi Lipowitz would return to Slobodka and renew his relationship with the rabbis and yeshiva heads and also give lectures on the preliminary steps of the Musar movement.

He spent some time in Berlin where he attended the lectures of Rabbi Raphael Hirsch of Frankfurt am Main, leader of German Orthodox Jewry. He was able to continue his Musar training with Hirsch's views and commentaries on the Bible.

In 1924, he settled his affairs and emigrated to Palestine where he settled in Tel Aviv and became a teacher in the Tachkemoni high school. Many Slobodka students also emigrated to Palestine with their rabbis, Moshe Epstein and Neta Hirsch. They established a yeshiva in Hebron, the city of the Patriarchs, and Rabbi Joseph Ze'ev was once again in their company on festivals while they would frequent his home in Tel Aviv. When the Tel Aviv yeshiva 'Agudat Torah' was established, he was among its teachers.

[Page 109]

The artist Avraham Izchak Goldberg, who was born in Riteve in 1910 and died in 1970. He studied painting at schools in Montreal, Canada and received a Decoration for Excellence from the directorate of the museum in Montreal. Before his emigraiion, he was a student at the Slobodka yeshiva and lived with a religious family. One day, the lady of the house noticed that Alter, as he was called, was drawing and she informed the head of the yeshiva. For this sin he was expelled from the yeshiva. His family was very upset, but his mother immediately approached the rabbi of the time, Rabbi Fundiler. The rabbi called Alter and granted the mother's request to allow him to return to the yeshiva on condition that he sign an agreement that he would not continue drawing. Aiter's answer was unambiguous. 'Truly I will promise never to draw again: however, I will not sign an agreement.'

Above right: A self–portrait of the. artist. A photograph of him in a group taken, at the Hebrew School – see page 41 – and the list on page 36 indicate that he became a teacher there briefly before emigrating.

In 1926, a society of yeshiva graduates was formed on 'the Grandfathers' initiative, and Rabbi Joseph Ze'ev was its moving spirit. His home in Lilienblum Street, Tel Aviv, was the centre of study and of minyanim for many years. He was among the founders of the Kollel 'Hechal Ha–Talmud' (palace of the Talmud) and was instrumental in getting the philanthropists Pollak and Olitsky to contribute

[Page 110]

a suitable site for this venture. He was principal of Yeshiva 'Or Zoreach' (a glowing light) at N've Shalom and lecturer to the Workers' Organisation of Agudat Israel in Tel Aviv. He was a great supporter of Rabbi Joseph Kahaneman's Talmudic enterprise, in memory of the Ponevezh yeshiva, at Bnei Brak. He was active in all the Ponevezh institutions in Israel and also in the field of memorialising Lithuanian Jewry, as for example at Kiryat Ponevezh.

He died in 1962 after a severe illness and was mourned by many. The orthodox press paid tribute to his numerous activities in Riteve, Ponevezh and, above all, in Israel. His friends had two of his works published: Nachlat Yosef, on the Book of Ruth, and a commentary on the Torah. In these two books the author quotes widely from the ideas of the Grandfather', Rabbi Natan Zvi Finkel, but he also adds original and logical arguments of his own.

Rabbi David [Dov] Zvi Heiman

Undoubtedly a pupil of rabbis Lipowitz and Fundiler was Rabbi David Zvi Heiman,8 born in Riteve in 1902. He was later to study at Slobodka and Telz and at Hebron in Eretz Israel. He was graduated as a rabbi in Jerusalem by the great rabbis Moshe Mordecai Epstein, Isar Zalman Melzer and Eliyahu Klotzkin. He emigrated to the United States in 1931 and became a rabbi in Minneapolis. In 1947, he was appointed head of the Yeshiva Chofetz Chaim in Baltimore. He was also a member of the Association of Orthodox Rabbis of America and Canada and a member of the executive council of the Mizrachi organisation of America.

Before completely leaving the period before the First World War, Abraham Shabtai Movashovitz should be mentioned. An anonymous writer recollected him around 1909.

Abraham Shabtai Movashovitz

There are people whose lives seem to be a riddle, who seem strange in their ways. Such an unusual person was Abraham Shabtai Movashovitz, who lived in Riteve in the period of the Revival, when the Zionist movement became active. If one had seen him going about his business in Riteve dressed in farmer's clothes, one would not have realised that he was someone extraordinary. His clothing – high boots and a short jacket of leather – made him look like one of the masses. But whoever knew him, knew that he was a very refined person. He was born in Kupishik (a small town 40 kilometres east of Ponevezh), studied at Slobodka and qualified as a teacher. He was well acquainted with Hebrew literature and was a devoted Zionist.

Rabbi David [DOV] Zvi Heiman

[Page 111]

He worked hard on behalf of the Hebrew school, both materially and spiritually. How sad that he died young after an operation in Koenigsberg. He was survived by his wife, three daughters ard a son. Many in Riteve honoured his memory and regarded highly his generous contributions to the building of the Hebrew school, which was a centre of culture in Riteve. His memory is enshrined as on a tombstone of marble, among the personalities of Riteve.

Athough Abraham Movashovitz qualified as a teacher, it seems unlikely that he followed this profession, or he would not have been able to make generous contributions to the Hebrew school nor would he have walked about the town dressed as a farmer. It is likely that he followed some sort of agricultural pursuit, possibly as a broker of agricultural produce. Editors.

Zalman Leib Levite – a teacher of the 1920s

Alter Levite (his brother)

Zalman Leib Levite, who was a man of great achievements and rare spirit, invested much energy in the Hebrew school the first in Riteve. In the days before Hebrew textbooks were published, he and Shimon Varkul and myself were involved in solving this problem. After much effort, some fairly simple methods were devised. One was a device used by the German underground at the end of the First World War, called a spirograph, in which the contents of the lesson were written in special ink on smooth paper and the written words would sink into the gelatine on the device. In our home, there would be meetings whose aim was to prepare the lessons by this method and copy them for the needs of the children.

Although Levite was not a qualified teacher, he fulfilled his duties with great dedication. I can still picture my brother in his classroom, teaching arithmetic and Hebrew. He married in Tavrig and the young couple emigrated to the Land of Israel.

[Page 112]

A photograph of Rabbi Joel Dov Saks, which appears to have been taken in the 1930s, was placed in the orginal book without explanation, suggesting that he was well known to the readers

Hillel Saks, another teacher of the 1920s

Alter Levite

Hillel Saks was bom in Riteve in 1899, the son of Riva and Simcha Saks. He excelled at school and was therefore sent to the Telz yeshiva where he also shone. He was gifted musically and played the mandolin which gave hours of pleasure to his audiences. He had a strong interest in people and a desire to improve their lot. After the First World War, he moved to Kovno and studied at the teachers' seminary of 'Tseirei Zion'. He taught in various places and was considered one ot the best teachers in Lithuania. During the Second World War, he died a martyr having suffered at the hands of the Nazis. May his blood be avenged.

Lastly, the touching reminiscence that Chanoch (Zundel) Prisman gave of her father, Rabbi Eliezer Ze'ev Prisman, a man born in Riteve who remained there and typified both the scholar and the townsman, for he became a shopkeeper and was also the typical keen Zionist.

Rabbi Eliezer Ze'ev Prisman

Chanoch (Zundel) Prisman

My father, Rabbi Eliezer Ze'ev Prisman, was born in Riteve. His father was Rabbi Yehoshua Klonimus Prisman. I did not know my grandfather, but he was reputed to have been a scholar and teacher in the Beit Midrash. My father absorbed from him his devotion to Torah and the fear of G–d. While I do not know the details of my father's youth, I assume that he studied at a cheder and at a yeshiva as did all the good students in Lithuania at that time.

During the dispute between the exponents of the Musar and their opponents in the Slobodka yeshiva, my father changed over from the'Knesset Israel' of the Musar movement to the'Knesset Beit Yittchak', which opposed the Musar faction. On leaving the yeshiva, he married my mother, Esther Gittel Bloch, from Plungyan. He then opened a shop for pharmaceutical products, where he earned his living up until the Holocaust that mowed down Lithuanian Jewry.

[Page 113]

From his youth he was a Zionist supporter and member of the Hibbat Zion movement. He did not hide these Zionist sympathies even in his yeshiva days. With the rise of the Zionist organisation, he devoted himself to it wholeheartedly. He worked for the Keren Kayemet and Keren Hayesod and was also active in per– suading people to 'Take the Shekel', namely, to donate regularly a small sum that served as a sort of membership fee in the Zionist movement. His home was the centre for Zionist emissaries who came from the centre in Kovno to enlist members and collect contributions to its funds.

The orthodox element was opposed to Zionist activities, but my father resisted their opposition and even the obstacles they put in his way and remained loyal to the Zionist ideal. He saw in the Balfour Declaration an important step towards the complete redemption of the Jewish people and looked forward to the rise of an independent Jewish state.

Rabbi Joseph Itzikowitz by his son, Itzchak Itzikowitz.

Rabbi Joseph Itzikowitz was born in the city of Shvckshna in Riteve. He studied at yeshivot until the age of 21. He was exceptionally talented, an able reader and an outstanding cantor with a beautiful voice. For many years, he was the teacher in the Talmud Torah. He interested his pupils in the stories of the Talmud, which flowed like gathering spring. All his paths and his ways were holy. His faith was his guiding principle from his earliest youth until the last moment of his life. He was killed in the Holocaust together with the members of his family

How sad that his dream was not fulfilled. He did not live to see the establishment of the State of Israel. Tragically he was murdered with all the inhabitants of Riteve by the Nazis and their Lithuanian collaborators on Tamuz, 1941.

[Page 114]

'May his soul be bound up with life' with all the martyrs of our people and may G–d avenge their blood.

Footnotes

1. Article in *Hapeless* (the balance.) in 1905, a rabbinical monthly edited by Rabbi Eliyahu Akiva Rabinowitch, rabbi of Poltave. Quoted by the anonymous writer of the brief item on Rabbi Yaffe in the original book.

2. This fact is known because in 1842 a book named *Ateret Shaul* (Crown of Shaul), written by Rabb: Shaul Luria, the head of the Rabbinic Court in Shavla, was published and, in a list of those endorsing it, is the name of Rabbi Bendel, son of Yoel, the rabbi of Riteve.

3. His career was extensively described in the original book, but as a is available in musical reference works has been omitted from this account as his connection with Riteve was tenuous.

4. Antanas Smetona, the president of Lithuania, governed with strong-arm methods from 1926 until 1940.

5. A leading yeshiva in Eastern Europe which was dedicated to the ideals of the Musar movement.

6. David Tidhar. *Encyclopaedia of the Pioneers and the Builders of the Vishuv*, Tel Aviv, 1959. Vol. 10, pp. 3743-3745.

7. Ibid.

8. Simcha Alberg. *HaPardess* (jubilee book). New York 1951, p. 97

[Page 115]

Chapter Seven

Public and Zionist Institutions

Townsfolk

'In a place where two Jews reside, one may find three synagogues' goes a famous Jewish saying which portrays a national characteristic: to be one nation or one community or even one family, with dozens of political, religious, cultural and other conflicting convictions. The Lithuanian shtetl had a special blend of orthodoxy and Zionism, Hebrew and Yiddish, socialists and a few rightists, reaching some kind of harmony despite the disputes. Also, the number of the various institutes, parties and youth movements existing in one small place is amazingly high.

DP

The Maccabi in Riteve

Alter Levite (Original editor)

With the flourishing of the Jewish autonomy in Lithuania, there grew up a new move– ment whose motto was 'a healthy soul in a healthy body'. This was the movement of Maccabi. In every village there were young people who said that if we want to be a nation like all other nations, we have to attend to the youth so that we will be healthy in body and in soul. In Riteve this movement found wide scope.

Harry Singer[1], who now lives in Sea Point, Cape Town in South Africa, gave me some important data about the Maccabi and I am relating it as I received it from him.[2] Harry Singer, or'Hirshke Nachoum, Yanke Mendes', gives the following account:

In the summer of 1924, I happened to be in Kovno. the capital of Lithuania, and I saw a football match between Maccabi Kovn, and Ha–Ko'ach (the Star) Vienna.

The entrance to the Oginski estate, drawn from a photograph by Dean Simon.

[Page 116]

'Athletics classes' were a popular part of Maccabi Riteve.
Above: Maccabi Riteve 'Pyramid'.

The girls of Maccabi Riteve with decorated Hoops among the equipment.

[Page 117]

Two groups of Maccabi boys in Riteve.

In the photograph above, they appear to be in the uniform used for athletic classes and in the photgraph below, most of them are dressed for football.

[Page 118]

I decided to organise a Maccabi Riteves.

When I came home, I told a few people about the idea to found this organisation. We appointed Moshe Zelker as chairman of the organization, Berka Freedman the secretary, and I. the captain of the football team. I taught my friends, my comrades, the rules of the game, and we started to train ourselves. We appointed Mendel Segal to be the referee and Aaron Eppel, the photographer, was a member of the committee.

The Graaf Zalutsky, the heir of Oginski, came to our assistance. He gave us a field where we could train and also boards to make benches for spectators to sit on. The Graaf also became the goalkeeper of Maccabi, although he was not a Jew. Our young people showed a great interest in the game and learnt, all the rules pertaining to it. We played against pupils of the Lithuanian Gymnasium and we were successful.

On Lag Ba'Omer 1925, we invited the Maccabi of the nearby village of Plungyan to come and play in Riteve against our Maccabi. This Lag Ba Omer turned out to be a great festival for us. Here all the people of the village turned out on the football field to see the game. We invited a special orchestra to accompany the players from the village to the sportsfield. I was very surprised to see young and old marching along with us on the way.

We, the Maccabi of Riteve, were defeated because our competitors knew the game and all its tricks very well, but our moral victory was very great. We showed the people that we were able to achieve something. Besides the moral victory, we also had a substantial income from the tickets sold, so there was enough money now to enable us to invite an instructor to come from Kovno to teach us gymnastics in general and football in particular.

Our Maccabi made wonderful progress until the day came when we lost our money and this happened as a result of the following incident. We were playing one Sunday against the pupils of the Lithuanian Gymnasium and an argument arose between one of our members and one of the Lithuanians. One of our members accidentally kicked one of the Lithuanians who demanded new gold teeth. We had no choice but to pay. Naturally, we became very poor and were unable to pay for the instructor from Kovno.

[Page 119]

**Ze'irei Zion (Youth of Zion) Committee of Riteve,
5684-5688 (1923/24 – 1927/28)**

I am unable to record what happened afterwards, because I left Lithuania to emigrate to South Africa, but I shall never forget those wonderful days. The Maccabi was an experiment for the Jews to put down roots in a country which did not belong to them. We thought that we had come to stay there, but all our troubles were in vain. A flood of fire came and earned those things away, and also those plans of Maccabi were destroyed by the murderers.

The Zionist movement in Riteve – 1909

Author unknown

At the end of the month of Elul (September), a Zionist congress was held for the provinces of Kovno and Suvalk. From the province of Kovno there were eight representatives including one from Riteve. This testified to the importance of the Zionist movement in Riteve since there were many places like Plungyan, Telz and Salant which only sent one delegate to represent all three towns. There were also large towns which were not represented at all. Riteve's delegate represented the Zionists of Riteve in their own right. One of Riteve's active members was the well–known scholar Rabbi Eliezer Prisman who, while still a student at the Slobodka Yeshiva 'Beit Yitzhak', had openly announced his membership in the Zionist movement, to the chagrin of his teachers. He stood at the head of a group of yeshiva students who were Zionists (and became well known for their Zionist activities many years later) and who obtained help from Kovno for their under– takings. He foiled an attempt by Ya'acov Lifshitz who had tried to gather a group of rabbis and ultra–orthodox activists to pursue anti–Zionist activities. Prisman and Ben–Zion Dinaburg (later Professor Ben–Zion Dinur of the Hebrew University and minister of education in the Israeli cabinet) were in close contact with the Zionists of Kovno (Isser Ber Wolf, Moshe Bramson and others). Thus the efforts of the anti–Zionists did not bear fruit.

[Page 120]

Among the people of Riteve, Joseph Levite contributed greatly to the Zionist effort. He later lived in Warsaw. Levite was born in Riteve and received a traditional education. In Warsaw he was the first of the Zionists to be chosen as an administrator of the Warsaw community in 1908, a time when the Zionists and the moderate orthodox leaders had united for the purpose of elections. Levite embarked on a project to improve the Talmudei Torah (primary schools) which were under the control of the community. However, he provoked the opposition of the assimilaiionists and also the Hassidim in his attempt to introduce the teaching of Jewish history in Yiddish and the teaching of Hebrew in the beginners' classes and in the girls' schools, which numbered 20 at that time.

Keren Kayemet – Jewish National Fund (JNF)

The dissemination of the Zionist ideal of redemption of the land and the collecting of funds were restricted to the 'plates' into which donations were placed in the synagogue on the eve of the Day of Atonement. The community contributed generously to the 'plate', decorated with blue and white. Another educational activity for the benefit of the JNF[3] was conducted among the school children, who acquired JNF stamps and contributed to the Blue Box. The day–to–day contributions were not large, but were given willingly. Nevertheless, it was necessary to go from house to house to explain the need for contributions.

Keren Hayesod

Keren Hayesod[4] conducted its fundraising by means of a special annual campaign at which funds were pledged. The number of Riteve inhabitants who contributed yearly kept increasing. The opening of the campaign was attended by important personalities from Kovno and all of Lithuania.

The chairman of the two national funds was Eliezer Prisman.

[Page 121]

Left: Rabbi Eliezer Prisman, worker and activist, Jewish National Fund

Right: Shimon Varkul, one of the communal workers of Rlteve, who became one of the first senior workers of the Tel Aviv Municipality

Left: Uri Berman, one of the communal workers and active people of the town, who emigrated to Canada, arriving at the home of Rabbi Zalmanovitz. Uri Berman was a slaughterer and inspector.

Right: Dr. Pikin, a very active communal worker in Riteve

[Page 122]

Hashomer Hatzair

Any member of the Hashomer Hatzair[5] (the young guard) youth movement who resides in Israel will recollect that period with a thrill. The movement in Riteve was a lively branch of a fruitful tree. Its influence on its members and their education to its cause can be gauged by the saying that was current: 'Once a "Shomer" [guard] always a Shomer.' The movement exerted a vitalising influence on the town. It served the youth of all sections of the town, the poor and the better off.

Activities in the movement began in the 'Ken' (nest), where they gathered. Each member already saw himself or herself as taking part in the building–up of the land, and the kibbutz became the goal of their efforts.

One of the main activities of the movement was the study of the Hebrew language. Newspapers and cultural evenings all contributed to the fulfilment of this aim. The movement had followers among the young intelligentsia and also among the simplest sections of the population. Each section contributed in its own way for their mutual benefit.

The summer camps, as well as the excursions in which outdoor training was the main goal, are well remembered. The youngest group was known as K'firim (the young lions) and the second group was trained for pioneering activities with great emphasis on the kibbutz and Jewish history. At the age of 18, the member received the badge of Chazak Ve'Ematz: 'Be strong and of good courage', and was then promoted to the seniors, who prepared (had Hachsharah) for emigration.

We were always very elated by news from the Land of Israel. A song sung by the pioneers about draining swamps or building roads was cherished by everyone. It was learnt by heart and sung with fervour. The leader of the movement in 1939 was Shmuel Shavit (formerly Hirshowitz) who is today a member of Kibbutz Ramat Hashofet.

Those who went on Aliyah

David Babchiks and family – parents of Getzel Zelikovitz

1905   Ber and Tovah Zusman and family

1906   Rabbi Baruch Marcus (later chief rabbi of Haifa)

1921   Shimon and Dvorah Varkul

Tsvi Nadel Machati

1922   Shmaryahu and Leah Cohani

1924   Rabbi Lifschitz and his wife

Leah Groslovski–Milman

Chana Gelman

Michah Singer

Leah Singer and her husband

[Page 123]

1925   Dov Birk and family

Rabbi Elijah, his wife Masha and their sons Avraham and Meir (later a scientist at the Weizmann Institute)

Rachel Varkul

Rivkah Yad–Shalom (formerly Auerbuch)

Reshl Prisman

Rivkah Zaltsman

(This is an incomplete list of the emigrants from Riteve to Eretz Israel up until the mid–twenties. Many more went on Aliyah later on.)

The Jewish People's Bank (Folksbank)

Rivkah Zaltsman

The Jewish People's Bank (Folksbank) was founded in the early 1920s and with its headquarters located in Kovno had branches throughout Lithuania. (At the beginning of 1931 there were 88 Jewish co-operative people's banks in Lithuania. They supported Jewish merchants and craftsmen, oppressed by the anti–Semitic government, by providing loans on convenient terms. Editors) The branches were constantly supervised by the central authority in Kovno. Its founder and manager was Zalman Schneur Abelov.

There was an annual shareholders' meeting and annual reports were submitted and plans laid for the new year as well as elections for the new head of the bank. Profits were invested in the various funds of the bank. The shareholders consisted of merchants, shopkeepers, small industrialists, etc. Loans were available to borrowers with suitable guarantees. The bank's staff in Ritcve included the manager, two young clerks and a messenger. Shoshana Berelowitz Babush, Leib Berelowitz and I were staff members.

The people had confidence in the bank and Lithuanians as well as Jews were its clients. Even though the Lithuanians had their own national bank, they were envious of the development and the stability of our bank as compared with the traumas their bank experienced. After Abelov's death, Zvi Levit represented the bank's headquarters as manager in Riteve.

The Linat Tzedck Society

The Linat Tzedek Society was a mutual help group that performed tasks which were of inestimable value to the community. These tasks were done with love and dedication and deserve to be remembered as among the most meritorious deeds of the community. Since there was no hospital nor nurses and of course no medical aid, people who fell ill had to be cared for at home so that the mother of the family had the additional responsibility of caring for the sick. Hardworking fathers were not able to assist in nursing the sick during the night, so volunteers from the Linat Tzedek would spend the night at the bedside of the patient to relieve the mother. Linat Tzedek has two connotations, the one being the 'house where righteousness dwells', and the second, the actual act of spending time on a righteous deed for the good of those in need, as for example lonely people without relatives.

[Page 124]

Four groups of the Hashomer Hatzair – Zilla, Chaya, Eta and Shoshana – emigrants to the land of Israel on 2 June 1933. There are some 30 people in this photograph and this must have touched many families in Riteve with parents realising that they were unlikely to see their children again.

Hashomer Hatzair group in Riteve before the emigration to Israel of Rachel Linder and Hadassah Katz Landsman, a photograph probably taken during the latter part of the 1930s.

[Page 125]

A Hashomer Hatzair group wearing uniforms not unlike those of the Scout Group

A group picture of the Hashomer Hatzair Association

[Page 126]

A group of ten emigrants to Israel from Riteve, photographed in the mid–1930s.
No names were provided in the original book.

Zalman Abelov, manager of the Jewish People's Bank (Folkslbank) in Riteve

[Page 127]

Footnotes

1. Harry Singer died in 1998.

2. This introduction was written by an editor of the original edition of this book.

3. The land purchase fund of the Zionist Organisation was founded on 29 December 1901 at the Fifth Zionist Congress of Basle.

4. The Palestine Foundation Fund – the financial arm of the World Zionist Organisation – was founded at the Zionist conference held in London in July 1920 in order to be a 'central permanent financial organ' that would help in the materialisation of the 'Balfour Declaration'.

5. Hashorner Hatzair was a Zionist–socialist pioneering youth movement established in Vienna in 1916 by the merging of two former youth movements: Ze'irei Zion (the youth of Zion) and Hashomer. Politically, the movement abroad was part of the Kibbutz Ha'Artzi, the Mapam settlement section in Israel. It was an active leftist, very anti–religious movement that cherished Marxist ideas for decades.

[Page 128]

Chapter 8

Holidays and Ceremonies

Townsfolk

The Jewish Sabbath and Holidays

The sanctity of life is the Torah of Judaism. Religious principles are its foundations. Can a person labour all his days without a rest? Therefore, we were given the Sabbath and Holidays as days of rest that are both days of study and relaxation.

Holidays were given to man in order that he should be with himself, with his thoughts and with his people. They give us an opportunity to maximise the expression of our thoughts and spiritual meditations. The Holidays exist not only as days of rest, but also as days of spirituality, for the reading of the works of philosophers, thinkers and. during the Days of Atonement, also for taking account of oneself. Each generation not only observes the national Holidays, but also adds something of its own personality. The generations keep the Holidays and the Holidays keep the generations and enrich them.

The customs, commands, prayers and folklore reinforce and enrich the human experience. The Jew takes off not only his everyday clothing, but also his mundane thoughts. He devotes his time to reading the Torah, to prayer and study of the Holy Books. In days like these he acquires an additional soul. This is sanctity with the joy of learning.

With the destruction of our shtetl Riteve, only a handful of the Jewish Sabbath and Holiday customs survive. We should not neglect our fathers' inheritance. We should instil in our children and grandchildren our traditions and it should be to our glory and fame.

Sabbath

The idea of one day of the week devoted to spiritual things is a sublime idea. Void of secularity, troubles and worries, the Sabbath was a day for the purification of the soul and devotion to the living G–d. The Sabbath was a part of the Jew – a part of his blood. Six days of work, with their toil and trouble, received their meaningfulness from the Sabbath. The Sabbath erased the tears from the Jews eyes. It made him forget his worries, straightened his posture and made him a 'prince'.

[Page 129]

The Sabbath had its own culture. A style of its own, customs, manners, a way of life: special food for Sabbath, special ritual objects. The people invented wonderful stories about the Sabbath, its observers and those rewarded for honouring her. In addition, there were beautiful sayings about the Sabbath and ritual articles were also created to decorate, to give pleasure and to glorify the Holy day: candlesticks, Kiddush cups, spice boxes, covers for Sabbath challahs. The Sabbath was the source of all sacredness, the origin of glory. The Sabbath eased the hardships of life and lightened the burden of exile.

If the weekdays in Riteve were mundane and filled with turmoil, with running and movement, the Sabbath was a princess. The welcoming of the Sabbath, even in the smallest and darkest alleyway, was felt in the air. All the stores closed down, not a soul was seen in the market. The old and the young, men and women, would wash and dress in their best Sabbath clothes and flock into the synagogue.

One could see in every Jewish home the preparations in anticipation of the dear guest: the Sabbath. On Friday afternoon people went to the public bath in honour of the Sabbath. The women who maintained the Mikveh would light candles with a blessing and warm prayers.

There were always those who would never leave the synagogue on Friday night without bringing home a guest. There was never a shortage of guests. Returning to his candlelit home, the master of the house would welcome the angels with song. According to Jewish legend, angels would visit every Jewish house on Sabbath eve. The Sabbath meal consisted of meat, fish, tshulent. tsimmes and other delicacies and it ended with the singing of 'Zmirot'.

Sabbath day was devoted to prayer, rest and sanctity. Afternoons were spent studying the Torah and Talmud and chapters from the moral books. The women would read the Tze'enah Urenah or Agadah books in Yiddish. These books were a source of spiritual upliftment for our mothers. They gave them the courage and integrity to withstand life's experiences. The three meals or the third Sabbath meal would exalt the spirit. The atmosphere was filled with holiness and prophecy. At twilight they would sing holy songs with longing, for they were unwilling to part with the holy Sabbath.

Passover

Preparations for Passover began the week before the Holiday. When the tasks of laundering and whitewashing ended, the job of taking out the furniture and dishes to be scraped and ritually prepared began. These tasks reached their climax on Passover eve, with the removal of leaven. Children participated in all the preparations. They would take down the Passover dishes from the attic, including the wooden mortar, for making matzah meal, and the cup of Elijah. Every dish was received with cries of joy.

[Page 130]

The synagogue and the shul (Beit Midrash) at Riteve and below, the Holy Ark with its artistic decorations.

[Page 131]

The synagogue was filled with light. Its floor was scraped clean. Its benches were whitened from cleaning. The faces of the congregation, who were dressed in festive clothing, radiated happiness. The excitement would grow until the tune of 'Ma'ariv' was heard.

Returning from the synagogue, the house was lit up and one could feel the spirit of the Holiday. All through the winter, the Seder night was longed for. Nothing could match the happiness and joy it inspired.

Father's seat of honour, the Hagadah, the four cups, the Passover table, eight days of merriment, would all stimulate our imaginations until each one of us saw himself leaving Egypt. Indeed, it was pleasant to expect Elijah the Prophet and in our childish imaginations we could see him drink his wine cup empty.

It should be noted that our town kept the beautiful custom of 'Maot Chittin'. Before the 'Sabbath Hagadol', our rabbi would prepare a list, with the help of the public workers, for soliciting contributions to aid the town's poor. This was done to fulfil the appeal: 'Let all those who are in need come and partake in the Passover festivities.'

An unforgettable Erev Pesach in Riteve

Rabbi Aharon Ben–Zion Shurin

My hometown Riteve, in what was then Jewish Lithuania, no longer exists. It was destroyed in the Nazi Holocaust, suffering the same fate as so many other Jewish communities of blessed memory. The only indication of its past Jewish life is the cemetery.

From time to time, especially on the eve of festivals, youthful memories of both joyous and sad events are evoked. I remember an event of 40 years ago, which threw the community into fear and panic. An unjustified accusation of a blood libel was levelled at the community when a young gentile boy suddenly disappeared. It happened on the eve of Passover and if I'm not mistaken in 1925 or 1926. It was well before my Bar mitzvah, but the events remain vividly in my memory. I remember clearly the fear and panic of the community as rumours and threats against the Jews were being spread by the local gentiles, in the event of the boy not being found before the festival. The issue was clear to them: a classic case of the blood libel, when it was alleged that Jews were unable to celebrate the Seder without the blood of the lost child for the baking of their matzot and the making of their wine. In short, all that was needed was for the priest to give the word to attack and kill the Jews of Riteve.

This is what actually happened. Two weeks before Pesach on the regular market day on Wednesday, hundreds of peasants gathered from the surrounding vil– lages to sell their wares to the local population in the Riteve marketplace. Due to the approaching festival of Pesach, the market was larger than usual. One of the peasants among the crowd had brought his young son, probably to show him the sights of the beautiful Jewish town and the Catholic church overlooking the marketplace. In the commotion of trading, the father did not notice his son's disappearance.

[Page 132]

As night fell and he was preparing to depart, he saw that his 'pride and joy' was not there. After much searching, rumours began to fly around. Seeing that Passover was close, who knew what could have befallen the boy at the hands of the Jews? The peasants put two and two together, and for them there could only be one explanation... Attempts were made to placate the anxious father with suggestions that the boy had probably gone home on his own. since there was no knowing what boys get up to! The father accepted this suggestion, since relations between Jews and gentiles in Riteve had been good for generations and no such event had ever been heard of before. However, the next day the youngster was still missing and, in spite of intensive searching by both the Jews and gentiles of Riteve. the child could still not be found. The matter was reported in the local newspaper, but which peasant could read a newspaper? There was no response.

In Riteve, there was a so–called 'intellectual' who was a known anti–Semite. He began to threaten that if the boy was not found all the Jews would be killed. He began a campaign of incitement, warning my father (Rabbi Moshe Shurin) that he himself would gather the importart Jews of the town, lay them out and cut off their heads with a scythe as revenge lor the blood of the boy. The atmosphere in the town assumed the character more of Tisha B'Av than the festival of Passover. The Jews were becoming more and more alarmed every minute, while he, the anti–Semite, was preparing, in his fanatical, bloodthirsty rage, for his great moment.

The Jews did their utmost to avert the disaster. They pleaded with the priest, they begged the police and sent emissaries to high places, but to no avail, for where was the child? The question remained unanswered and they were at their wits' end.

In the first few days, there were rumours that the child had been seen here and there. However, the community was already anticipating a bitter outcome, rather than a joyous festival. Their anguish grew day by day and no amount of pleading with the authorities could avert their evil fate. But Jews are a people who trust in miracles and they awaited a miracle to save them. And indeed, a week later, one occurred.

I remember the great joy when it was discovered that the hoy was safe and sound. He was found in a remote village by a Riteve youth who was completely unaware that the threat of a blood libel was hanging over his home town. It so happened that the young man, Leibe Itzik Maze by name, who is to this day living in Cape Town, South Africa (Louis Maze), being a peddler by occupation, had come across a strange face in a small village whose inhabitants he knew well. He had not heard that there was a search for the young lad. since no newspapers reached these remote parts. On his return home, he became aware of the very serious situation due to the boy's disappearance and the fate awaiting the Jewish community. Suddenly it struck him that he had seen a boy answering to this description in the remote village. In no time horses and carts were made ready and Leibe Itzik directed them to the village, where the boy was found. When questioned as to why he had disappeared on that market day, he replied that he felt like working away from home. Thus a thoughtless act by an illiterate, ignorant, Lithuanian peasant boy almost brought calamity to a whole community.

[Page 133]

That Passover, not only was the Exodus from Egypt the cause for celebration, but also the miracle brought about by a local Jew named Leibe Itzik Maze.

Lag Ba'Omer

During the 49 days of the counting of the Omer, the community would mourn. On the 49th day 1, Lag Ba'Omer, all limitations in force during the period between Passover and Shavuot were lifted. Marriages, haircuts and washing in the river were permitted. The greatest joy for the children was going to the forest with bows and arrows, accompanied by teachers and movement guides. Sometimes, the youth would hold a parade and each movement would have its own flag. They would dance and sing until the end of the day. Occasionally they would make bonfires and the children would receive coloured eggs from their parents.

Lag Ba'Omer – a meeting of the. schools of Vorna, Keidan and Ritev near a forest, possibly on the Oginski estate.

[Page 134]

Shavuot

Although Passover was considered a nature holiday, when the earth awoke from its winter sleep, the Shavuot festival carried the true grace of the awakening of nature. The swamps in the shtetl would dry. The earth would grow flowers and grass. The trees would blossom and the birds would sing.

Despite being a religious holiday, the giving of the Torah, it was a day free of all limitations. As the saying goes: On Passover a man can enjoy himself wherever he wishes, but not everything that he wishes for fear of leaven. On Succoth a person can enjoy anything he wishes but not anywhere he wishes, because of the ban on eating outside the Succah. But on Shavuot a man can enjoy everything, anywhere. On the eve of Shavuot, our father observed a custom of bringing trees and putting them in the synagogue and in private homes.

The traditional tune for the 'Acdamoth' (a long mystical ancient poetic prayer, written in Aramaic and sung before the Giving of the Torah ceremony) is one of the most cherished and beloved tunes, with its special flavour, so befitting the festive spirit of giving the Torah. This tune preserved a remnant of an ancient melody with a glorious echo of togetherness, pathos, a lofty tunc and solemnity.

Dairy delicacies were served on Shavuot, because of the logical belief that when the People of Israel got the Torah they did not have kosher meat at once ... On the second day of the holiday the story of Ruth was read, because it speaks about King David who passed away on that day.

Ninth of Av

The Ninth of Av is a fast day. It commemorates the destruction of the two temples. This custom was dutifully observed in Riteve. The fast, the ban on working and the obligation to mourn made the Ninth of Av a day devoted completely to the reading of the Book of Lamentations, to listening to the sermons about the destruction and to the telling of events and legends.

The people of Riteve would reduce all joyful activities from the start of the month. During the first nine days they were quite strict about the mourning customs: avoiding the eating of mcat, the cutting of hair, the washing of oneself in the river, the laundering of clothes, the wearing of new clothing and the holding of any family feast such as a marriage or housewarming, etc.

[Page 135]

All along the street in which the synagogue was located, one could hear the sad melody of Lamentations. The benches in the synagogue were turned upside–down and the community would sit as mourners. Into this web of grief and sadness sneaked an episode of frivolity. The young people adopted the custom of picking brambles on the eve of the mourning day and throwing them at the beards of the older men and into the hair of the women. It was very difficult to extract the brambles without pulling out one's hair.

On the eve of the Ninth of Av, after evening prayers, people would sit in darkness on the ground or on an overturned stool or bench with only one candle lit. Every person held in his hand one small candle in order to read the Lamentations.

A widespread legend said that every Ninth of Av, at midnight, the skies would open for a minute and whoever made a wish at that moment would see it come true immediately.

Rosh Hashanah

The modest quivering voice of the shofar could be heard. These were days of introspection. The Jews awoke early and hurried to the synagogue. The town stood to attention. When the year neared its end, all thought about their own end. With the blowing of the shofar, every Jewish heart would awaken to self–examination.

A week before Rosh Hashanah, the shammas would call everybody to 'Slichot' (prayers of forgiveness). The mood in Riteve was one filled with grace and charity.

The challahs for Rosh Hashanah were baked in the shape of ladders to symbolise that every person would either be sentenced to poverty or rewarded with riches, to go up or to go down. Some baked their challahs in the shape of birds, symbolising G–d's mercy – 'As birds hovering so will the Lord of Hosts protect Jerusalem' (Isaiah 31:5). Some also baked their challahs in the shape of crowns symbolising the crown of honour. A piece of challah from the 'Hamotzi' blessing (he who provides us with bread) or a sweet apple would be dipped in honey: 'It should be Your will that a new and sweet year will come to us.' People would go to 'Tashlich' to throw away their sins as if from their pockets to the bottom of the river.

The common form of prayer was not enough to express the spirit of the people and so they added different lyrics. The lyrics were songs of praise to G–d and the 'Slichah' was the pouring out of one's soul in confession and lamentation accompanied with supplication and hope.

Nothing could compare to the depth of thought and the elevation of the spirit during Rosh Hashanah in Riteve.

[Page 136]

Yom Kippur – the Day of Atonement

If the Days of Awe resembled a tall ladder with many rungs for reconsideration, repentance, introspection and censure of deeds between man and his G–d and between man and man, then the Day of Atonement resembled the highest rung in that ladder, the epitome of sanctity and purity. Before the Day of Atonement were the Ten Penitentiary Days when Slichot were recited.

A widespread custom at the time was 'kapparot': a chicken would be selected (a rooster for a man and a hen for a woman and one of each for a pregnant woman) and while verses from the Book of Psalms and Job were recited its head would be wrenched off. With this the following saying would be recited: 'This is my replacement ...'

The Torah commands that we eat heartily during the evening meal of the Day of Atonement. Overeating would balance the fast of the following day. The food consisted of kreplach, fish and honey cake. The custom of lashing was also fol– lowed by which every Jew would prostrate himself on the floor of the synagogue as the shammas lashed him 40 times minus one. Another custom was the 'bowl' or 'plate' in which contributions were collected to support the synagogue. In later years, this system was used by the Zionists for their fundraising.

The most pleasant of customs was the reconciliation between friends and neighbours on the eve of the Day of Atonement. This was done because there was no atonement for sins affecting the relationships between people. Before leaving home for the synagogue, mothers would prolong their blessing over the candles with bitter crying. This was followed with the blessing of the children. It was also customary to pay visits to homes of relatives and neighbours and greet them with: 'May you be inscribed and sealed with happiness.'

Most memorable was the 'Kol Nidre' prayer. The sad melody would envelope the congregation casting its spell over every Jew. Its force and beauty were heart– rending. Twenty–five hours would follow – hours filled with the splendour of holiness, and the excitement of sharing the ancient traditions.

The entire day would he spent in synagogue. It was not surprising that this day is deeply etched in one's memory. Suffocating heat, light, memorial candles on every table and in every window, fainting in the women's gallery –

all memories. Finally, with the concluding prayer of 'Neilah' the people would give a last vent to their emotions. The fast was forgotten, the fatigue overcome and with the final chant of the cantor, 'Open for us the gates of mercy', the heart would melt and the devoutness would reach us pinnacle. The final sound of the shofar and the words, 'Next year in Jerusalem' would end the service.

[Page 137]

Succoth – the Feast of Tabernacles

The evening after the Day of Atonement, the community would begin building the Succah. The thatch would be made of branches and straw. The Feast of Tabernacles was really the main Holiday. Rosh Hashanah and Yom Kippur were not real festivals, they were days of awe and days of judgement.

The Succah was a source of pleasure. The rich would reserve a room as a per– manent Succah. In place of thatch, it would be made of wooden planks and its roof could be raised or lowered. Building a Succah was not a difficult task. Unused windows and discarded doors, a broken bench and an old blanket would all find their way into the Succah. The Jews would actually rejoice sitting in the Succah catching glimpses of the twinkling stars. The children, of course, were most involved in building, thatching and decorating the Succah.

Hashanah Rabbah, the seventh day of the Feast of Tabernacles, was called alter the 'Hashanah' lyrics. It was like pan of a note written on Rosh Hashanah and signed on the Day of Atonement. Therefore, on the eve of Hashanah Rabbah. people would sit up until late at night in the synagogue. In the morning they would pray with the melody of the Days of Awe. The main custom was the heating of willows.

Shmini Atzeret and Simchat Torah were considered Holidays unto themselves. On Shmini Atzereth the prayer for rain was said in the Mussaf prayer. The day of Hashanah Rabbah was a day of preparation for Simchat Torah.

Since there can be no rejoicing without wine, a Kiddush Rabbah was made during the day of Simchat Torah. Wine would be drunk in the synagogue and at home. Some people would even get drunk. Circling the synagogue with the Scrolls of the Law was a happy event. A big crowd of men, women and children would stand in two rows surrounding the pulpit. The children would carry decorated llags, topped with an apple and a candle. This was not done If Simchat Torah happened to fall on the Sabbath.

The cantor would begin with the chant. 'Please G–d, help us', and each of the attendants would be honouretl by circling around the pulpit with a scroll. The crowd would kiss the Torah and bless its carrier. This was considered a Miizvah. Overexcited with enthusiasm, the crowd would sing, clap hands, dance and be merry. Simchat Torah was a democratic holiday. Men, women and children par– ticipated equally. Most cherished, both for children and adults, would be the parade with the candlelit flags.

Every synagogue had its patron who would gather the children to one corner of the synagogue and call out: 'Innocent ones.' The children would answer confirming their presence. The young were called to the reading of the Torah. All the boys were even offered their own Aliyah, the reading of the Torah while standing on the podium.

For the benefit of the children, the 'Redeeming Angel' would be read while they were covered with the 'tallit'. At this moment one could feel that the 'Redeeming Angel' himself was blessing the children and that the heavens were opening. The crowd would then sing. 'Be happy and rejoice on Simchat Torah and give honour to it.'

[Page 138]

The Simchat Torah which was brought to a close

Alter Levite

Life in our little town of Riteve was desolate and sad. Each day resembled the next, and there was nothing to relieve the monotony. Cinemas and theatres had not yet arrived in town and so the young people had no form of entertainment. Nature, too. did not bestow great beauty on the town. In winter the rains created great puddles which made crossing the streets difficult, and in summer the thick dust choked us. We swam in the river which flowed through the town. But the swimming days were restricted: during the seven weeks of Sephirah1 and during the three weeks of mourning for the destruction of the Temple, swimming was forbidden. Thus much of the summer went by. Then the water became too cold. Furthermore, the days when one could swim were filled with fear and trembling because ihc priest's dogs menaced us on our way to the river.

Only on one day in the year was our joy full and undimmed. That day was Simchat Torah. On this day, young and old, men. women and children rejoiced. The rich men of the town who sat each day at the long tables in the Beit Midrash and pored over the Gemara would gather at the rabbi's house and enjoy a glass of brandy. The poorer folk were invited to the home of the president of the Chevra Kadisha, where the drink flowed freely. We, the young ones, took pleasure in seeing the adults inebriated. In the synagogue all restrictions were waived and there was no difference between rich and poor, young and old. If you wished to stand at the eastern wall, you were welcome. If you wished to stand on the benches, there was nothing to stop you. We were all overjoyed and. if one managed to take hold of a Scroll of the Torah and do the rounds with it along with all the important people, there was really no limit to one's joy.

On one occasion this great day of joy was marred. But we, the young ones, were not at all upset about that. On the contrary, we derived much pleasure Irom it. It was for us a Simchat Torah of victory, of great success. But first, I must tell of my friend Nathan. He was a dreamer and had a wonderfully fertile imagination. From his teacher in the modern cheder he had heard of the near–yet–far Land of Israel. He was very moved and concentrated all his thoughts on the revival of the land and the return of its people.

During the First World War, we were cut off from the outside world by the German occupation. After the war, a rumour reached us that a Jewish state had been established in the Land of Israel with a Jewish government. Those who spread the rumour had magnified the Balfour Declaration until it became a declaration of independence. But this rumour served to fire the imagination of the Jews of Riteve and especially of Nathan, my friend. What could a Jewish boy do, wishing to help in the establishment of the land?

[Page 139]

He decided to work hard for the Keren Kayemet (Jewish National Fund) and went around the town urging each household to take the 'Blue Box', and pleading with the women to put coins into it every Sabbath eve. Many of the inhabitants of the town laughed at him and his dream. However, they could not refuse him, especially as he was of a good family, and so they took the Blue Boxes reluctantly. However, he soon realised that the contributions were too meagre. How could one rebuild a land with only pennies?

He thought of other ways to raise money more effectively. He knew that on Simchat Torah every Jew goes up to the Torah and donates money to the synagogue and the Beit Midrash and all the communal institutions, so why should they not do so for the Keren Kayemet as well? He found a solution. He prepared a large sheet of white paper on which he drew a blue Star of David and in the centre he wrote Zion in gold letters. Above he wrote in bold letters: 'When you go up to the Torah, remember the Keren Kayemet.' All this was executed in the best of taste, and he planned to stick his poster on the synagogue door. Bui how could he ensure that it would not be removed? As luck would have it, that year the festival of Shmini Atzeret fell on the Sabbath, and no one would desecrate the Sabbath by removing the poster. So he put the poster in its place on the door of the synagogue. Soon the congregation started to assemble and the poster was seen by all. No one had ever seen such an unholy thing in a holy place. The rabbi, on arrival, was about to remove it and then he remembered the Sabbath, so the poster remained in its place. All of the next day, people were curious to know who had desecrated the sacred place, but my friend kept his secret.

That day the congregation did not indulge in drinking or in dancing, as was their custom on Simchat Torah. They were upset because, in their eyes, the synagogue had been desecrated by the poster. They were depressed and downcast. That evening, the eve of Simchat Torah, the prayers were said hurriedly and they began the circuits around the bima (the podium). The chazan was chanting the well–known verses of the prayer and awaited the usual responses, when suddenly the young men took over and sang out together, 'Our hope has not yet been lost', the first words of Hatikvah, the Zionist anthem. The older men were stunned at first and were unable to accept that Hatikvah had been sung within the walls of the synagogue. But in a moment they themselves began singing: 'You are one and Your name is one.' The young people were not intimidated and broke into a new song: 'There in the pleasant land of our forefathers.' The crowd was divided into two competing singing groups. From the one, came the strains of 'How good is our lot and how happy we are', and from the other 'We shall be the first' rang out in reply. The voices of the youth prevailed over those of the older folk, so that the synagogue was filled with the singing of the songs of a young and vigorous generation in praise of a new life in a new land. Slowly the old people returned the Torah to the Holy Ark and one by one they left the synagogue as if they had been defeated in war.

[Page 140]

On the following day, something happened which my friend Nathan had not anticipated. The community which had recovered overnight from the confusion of the Simchat Torah evening, paid attention to the appeal made to them by the poster, and all, to a man, contributed generously to the Keren Kayemet. My friend Nathan was overjoyed. He guarded his secret of the forbidden poster which was the source of 'impurity'. Only to me did he reveal his secret. The whole town felt, however, that the poster had brought about a revolution in their lives, calling them to the banner of the Land of Israel.

My dear friend Nathan did not live to see the realisation of his great dream – the Return to Zion. When the Second World War broke out. he wandered off to far Siberia, where he died in the prime of his life after a long illness and found his last resting place in a cold land far from any Jewish habitation.

Hannukah – the Feast of Lights

Hannukah was celebrated with praise and thanksgiving. Warmth and excitement were typical of the spirit of this Holiday: parties, psalms, and melodies. The lighting of the Hannukah candles was the centre of activity. The lighting ceremony was accompanied before and after with liturgical singing. The adults would play cards and eat 'Latkes' and the children played with a metal or wooden 'dreidel' (spinning top). They would receive Hannukah gifts, usually money, which would make them very happy.

The Fifteenth of Shevat

In the middle of the month Shevat, when it was cold and there was still snow, this Holiday would be celebrated. This was the Holiday for the revival of nature in Israel and it was known in Riteve as the Fifteenth. The teachers would explain to their students that this day was the day for planting trees in Israel and it was customary to eat the fruits of Israel: carobs, figs, dates and raisins. This holiday emphasised our attachment to Israel and the desire to emigrate and build the country and enjoy its fruits.

[Page 141]

Above: A Purim party at the Hebrew School in 5689 (1928/29) and, below, a later party in the same venue, with the children dressed up, with their teachers, Miriam Levite (second row from the front, extreme leftj), Izchak Paktor (extreme right, front) and Alter Goldberrg (second row from the front, with glasses, wearing a hat.)

[Page 142]

Purim

The legendary literature has many shades and nuances: research, commentary, prophecy, morals, mysticism, charity preaching, etc. And all these features of a legend can be found in the Feast of Purim. This holiday was celebrated with great joy in Riteve. Preparations would begin at the beginning of the month of Adar: 'With the beginning of Adar. we must multiply our rejoicing.' The children were the ones who would prepare most industriously for the celebrations. It was a day when no one worked and it was customary to send Purim presents to one another. It was a day in which the heart would fill with joy.

Many relatives would be invited to the Purim meal which was eaten by candlelight in order to fulfil what was said in ihe 'Megillah': 'And Jews had light and joy and mirth and honour.' It was said in our folklore that when the Messiah comes, all Holidays will cease except Purim.

Reading the Megillah in a festive way was an open invitation for merriment. Whenever Haman's name was mentioned, the silence was broken by hundreds of noisy rattles and sticks. It was as if the air was touched by a magic baton.

The Purim songs were popular and well liked, especially the song 'Shoshanah Yaa'kov' that was widespread as a folk song. The special food for Purim were those reminders of Haman's hat, Harmntaschen. Triangular shaped, they were filled with poppy seeds. Twisted loaves with crocus (saffron) were especially liked and they were called 'Purim Koiletch'.

It was said in Riteve that during Hannukah an open miracle occurred and so we ate latkes, but during Punm a hidden miracle occurred and so we ate Hamaniaschen. During Hannukah the awakening came from above and therefore one held the dreidle with its handle turned upwards; during Purim. the awakening came from below and one holds the rattle with its handle turned downwards.

Footnote

1. Sephirat Ha-Omer - counting of the Omer: a Pentateuchal injunction to count 49 days from the first offering of the Omer sheaf of corn - in the Temple. The counting starts from the 16th of Nisan until Shavuot (Pentecost). On each day the counting must mention both the number of days and the number of weeks. The days of the Omer are also characterized by semi-mourning customs. It is a very old tradition normally associated with the death of the disciples of Rabbi Akiva. The solemnisation of marriages, as well as haircutting and the playing of musical instruments arc prohibited during thcsc days.

[Page 143]

Chapter Nine

The Holocaust in Riteve

Dina Porat

This chapter includes an historical survey of the Holocaust in Lithuania and in Riteve, a number of survivors' testimonies, lists of the victims and finally a Yizkor. It was not easy to establish the chain of events in Riteve during the Holocaust, since very few people survived, each having experienced hardships in other places and forms, after the evacuation of the place by the Germans. The killing was almost total, as in most other Lithuanian shtetlakh. Today there are no Jews in Riteve, and only one survivor lived in another town in Lithuania until his death a couple of years ago. The rest of the few survivors reside in Israel, South Africa and the USA. Although the once neglected old Jewish cemetery has been put in order, the Beit Midrash was turned into a cinema and the beautiful synagogue is gone.

DP

The Holocaust of Lithuanian Jewry

by Roni Stauber

On 22 June 1941, the German army invaded the Soviet Union. This date marks a turning point in the anti–Jewish activity of the Nazi regime. Two or three months earlier Hitler had decided to adopt new and drastic measures in his war against the Jews. He ordered Heinrich Himmler, the SS supreme commander, to take the necessary steps towards the destruction of the Jewish inhabitants of the Soviet territories.[1] As a result, Reinhard Heydrich, Himmler's deputy and head of the main office for security of the Reich (Reichssicherheitshauptamt – RSHA), formed four specialised units for this purpose – the Einsatzgruppen. Their task was to move from town to town in the occupied areas and to kill Jews as well as other 'ideological enemies', such as officials of the Communist Party.[2]

The total strength of the Einsatzgruppen was about 3,000 men. Each group was composed of several operational units, Einsatzkommandos and Sonderkommandos. Their commanders were senior officers in the RSHA. Most were from while–collar professions – lawyers, economists, a physician, a professional opera singer and even a Protestant pastor. The personnel, made up partly of volunteers, were drawn from the Security Police (Sipo), the Security Service (Sicherheitsdienst – SD), the Law and Order Police (Ordnungspolizei), and the Waffen–SS. While the Einsatzgruppen operated in the occupied areas, they were reinforced by indigenous units of Lithuanians, Estonians, Latvians and Ukrainians.[3]

[Page 144]

As early as the end of March 1941, after a series of discussions, Heydrich, as the representative of the SS, and General Edward Wagner, the general quartermaster of the Wehrmacht, reached an agreement regarding the relationship and co–operation between the Einsatzgruppen and the army in the occupied areas. The army gave the SS a 'free hand' to carry out their 'special duties'. The co–operation with the army was an essential condition for the SS operations in the east. The small killing units could not fulfil their tasks without the logistical support of the Wehrmacht.[4] On 23 June 1941, they crossed the border into the Soviet territories, moving behind the advancing German army. Each Einsatzgruppe was attached to one of the army groups. Einsatzgruppe–A operated in the Baltic countries. Einsatzgruppe–B in Byelorussia and the Smolensk district, Einsatzgruppe–C in north and central Ukraine, and Einsatzgruppe–D in south Ukraine, Crimea, and the Caucasus.[5]

The Einsatzgruppen were not the only SS forces that participated in the killing operations. An additional force, composed mainly of two mechanised SS brigades and SS cavalry regiments, was sent to the occupied areas. Their assignment was to operate in areas not covered by the Einsatzgruppen because of their lack of manpower. Altogether some 23,000 men were sent to the east in order to carry out the orders of the Fuhrer. This large force was equipped according to army standards.[6]

The first phase of the mass executions, which had begun in June 1941, was completed toward the end of the year. During this period about 500,000

Jews were killed in ihe areas taken from the Russans. The killing units succeeded in covering most of the occupied territories. They moved very rapidly behind the advancing armies and were frequently sent to the front line. More than once they even entered occupied cities with the advance units of the army. They used this strategy in order to reach the Jewish communities before rumours of the mass killings could spread.[7]

The operation of slaughter was standardised. In every Jewish community the Einsatzkommandos used the same procedure. The Jews were forced to assemble in a central place. Those who did not present themselves were rounded up from their houses. From this central place, they were taken by a well–armed unit to a killing site not far from the town or the village. Occasionally the Germans used anti–tank ditches or shell craters as graves, but in many killing sites the graves were specially dug a day or two before the massacre. Before their deaths the victims were made to hand over all their valuables to the murderers. They were forced to remove their clothes and stand in front of tie graves or lie in them. They were then killed on the spot by the killing unit.[8]

[Page 145]

The destruction of the Lithuanian Jews began on the day of the German invasion. Throughout the country thousands of Jews were slain by Lithuanians. In many cases pogroms were organised immediately after the flight of the Red Army, even before the entrance of the Wehrmacht. Documents published after the war show that the first directives to persecute the Jews were sent to the nationalists in Lithuania even before the beginning of the German–Soviet war. These directives were sent by the members of the Lithuanian Active Front in Berlin to their secret organisation in Lithuania.[9]

The Germans encouraged the brutal pogroms. The concept of this policy was explained by Franz Stahlecker, the commander of Einsatzgruppe–A, in his report to Berlin on October 1941: 'It was no less important, for future purposes, to establish as an unquestionable fact that the liberated population had resorted to measures against the Bolshevist and Jewish enemy on its own initiative and without instructions from the German authorities.'[10] Einsatzkommando 2 and Einsatzkommando 3, operating in Lithuania, were divided into smaller units in order to reach all the Jewish settlements. During the annihilation operations, they were assisted by Lithuanians. In many cases the massacres were carried out mainly by

Lithuanians under the supervision of the Germans. 'The active anti–Semitism which flared up quickly after the German occupation has not abated. Lithuanians are voluntarily and untiringly at our disposal for all measures against Jews. Sometimes they even execute such measures independently,' wrote Stahlecker in his report.[11]

Before Yad Vashem was established, a commemorative site to honour victims of the Holocaust was established on Mount Zion, Jerusalem, the many memorial tablets being placed under the collonade seen above. Israelis and others with Riteve origins or connections are seen in front of this in 1965 after the unveiling of the tablet to the martyrs of Riteve. The main focus of the site, however, is in the basement of the nearby old building on Mount Zion, referred to in the original book as the Holocaust basement on Mount Zion, Jerusalem.

[Page 146]

כ"ז
זכ

לזכר
לקדושי
ליטא (ריטעווע)
(ליטא) הי"ד
שחטו ונקברו חיים
גרוריהם ימ"ש
ימוש מקרבגו לנצח
ול חי"ג צי ב"ה
א בישראל ובתפוצות

עולם
קהילת

ישראל

**The monument in the martyrs of Riteve that was unveiled on
Mount Zion in 1965. The design in the centre is a reproduction
from the photograph of the old synagogue in Riteve.**

During July the majority of the victims was male, while the killing of
women and children began in most places in August 1941. Most of the Jewish
communities were destroyed by the end of the year. About 175,000 Jews,
more than 80 per cent of Lithuanian Jewry, were killed within four and a half
months.[12]

By the end of 1941 the systematic murder of the Lithuanian Jews was
suspended as a result of intensive pressure from the Wehrmacht and various
elements in the civilian administration who wanted to utilise the skilled
Jewish manpower. About 50,000 Jews were concentrated in the large ghettos
of Vilna. Kovno and Shavli (Siauliai) and in smaller ghettos in Sevencionys and
in other small towns. In his report concerning the executions carried out in
Lithuania up to December 1941, Karl Jager, the commander of
Einsatzkommando 3, wrote: 'I can state today that the goal of solving the
Jewish problem in Lithuania has been reached by EK 3. There are no Jews left

in Lithuania except for the work–Jews [in the ghettos] ... I intended to kill off these work–Jews and their families as well, but met with the strongest protest from the civil administration (Reichskommissar) and the Wehrmacht, which culminated in the prohibition that stipulates that these Jews and their families may not be shot dead. The work–Jews and Jewesses left alive for the time being are badly needed, and I presume that when winter is over this Jewish labour force will still be essential. I am of the opinion that it is imperative to start at once with the sterilisation of the male work–Jews to prevent propagation. If in spite of this measure a Jewess still happens to fall pregnant she is to be liquidated.'[13]

[Page 147]

Fellow townsmen of Riteve in the basement of the Holocaust memorial on Mount Zion. Names of the concentration camps are engraved on the black marble slab

Harry Singer Collection

The lull in the process of total annihilation continued until the summer of 1943. Nevertheless, throughout this period, individual Jews and groups of Jews were murdered in the ghettos. Mostly they were killed as punishment for even minor offences like smuggling food into the ghetto or failing to wear the yellow badge. In February 1943, 45 Jews were murdered in Kovno for such slight transgressions as an act of 'revenge' by the frustrated Germans for the defeat of the Wehrmacht in Stalingrad.[14] In March and April 1943 several small ghettos and labour camps in east Lithuania were liquidated. In one day, 3 April, the Germans murdered about 4 000 Jews at Ponery near Vilna. The 'operations' were reported immediately to RSHA in Berlin. It was reported that '...the Byelorussian areas incorporated into the General District of Lithuania ...have been cleared of Jews ...The Jews who were found to be not fit to work, some 4,300, underwent special treatment.'[15]

The liquidation of the three big ghettos in Lithuania, Vilna, Kovno and Shavli, began in the summer of 1943 following Himmler's order on 21 June of that year to liquidate the ghettos in Ostland and set up concentration camps.

[Page 148]

The decision was made to send the surviving inmates of the ghettos in Lithuania to camps in Estonia and Latvia. During this process all those unfit for labour were to be exterminated.[16] The liquidation began with the deportation of the inmates of the Vilna ghetto to camps in Latvia and Estonia during August and September 1943. Four thousand women, children, the sick and the elderly were sent to death camps or murdered in Ponery. During the autumn and winter of 1943 thousands of Jews were deported from the ghettos in Kovno and Shavli to labour camps. The ghettos were converted into concentration camps. Children and adults who were found to be unfit for work were sent to the death camps in Poland.[17]

The annihilation of children and old people continued in March 1944. Hundreds of children and elderly people were sent to the death camps or killed in death sites such as the Ninth Fort near Kovno, where most of the Jews of Kovno and at least 5,000 Jews from the Reich as well as smaller numbers from other countries had been killed. The process of liquidation continued during the German evacuation of Lithuania in the summer of 1944. Two thousand Jews from the camps in the Vilna area were executed in Ponery. Most of the Jews who survived the camps in the Shavli and Kovno districts were deported to camps in Germany and many died during the last stage of the war. Out of the 220,000–225,000 Jews who lived in Lithuania before the

German invasion, only 2,000–3,000 survived in the forests of Lithuania and a few more thousands in the concentration camps in Germany.[18]

Lighting a candle in the Holocaust memorial basement on Mount Zion, for the raising of the martyrs of Riteve on the Day of Remembrance in 1965.

[Page 149]

About 95 per cent of Lithuanian Jewry was killed during the Holocaust, the highest rate among European communities. They were killed in Lithuania, not in any of the extermination camps in Poland. Most of them – about 80 per cent – were killed during the summer and the autumn of 1941; their bodies were thrown into pits and mass graves. The scope and speed of the killing could not have been attained without the enthusiastic assistance of the local population, which did most of the killings, sometimes even without the presence of Germans, especially in the small shtetlakh in the countryside.

Lithuanian Jewry was as unique in its death as it was in its life.

Footnotes

2. The decision concerning the Final Solution has been the subject of differing historical interpretations and serious debate. See for example Tim Mason: Intention and Explanation: A Current Controversy about the Interpretation of National Socialism, in Der Fuererstaau Mythas und Reahtat (eds. G Hirschfeld and L Kettenacker), Stuttgart, 1981, pp. 210–40; Christopher R Browning, Fateful Months. NY, pp. 8–38.

3. Raul Hilberg, The Destruction of the European Jews. New York, 1961. p. 186: Trials of War Criminals before the Nuremburg Military Tribunals (1M1). Vol. 4. p. 130; Documents on the Holocaust (eds. Y. Arad, Y Gutman: A Margollot). Jerusalem, 1981, p. 377.

4. IMT, Vol. 4. p. 414.

5. Helmut Krausnick, The Persecution of the Jews in Krausnick et.al., Anatomy of the SS State. London, 1961, p. 61.

6. The Einsatzgruppen Reports (eds Y Arad, S Krakowski, S Spector). New York. 1989. p.vi.

7. Yehoshua Buchler. 'Kommandostab–Reichsfuhrer–SS: Himmler's personal Murder Brigades in 1941'. Holocaust and Genocide Studies. Vol. 1, pp 11–25.

8. Hilberg, p. 225.

9. Ibid. p. 209.

10. Documents Accuse (ed. R Rozauskas). Vilnius. 1970, p. 124.

11. Hilberg. p 203.

12. Hilberg. p. 205: IMT. Vol. 4. p. 164.

13. Yitzhak Arad, –The "Final Solution" in Lithuania in the light of German Documentation. Yad Vashem Studies II. 1976, p. 246.

14. Documents Accuse. pp. 238. 240

15. Avraham Tory, Surviving the Holocaust: The Kovno Ghetto Diary. London & Massachusetts. 1990. pp. 189–195

16. Documents Accase, pp. 271–272.

17. Documents on the Holocaust, p. 546.

18. Arad, p. 264.

19. Arad. p 272.

———

The destruction of the Riteve community

by Roni Stauber

The fate of the Jewish community in Riteve was similar to that of most small communities in the occupied Soviet territories which were destroyed during the first phase of mass executions. In many small towns and villages the annihilation was total and not a single Jew survived. The story of the last days of these communities will remain forever vague.

The Jewish community in Riteve was destroyed shortly after the German invasion of Lithuania. During the summer and autumn of 1941 most of the Jews of Riteve were killed by Germans and their Lithuanian collaborators. Very few succeeded in escaping this fate.

Some of the survivor gave testimony about the destruction of Riteve immediately after the war, while they were still in the DP (displaced persons) camps in Germany. These testimonies and many others were collected in the camps by the Jewish Central Historical Committee, and can be found today in the Yivo and the Yad Vashem archives. Other survivors testified three decades later, during the compilation of the Hebrew edition of the Riteve book. Some of the details given in these testimonies are inconsistent, particularly when describing what they had heard about the death of Rabbi Fundiler. It is only natural that there be some diversity in the recollections of such traumatic events. However, careful examination and comparison can provide a comprehensive picture of the end of the Jewish community of Riteve.

It is difficult to establish with certitude the exact number of Jewish inhabitants in Riteve on the eve of the destruction. According to some evidence, we can assume that between 800 and 1,000 Jews were living in the village when the SS killing units crossed the Soviet border.[1]

[Page 150]

As in most other Jewish communities, the Lithuanians in Riteve did not wait for the arrival of the Germans to begin their persecution of the Jews. The persecutions apparently began immediately after the first news about the

German invasion was received. According to one testimony, the first action of the Lithuanians was to plunder Jewish property.[2] Hearing the news about the advance of the German army and fearing their neighbours, most of the Jews escaped from Riteve and looked for shelter in the surrounding villages.[3] The day after they fled, on 23 or 24 June 1941, most of their houses were burnt. Some available evidence indicates that the Russians set fire to the small town when they retreated from this part of Lithuania, whereas some survivors testified that the fire was caused by a German air raid.[4]

In keeping with what was happening in Lithuania as a whole, 'patriotic' Lithuanians in Riteve were organised to help the Germans as an auxiliary force. The Germans, as has previously been pointed out. encouraged the phenomenon of 'spontaneous' violence against the Jews. A collaboration committee was set up, headed by the local pastor. One of its first instructions to the population of the surrounding villages was to drive away any Jew who sought refuge there. They were given a sanction to confiscate the property of the Jews. The committee also ordered the Jews to return to Riteve. According to one testimony, they declared that accommodation would be found for every Jew.[5]

A few days later, probably on 27 June, all the Jews of Riteve were concentrated in Oginski's estate. Sadistic conduct, mainly against the men, preceded the concentration. One of the most painful memories, which not one of the survivors from those first days neglects to mention, was the severe humiliation of Rabbi Shmuel Fundiler, the rabbi of Riteve. Half his beard was cut off, he was forced to burn ritual articles and holy books and he was harnessed to a wagon loaded with garbage. The tortures continued until the Lithuanians shot him dead.[6] According to one of the survivors, the Lithuanian atrocities were filmed, presumably by Germans. Similar incidents occurred in other places in the Baltic States.[7] The Germans, as Stahlecker, the commander of Einsatzgruppe–A, pointed out, wanted to display the severity of the local treatment of the Jews.[8]

The annihilation of the Jews of Riteve was a microcosm of the process of destruction in Lithuania as a whole. The first victims were those accused of being Communists. This was the implementation of the instructions given by Heydrich to the commanders of the killing units just before the invasion.[9] In Riteve four to six young Jews were selected as Communists and were stabbed to death by Lithuanians.[10] About ten days later the Jews of Riteve were evacuated and sent to a camp in Vishtevian near Telz, which was set up by the Germans in order to concentrate Jews from several places in the district of

Telz.[11] It appears that not all the men were sent to Vishtevian. According to one testimony, men from Riteve were taken to labour camps in the environs of Heidekrug. near Memel. This occurred in several communities in west Lithuania, mainly in the districts of Tavrig anil Telz. Males, even small boys, were deported by SS men and Lithuanians to Heidekrug, where they were forced to perform such hard labour as draining swamps and paving roads.[12]

[Page 151]

In Elul 5730 (1970), another memorial tablet was unveiled on the Day of Remembrance, on this occasion in the forest planted to the memory of the martyrs of the Holocaust – the Forest of the Sacred in Jerusalem. Seen here are People of Riteve in Israel on this occasion.

[Page 152]

The conditions in Vishtevian were terrible. About 1,500 Jews from a number of towns were herded together in stables and suffered severe hunger. There, in Vishtevian, the second stage in the process of annihilation was carried out. On 15 and 16 July Germans and Lithuanians executed all Jewish males over the age of thirteen. The murderers killed the men first, acting in accordance with the procedure followed by most of the killing units.[13] The victims in Vishtevian were part of the 13,000–14,000 Jews massacred by Einsatzkommando 2 in the Shavli area in northwest Lithuania during July 1941.[14] The rest of the community the women and children, were forcibly removed from Vishtevian to the village of Giroli near Telz. Here there were also women and children from other communities in the Telz district. In Giroli they were kept alive for six weeks, living in open barracks under inhuman conditions. Many children died from an epidemic which broke out and young women suffered the importunities of the Lithuanians.[15]

The third stage in the process of the annihilation of Riteve's Jews was carried out by the end of August. This was the implementation of Helnrich

Lohse's directive to complete the destruction of the Jewish communities in the countryside (Flachesland).[16] In Giroli, on 29 August, all women over the age of 50 and all the boys were killed. Before the execution, the Lithuanians extorted money from the helpless women, promising in exchange to keep them and their children alive.

The women under the age of 50 and the girls, about 450–500 in number, were sent to the ghetto in Telz. At first they were unaware of what had happened to the mothers and siblings from whom they had been separated in Giroli. But on the following day they heard the terrible news from a woman who had succeeded in escaping from the death site.[17] Rachel Zinger–Taich from Telz remembered her telling them that the mothers were forced to see the murder of their own children.[18]

From the ghetto in Telz they were sent every day to the surrounding villages to work in the fields. It is possible that the need for manpower brought about the postponement of the extermination of the young women. However, the suspension of mass killings was terminated at the end of three months. At the beginning of December, the last surviving remnants from Riteve and other communities in the Telz district were taken to Rayin and murdered. Only a few survived. The survivors were hidden by peasants or managed to escape to the Shavli ghetto.[19]

The same tragic fate overtook the men who were deported to Heidekrug. About 800 men were brought to the camps in July 1941. More than half of them were murdered after several 'selections' that took place in the camps during the first six months. Many died as a result of the difficult conditions and cruel treatment. Those who managed to survive, some 300 men, were evacuated in the summer of 1943, first to Auschwitz and. after selection, to Warsaw for slave labour. From Warsaw they were transported to the Mildorf camp near Dachau and only a few were still alive at the end of the war.[20]

[Page 153]

The tablet to the memory of the martyrs of Riteve unveiled in the Forest of the Sacred in 1970 with, below, a small group standing next to it which gives some idea of its setting.

Footnotes

1. This estimate is based on diffenent figures given by survivors and people born in Riteve. See, for example, testimonies by Shaul Shenker and Yentel Gershovitz, Yad Vashem Archive (YVA) M–1/Q/1322/136: letter from Harry Singer to the editors in May 1991; see also Lithuanian Jewry, Tel Aviv. 1967, Vol. 3, p. 359; Lithuanian Jewry. Tel Aviv, 1984, Vol. 4, p. 489; Ibid., p. 359. according to which about 400 Jewish inhabitants lived in Riteve before the destruction. but this figure is far less thian in all the other estimates.

2. Testimony by Shaul Shenker YVA, M–I/Q/2/1322/136.

3. Testimonies by Shaul Shenker and Yentel Gershovitz YVA. M–1/Q/1322/136; see here. testimonies by Ethel Levinson–Friedman and Zlatta Olshwang.

4. Testimony by Zlatta Olshwang, op. cit.; testimonies by Paul Shenker and Yentel Gershovitz YVA. M–1/Q/1322/136.

5. Testimonies by Shaul Shenker and Yentel Gershovitz, YVA. M–1/Q/1322/136.

6. Testimony by Ethel Levinson–Friedman. in op. cit. testimonies by Shaul Shenker and Yentel Gershovitz YVA. M–1/Q/1322/136

7. Testimony by Yentel Gershovitz, op. cit Raul Hilberg. The Destruction of the European Jews NY. 1961. p. 204.

8. See 'The Holocaust of Lithuanian Jewry', at the beginning of this chapter.

9. Documents on the Holocaust, p. 377.

10. Testimonies by Shaul Shenker and Yentel Gershovitz, op cit.; testimony by Zlatta Olshwang. op. cit.

11. The survivors gave different estimates of the number of days they were locked up in Oginski's estate. According to one of the testimonies, they were kept there for only four days, testimony of Yentel Gershovitz YVA. M–1/Q/1322/136; but other survivors testified that the period was much longer – about 10–14 days; testimony by Shaul Shenker YVA. M–1/Q/1322/136; testimony by Ethel Levinson–Friedman, op cit.

12. The information about the deportation of males from Riteve to Heidekrug was given by one of the survivors immediately after the war. According to his testimony, the men were separated from the women and children in Riteve, before the evacuation. Every group was sent to a different place: the women and children to Vishtevian and the men to Heidekrug – testimony by Shaul Shenker YVA. M–1/Q/1322/136. This information conflicts with the testimonies given by all the other survivors. They emphasised the fact that the entire community, men, women and children, were evacuated to Vishtevian. However, a very careful reading of Shenker's testimony may bring us to the conclusion that only some men were separated from the rest of the Riteve Jews. Ethel Levinson–Friedman's testimony supports this assumption. She had to beg the Germans or the Lithuanians to allow her husband to accompany her to Vishtevian. Moreover, the fact that Jewish males from various small communities in west Lithuania, near Riteve, were deported to Heidekrug, gives Shenker's testimony plausibility. On the labour camps in Heidekrug, see Israel Kaplan, 'The camps in Heidekrug' Lithuanian Jewry, Vol 4. pp. 387–390 (Hebrew).

13. This fact leads some of the Holocaust researchers to the conclusion that the killing units had received more than one order concerning the annihilation of the Jews. The first order was to kill Communists and Jewish males and, a month later, Himmler and the Nazi leadership gave orders to begin the annihilation of all Jews, including women and children. See Christopher R Browning. Fateful Months. NY, 1985. pp 8–38

14. Yitzhak Arad, 'The "Final Solution" in Lithuania in the light of German Documentation', YVS, 11, 1976.

15. Testimonies by Shaul Shenker and Yentel Gershovitz YVA. M–1/Q/1322/136; testimony by Rachel Zinger–Taich., Telsiai Book, 1984, p. 364.

16. Documents on the Holocaust, pp 378–383

17. Testimony by Mina Kershtat, Telsiai Book, 1984, p. 381; testimony by Yocheved Huler. op. cit.. pp 341–342; testimony by Zlata Olshwang, op. cit.; testimonies by Shaul Shenker and Yentel Gershovitz, YVA. M–1/Q/1322/136.

18. Testimony by Rachel Zinger–Taich, Telsiai Book, 1984, p. 364.

19. Testimony by Zlata Olshwang op. cit., Yentel Gershowitz YVA. M–1/Q/1322/136; testimony by Yocheved Huler, pp. 341–342; 180 Lithuarians were deckared as Righteous of the Nations – people who saved Jews during the Holocaust – by Yad Vashem until the beginning of 1992.

20. Shaul Shenker YVA. M–1/Q/1322/136, Kaplan, op. cit.; pp. 387–390.

[Page 154]

Testimonies

by Roni Stauber

The death of Rabbi Fundiler, the last rabbi of Riteve

Author unknown

When the Second World War broke out, the Soviet authorities annexed Lithuania. At first conditions remained stable. In a letter which Rabbi Fundiler wrote to his brother–in–law in America in 1940 he said: 'For the moment peace reigns here and with the help of G–d we hope for peace in the future.' But with the approach of the enemy eastwards, the end of Jewish Lithuania in all its glory was imminent.

On the morning of 23 June 1941, Nazi aircraft dropped their first bombs on Kovno, the capital, and on that day the German army entered Riteve. In his book The Destruction of Lithuania, Rabbi Ephraim Oshri writes: 'With the arrival of the Germans in Riteve, the great misfortune and sufferings of the Jews began. Rabbi Fundiler was treated brutally. He was ordered to tear up the Scrolls of the Torah and other holy books. Unable to endure this humiliation, he suffered a heart attack and died in the Beit Midrash. The Germans then set the Beit Midrash alight and his body and those of other Jews were destroyed in the flames.[1]

In the book Lithuania, a survivor of Riteve, Ethel Levinson–Friedman, relates that the worst oppressors in Riteve were a Lithuanian tailor, Baranauskas, who had lived in Memel and who knew German, and another Lithuanian called Juadaikis. They rounded up 70 Jews including Rabbi Fundiler. They forced the rabbi to burn the holy books and this cruel command led to his death.[2]

Thus Rabbi Fundiler's life came to a tragic end. He was one of the most revered and influential teachers of his generation.

The destruction of Riteve

Ethel Levinson–Friedman

Dawn broke on 22 June 1941 and we were all asleep, unconscious of what lay ahead of us. Suddenly, a neighbour knocked at the door and told us that Germany and Russia were at war. We dressed hurriedly and ran outside. The pale faces testified to the confusion and fear in all our hearts. We were particularly badly off, because our son, Moshe Zavlav, was then at a forced labour camp 80 kilometres away.[3] Our mother, who usually gave good advice, was also confused. Everyone believed that the end had come and we and some neighbours decided to leave town and seek refuge in the nearby villages. We loaded a wagon with as many of our possessions as we could and in the afternoon left Riteve, fearing that we would probably never see it again.

We walked silently behind the cart like at a funeral and so we reached a village 3 kilometres away where the villagers received us quite happily, taking pleasure in the Jewish misfortune. They offered us accommodation in their summer rooms, thinking that soon they would possess our belongings, acquired with toil and sweat over many years We slept on the hard floor that night. In the morning we heard the sounds of firing coming closer. Bombs rained down on our town and destroyed it completely.[4] I and an old lady went the following day to see what damage had been done and found only debris and stones. On the roads were German soldiers on foot and in tanks and, in our hearts, a feeling of approaching destruction. The Lithuanians, with whom we had grown up and who had been our friends, changed overnight and became our enemies. We looked heavenwards and asked: 'Whence will my help come?'

We roamed desperately from place to place, enemies all around us. Wherever we went we were told by the Lithuanians that they could not shelter us because there were heavy penalties for sheltering Jews.[5] We were at our wits' end and decided to return to our town. I cannot describe what befell us there. The gun and the sword ruled and life was cheap. Our honoured citizens, our sons and daughters were humiliated by the enemy, forced to carry out the most despicable work. The Germans believed that in six weeks they would be in Moscow and so the Jews were the object of their sport. On 26 June 1941, Jews returning home from work were caught and put into a concentration camp.[6] All night the cries of the unfortunate women suffering at the hands of the SS could be heard. On the Friday Jews were brought in from different places and put into the camp and the town was emptied of its Jews.

[Page 155]

'For he will avenge the blood of his servants, and will render vengeance to his adversaries.'
A view of the mass grave site of the women put to death at Giroli, 7 kilometres from Telz

Standing, right to left: David Salzman (see recollections pages 158–160), Rifka Levit-Berelowitz, Chaya Movshovits and 'name unknown'.

[Page 156]

After three days of hunger, dried fish left over by the Russians was thrown at us. We fell upon it, lit fires and devoured the fish with dire consequences, as we all became very ill with diarrhoea. We lay on the ground wishing to die. We were then made to stand up as 'visitors' were expected. We dreaded this because after these visits new and crueller regulations were instituted. I remember when our rabbi[7] was singled out by these murderers. Half his beard was torn out and he was ordered to burn the holy books and his talit and tefilin. They filmed this event. We asked our captors what the future held for us. They replied that they were awaiting higher orders. Then days later the orders arrived. We were to leave Riteve and be taken to a central camp at Telz. We knew that we would not see Riteve again but we did not know what awaited us.

I shed many tears before I received permission for my husband to accompany me to our new destination. At 5 o'clock in the morning, 40 carts arrived to transport the old and the sick to Telz. The Lithuanians stood around rejoicing at our sad fate and helped to load the Jews. As we departed we were ordered to surrender our silver and gold on pain of death. Out of fear and panic we did so, surrendering the fruit of generations of hard work. A Lithuanian saw my wedding ring and demanded it from me. I pleaded with him but he threatened thai if I did not surrender it. he would take the finger too. Finally we were ordered to proceed – the old and the sick in the wagons and the rest of us following on foot. Surrounded by guards we marched on while a German took photographs for the next generations to see.

The Jewish community had dwell for generations on Lithuanian soil, lavishing on it sweat and toil. Now within a few days it was totally destroyed.

Riteve

Shaul Shenker

Based on the testimony given by Shaul Shenker in the Displaced Persons camp Feldafing immediately after the war. This testimony, like many others, was collected by the 'Jewish Central Historical Committee' in the American zone in occupied Germany.

Riteve, like all the cities and villages of Eastern Europe, experienced its own particular martyrdom. The population of Riteve consisted of 250 Jewish families. In this smallish town, scores of young men had been ordained as rabbis. There was a Junior Talmudic College, a large Hebrew school and two Batei Midrash.

The martyrdom of the Riteve Jews was reminiscent of the martyrdom of Rabbi Akiva and other great rabbis. On that well–remembered day, the Lithuanians began to organise themselves against the Jews.[8] Their first action was to plunder Jewish possessions and by evening the community had fled into the surrounding villages and forests. Then the Lithuanians began to threaten the peasants that if they harboured Jews, their lands would be set alight.

[Page 157]

On the Tuesday, as the Russians were retreating, the Germans bombarded the town, reducing it to flames.[9] On Wednesday, the Jews were ordered by the Lithuanians to return to the town and were promised that they would be given houses. When the Jews returned, the organised persecution began with beatings, hard labour and starvation.

In the first week, the Lithuanian murderers – the brothers Kazis and Stasis Rimayke – picked out the Jews Nachman Smoller, Moshe Katz, Felix Radiskansky and my own brother–in–law Herschel Gerber. They were taken to the Kuter Road behind the Lithuanian cemetery where these martyrs were forced to dig their own graves. They were then stabbed to death and thrown into the graves.[10]

Shmuel Fundiler, the rabbi of Riteve, who was a prominent member of the Kelmer (of the town Kelm) Musar movement, also lost his life. He was subjected to great humiliation. He refused to desecrate 'holy vessels' and was later put to death most cruelly.

The esteemed scholar, Reb Fishel Zilber, aged 90, was also cruelly humiliated before being beaten to death. He had refused to be parted from his Torah scroll, which was a family heirloom, having been written by his father. He was buried where he had succumbed, in the shul yard, still clasping the Torah scroll.

By the second week, the Jews of Riteve were in great pain and anguish, for their Lithuanian countrymen turned out to be more bloodthirsty and cruel towards them than the Germans. An order was received to separate the men from the women. The men were sent to Heidekrug[11] where there were also to be found men from Chvaidan, Luykeve, Shveksne, Neustadt, Weinuta, Varzan, Shilel and other small towns.[12]

The women were sent to Telz, the young ones on foot and the other ones and small children in wagons. On the road, the women were forced to bow to dead German soldiers. The devout daughters of Rev Yossel, who refused to bow, were beaten to death. From Telz, the women were driven to Vishtivian, 8 kilometres away, where other Jewish men and women had been brought. Here they were housed in stables. Three days later, when the Lithuanians were very drunk, they inflicted upon their victims all manner of humiliation. Fifty strong men were selected and they were sent to dig graves in a wood. The next day all men over the age of 13 were put to death and thrown into these graves.

The women were sent to a village, Giroli,[13] where there was a military hospital facility. Here there were also women from Varne, Alsiad, Nevaran, Zaran, Lukeve, and also refugees from Plungyan.[14] The women were told that a ghetto was being built in Telz, so they waited there for six weeks. Early one Saturday morning, they were ordered out into the square. Thirty wagons had arrived. Five hundred women were selected to be sent to Telz. All the others were ordered to kneel, and suddenly a hail of bullets from machine guns mowed them down. With heartrending cries and the sounds of 'Shema Israel' on their lips, the women and children died. On that spot stands their mass grave. This massacre occurred on the 7th of Elul (September 1941). The writer sadly relates that among the martyrs were his mother Feige Chave, his sister Sarah, her daughter Miriam and his brother Feivel Wolf. He alone remains.

[Page 158]

In Heidekrug, after a three weeks' stay there was another selection, the old being separated from the young. The former were told that they would be sent home, but instead were killed in Neustadt. After Rosh Hashanah, the weaker men were put to death, but 750 remained in Heidekrug for two years. From there they were sent to Warsaw, Auschwitz and Mildorf. In the end only 30 survived these ordeals.

This is a short and lamentable account of the destruction of Riteve. In deepest sorrow, we pray that these martyrs shall not be forgotten.

In the hands of the murderers

David Salzman

A feeling of horror overwhelmed me when I came face to face with my hometown Riteve. A stillness reigned as in a cemetery, little children were not to be seen any longer. I had not expected to see any of the townsfolk, but their absence cried out to me with a thousand voices. The streets were desolate, but I had a feeling that hundreds of ghosts were present. As I walked on, my footsteps echoed through the dead town, until my legs were unable to carry me any further. I was born in Riteve, which had a vibrant and lively Jewish community. Up until 1933, I was at a Hachsharah (preparation for life in a kibbutz in Palestine) camp in Shavli. From 1933 onwards I worked in Memel in the flax laboratory.

I left Riteve in 1941 and was employed as an electrical technician. I worked together with my wife and her sister in the region of Yokutska. I parted company from them and went to the front, where I took part in various battles from which I miraculously emerged in one piece. On 16 June, I was wounded and was laid up for six to seven months. I was wracked with pain and found no peace as I was very anxious about the fate of my family. Thus I was homeless in Samarkand – a fugitive till 1945. Finally I reached Vilna, where I was reunited with my wife and I worked there in a pharmaceutical laboratory till 1971.

Returning to Riteve after its destruction, I looked in vain for familiar faces, young and old; for the familiar faces of my dearly beloved countrymen. Perhaps I'll see them in shul? I thought. Fortunately the shul building was still standing, but no sounds of Torah chanting were to be heard. There was simply no trace of Jews. The Lithuanians had converted the shul into a grain store. I walked on to the school and here too there were no Jewish children; only Lithuanian gentiles were to be seen.

[Page 159]

No longer were there traces of little shops which the Jews had owned, and there were no more Jewish artisans. I looked into the courtyards where I saw houses which I had previously known, but their owners were not there. And so I went to the graves. Maybe there I would uncover something... But I fled from there with sorrow in my heart.

In Riteve I met Chanan Shapiro and his wife, and also Rivka Lou who told me that Mishka Feivish had survived. They told me that many of the young people had been killed or had been buried alive. Rabbi Fundiler – may his blood be avenged – suffered pain, anguish and humiliation at the hands of the Nazi murderers. Half his beard was cut off and he was forced to dance in public. On the Sabbath on Poniver Road, alongside a little chapel, the revered rabbi was forced to chop wood in the forest and to drag the logs. He did not survive this great torment and humiliation and there he departed this life.

Riteve, a small and vital town with little shops and small traders, was also possessed of great humanistic feelings and a zest for life. The people of Riteve had confidence in themselves and in the future. Generations of peaceful living had permitted the nurture of qualities such as scholarship, community life, love of Israel and strong family feelings. Their contribution to Jewish life was immeasurable. Wherever Riteve folk are found today, they are noted for having these fine attributes.

But the executioner came and with unimaginable brutality mowed down this vital community. All the Jews of Riteve were utterly annihilated and were buried in two mass graves, one for the men and one for the women.[15] Each grave measures 18 metres in length and 5 metres in width. The women's grave is situated in the woods, and the inscription in Russian and Lithuanian reads: 'Here lie those who perished by the hand of the Nazi murderers and their Lithuanian accomplices.[16]

Chayka Mabush (may her memory be blessed), who died in Vilna, told me that she was lying in a pit with her mother and her niece. Everyone had been shot but the bullets had missed her. The Lithuanian guard, noticing that she was alive, whispered to her to lie still, and advised her to escape when it became dark. It was fortunate that he had recognised her as a sometime fellow worker under the Soviets.

Words cannot describe the pain and suffering which we endured. More than once, I despaired of life. I wanted desperately to lead a normal and independent life. We packed our bags and took to the road which was fraught with danger. We were smuggled over borders, crossing snow–capped mountains. We endured hunger and cold and, after much suffering, we arrived in our sun–drenched land, the land of our fathers. Today I am a citizen of Beersheba and I frequently take stock of my life. I consider the path that my life has taken, and those things which I myself have seen.

The Germans, in their barbarism, killed, burnt and murdered helpless victims.

[Page 160]

Thousands roamed around, hungry, fearful, nol knowing what the morrow would bring. I think constantly about the black day when Riteve was destroyed. Can there be any consolation for our pain?

A community deeply rooted over many years has been cut down. And the Heavens looked on and were silent, while the Earth swallowed all with their last sighs and cries of anguish. And afterwards the pale moon, silently and placidly shone over the mass graves in the ruined town. No, we cannot, nor will we ever forget. We shall always remember our fathers and mothers, brothers and sisters. May their illustrious bravery be an inspiration.

Bereavement and homelessness

Yentel Gershovitz Alter

On 22 June 1941, when the Russians entered the war, all the Jews of Riteve fled to the surrounding villages. On 23 June, the Russians in their flight from the Germans set fire to Riteve. The town was almost totally destroyed except for a few houses. When the Germans invaded Riteve, they immediately issued a decree that no Lithuanian should give refuge to Jews and all the Jews had to return from the surrounding districts to Riteve.

The Germans immediately set up a committee, in which there were Lithuanian collaborators. The new committee ordered that all the Jews should register, with the result that all those who registered were not permitted to leave. They were locked up in a barn. The men were subjected to severe beatings and humiliation. Rabbi Shmuel Fundiler had half his beard cut off. His hat was torn off and replaced with an umbrella. He was then forced to burn his talit. The rest of the people were beaten and tormented. They suffered severe hunger and thirst, since they were not permitted to take any possessions along with them into the barn. We were kept in the barn for three days. On 27 June we were moved to Oginski's villa on the main street, where we were kept for four days.[17] We suffered hunger continually, since the bread which the Lithuanians reluctantly distributed was mouldy and the so–called soup was water.

The strong ones among the men and women were sent to work in the town, to clean up the debris of the fire. They were ordered to gather all the religious books and talits and tefilin. The rabbi was forced to set fire to these religious treasures. Afterwards he was harnessed to a wagon loaded with garbage which he was then made to pull. He collapsed under this load, and suffered a heart attack. A Lithuanian collaborator shot him dead on the spot. Six young men were removed from the villa, accused of being Communists anil three of them were shot immediately. They were Felix Radiskansky aged 20 years, Herschel

Gerber aged 29 years and Nachman Smoller. The rest had to dig their own graves and were then stabbed to death and thrown in. One of them was Moshe Katz.[18]

[Page 161]

Most of ihe Jewish refugees were gathered in Rayin, a good 5 kilometres from Telz, where we met other people from the Lithuanian shtetlach. On 4 July many refugees were selected to go to Telz, the able–bodied on foot, and the weaker ones and children in wagons. We found on our arrival in Telz that many other Jews were gathered from the surrounding region. We were well received by them and given food and drink. That evening we were taken to Vishiviyan, since Rayin was earmarked for the people of Telz. We found Jews from areas such as Nornetver[19] and others, totalling about 1,500 people. Here we again suffered hunger. The strong ones were sent to do hard labour in Telz.

On Monday 13 July, a truckload of Lithuanian collaborators arrived and hounded their victims backwards and forwards. They shot Yaakov Ber Girshowitz from Riteve and also Dr. Traub from Tvert and Itzikson from Telz. Two days later, on 15 July, a carload of Lithuanians and Germans arrived. They ordered the men and boys from 13 years of age and upwards to leave the barracks. They were driven to a nearby wood where they were put to death and buried in the previously dug graves. The next day documents and papers of the victims were found lying around the area. The women and children were driven to a village called Giroli, 7 kilometres away from Telz.

We remained there for six weeks. Our situation was appalling. We were kept in open barracks; the weather was bad; an epidemic broke out and many children died. We lived through terrible times and constant bad news added to our despair. Since there were no men among us, the women undertook every kind of work. They would travel into the town of Telz, accompanied by their Lithuanian captors, to obtain food. At the same time they secretly approached the bishop and pleaded with him to set up a ghetto for them in Telz. He promised to do whatever he could. Every night women took turns to be on guard duty at the barracks, because often the collaborators came in search of young women. When those on guard noticed the presence of these prowlers, they immediately sent a warning ahead, so that the young women had time to hide.

Friday, the 6th of Elul (September), when the women returned from the market, they reported hearing that the ghetto in Telz was ready and it had been decided that they would be transported there on Sunday. The mood in the barracks improved. On Saturday the 7th of Elul at 5 o'clock in the morning, our representative, Esther Bloch, entered, accompanied by one of the collaborators, and announced that Commandant Platokis demanded a sum of 30,000 roubles or else we would be shot. A great panic ensued, since we did not possess a sum of such magnitude. Everyone gave whatever she possessed in order to avert this evil decree. This sum was collected with great hardship, since we gave of our personal treasures in lieu of money. At seven o'clock, everyone was ordered to gather at the commandant's office. Here, the chief murderers of Telz awaited us, namely Vladas Yodakis and Vlodos Metkutzki. We were urged to remain calm as we were being sent to a ghetto in Telz. They promised a kindergarten for the children while the adults would be given work. Now we were told to return to the barracks and to pack our bags for the trip, since the vehicles were standing by to transport the older women and the children. This was greeted with mixed feelings, since not everyone trusted their smooth promises.

[Page 162]

The children were cheered up somewhat. They had been living with danger and threats of death. Now they were promised kindergartens. When everyone had packed, we were ordered to meet at the commandant's office and here we were ordered to kneel. Out of the whole crowd, 500 women under the age of 50 were selected to be sent to Telz. Young mothers were not allowed to take their male children with them. Some disguised their sons as girls and so got them through. Suddenly we heard shooting. There was great panic. The remaining 700 were all shot on the spot.

In Telz we were housed in a ghetto surrounded by barbed wire. A committee of five women was elected, with the Telz Rebbetzin (wife of the rabbi, generally active and acknowledged in her own right), Rachel Bloch, as chairman. Other members included Esther Bloch, Leah Koppel (now in Philadelphia) and Leah Fleisher. Women police maintained strict order. Many women were sent out to the surrounding districts as farm hands. This location was better than in Giroli because it was situated near the marketplace and the women were able to barter their last possessions with the Lithuanians through the wire fence.

On 2 December an order was issued to Lithuanian employers of Jewish workers that they be brought back to the Svekotos Potikrinti ghetto for medical inspection. The promise was that, after the New Year, the employers would be able to reemploy them. So, many women were returned to the ghetto. Some women, suspecting what lay ahead, managed to take refuge in other villages.

Back in the ghetto, no one was allowed out again. A message was received in the ghetto, warning that they would all be shot and a great panic ensued. Many tned to escape into the town. The guards turned a blind eye, because they knew that they could be rounded up quite easily. And so it was. On the evening of the same day, many of the escapees were brought back. Some managed to save their lives by taking refuge in villages among the peasants. Some managed to reach Shavli ghetto. On 14 December, the remaining women and children were transported to Rayin where they were all murdered.

I am one of those who escaped to Shavli.[20]

Thus the town was destroyed

Zlatta Olshwang

In 1940 the Russians arrived. All the shops closed. Property was nationalised, goods sold off, only one school remained. The library closed down. No kosher slaughtering was available any longer. A co–operative was set up. Parcels of land were given out to the disadvantaged, the youth went to work. Some people got up at 4.00 am for the morning prayers. Uri Gross, owner of the wealthy homestead, was replaced by the Communists who had intended taking the Zionists, but took the bourgeois instead. Slowly but surely the town emptied out; all the Jews' goods were sold off until all trade was discontinued. Anyone with a little money left to buy provisions was arrested.

[Page 163]

**Moshe, the son of Rachel
and Avraham Meir Olshwang.**

On 22 June 1941 the Germans entered Riteve. It was 4.00 am. The town began to reverberate with the sound of cannon fire. Verza, near the border, refugees began arriving in town, penniless and barefoot. We began packing whatever we could put our hands on and loaded up the wagon to ready ourselves for escape. Our neighbour, Gershke Wolfovitz, helped my brother and me get on his wagon. We barely made it out of the village, reaching the town of Boderick where the neighbour had a sister. But it had already been destroyed and we managed to escape to the next village. It was from there, with much grief, that I saw our village go up in flames.

As a young woman, I personally experienced all the details I recall, and hereby record them from memory, in order to comprehend the extent of the tragedy.

I believe that to my dying day I will not be free of my memories. I review in my mind the efforts and prudence that were needed to keep my head above water, to survive, until the storm passed. I find it especially difficult to relate the details of the story which I personally went through, from the Russian occupation to the Nazi conquest to the day on which Riteve was destroyed.

How shaken I was in my grief to see the good citizens of Riteve, gentle, kind and loving mankind, give up their lives before their time, cruelly tortured. The first victim was my brother, Moshe Olshwang, may his blood be avenged. The second was Buka Babuv. The third was Rivkin. the husband of Rivka Schweitzen.

We returned to Dobrik. There were soldiers all along the way. Many Jews had hidden in the silo. Penniless, hungry and needy we wandered, barely walking the 4 kilometres to Riteve. Behind me walked a German; in one of the yards in Riteve we found a lot of Jews, some of whom managed to escape from time to time.

Many of the Jews of Riteve went to work in the Germans' kitchens. Jews were not allowed to walk on the town's sidewalks. Any goy who hated Jews, and there were plenty of those, joined the murderers. The Jews were sent in groups to Telz. I started wandering again – 49 kilometres on foot, without food or water. A few hundred people would fight over one loaf of bread.

It went on like this for quite a long time – new decrees each day, new actions, new victims. From far and rear terrible reports arrived of slaughter and the liquidation of ghettos. The tired and homeless souls, wavering between life and death, retained their hope. So long as they deceived themselves with false hopes while heroically bearing the weight of the decrees, the wished–for miracle and salvation had a chance of coming true.

[Page 164]

In the meantime, the fire raged on in Riteve, the synagogue burned, the Beit Midrash remained standing. While they were still in the camp in Riteve, five girls were sent to clean up the Beit Midrash and were forced to burn the holy books kept there.

Then the 'Aktionen' began in Telz. Near Telz was the Ravin homestead where the people of Riteve were taken when the citizens of Telz were already in the camp. The first 'Aktion' was personal revenge on the part of the 'nationalists' from Riteve who got even with the youth of Riteve who held progressive views. From Rayin they were sent to Yasavian near Telz. And on the 20th of Tammuz all the men of Riteve were taken together with Jews from other towns; they were brutally tortured and gunned down.

After this cleansing action, the Nazis came, rounded up all the women left in town and lectured them on the Jew, the criminal, because of whom this whole disaster had come about. Because there were camps in the vicinity of Telz they were to be sent there. The old and weak women were sent to Giroli near Telz where they met their death. There were five work camps near Telz and any woman who fell ill or who was unable to work was immediately sent to Giroli. We faced fear, danger and death every minute of the day.

On 30 August 1941, the 7th of Elul, all the women in Giroli were put to death in the camp. Those at the homestead were brought to the 'ghetto' at Telz. Their names were put on a special list and they were put under the jurisdiction of the Lithuanian police. On the 4th of Kislev, late 1941, the murderers liquidated the ghetto of Telz as well, including the women working in the camps. The sword of death hovered over them all.

Then a messenger arrived from the ghetto of Telz and told my landlord that I was to go to the ghetto of Telz for a medical examination. My landlord, who took pity on me, said: 'We are going to sleep. Take whatever you want, and go where you wish.' Then I began wandering, until the Red Army came.

The moral suffering of the Jews in the ghettos was great. From behind ihe fence they saw how the Lithuanians took pleasure from the property of the Jews and built themselves from their ruins, while the wearers of the Yellow Star of David, the members of the cursed race, were imprisoned, hopeless, exhausted, awaiting their end. Anyone who did not personally experience the atrocities of the Nazis is incapable of fathoming what happened to us then. The days were grey and the nights were black–grey.

Trembling, I record these memories of Riteve, the memory of my never–to–be– forgotten loved ones. My heart, my heart goes out to you!

For those for whom I cry

The martyred of Riteve

May the Lord revenge their blood

They fell on 21 Tammuz 1942 – on the day of the massacre and on all the days of the Holocaust. Their graves are to be found in the foret of Goroli.

ABILOV	Manja (daughter of Rev Ephraim Wolfson)
ABILOV	Abram and family
ABRAMOWITZ	Aharon and family
ADELMAN	family
AVERBUCH	Avraham and family
AVERBUCH	Avraham Izhak and family
AVERBUCH	Freide
AVERBUCH	Moshe (Mauke) and family
BABUSH	Elchanan and family
BABUSH	Jacov Wolf and family
BABUSH	Shlomo and family
BABUSH	Shmuel and family
BALLIN	Jirmeyahu and family
BALLIN	Moshe and family
BERELOWITZ	Blume Eide
BERMAN	Chaie
BIRK	Sheine
BIRK	Shmuel and family
BRICK	Kroshe
BUCHMAN	Chaie
DAVIDOWITZ	Aba and family
DAVIDOWITZ	Shalom Leib and family
DORFMAN	Jacov and Chana

DRUZIN	Elchanan and family
DRUZIN	Sarah
DUSHIN	Sarah Rive
EPEL	Aharon and family
ERMAN	Leibe and family
ERMAN	Preide and family
FEIN	Baruch and wife
FIG	Hirsh and family
FRIEDMAN	David and son Ze'ev
FRIEDMAN	Kroshe and family
GARBER	Asher and family
GARBER	Chaie
GARBER	Ettel and Esther (Minna's daughter)
GARBER	Hessel and family
GARBER	Mendel and family
GARBER	Selig and family
GENISS	Chaim Jacov and family
GENISS	Chana Gute
GENISS	Friedman, Chaja Rive and son
GENISS	David and Chana
GENISS	Lieber and family
GLAUN	Chaie
GLAUN	Moshe and family
GLAUN	Shmuel and family
GROLL	Chaim Hirsh and family
GROLL	Chone and family
GROLL	David and family
GROLL	Jecheskel and family
GROLL	Pesse
GROLL	Sarah Hinde
GROLL	Taube Mire and family
GROLL	Ure and family
GOLDBERG	Alte and family
GOLDBERG	Taube
GOLDIN	Zipe and Sheidke
GRIKSHT	Alte and family

GRIKSHT	Moshe Yudel and family

HANTMAN	Jude Leib and family
HEIMAN	Moshe Aron and family
HEIMAN	Wolf and family
HIRSHOVITZ	Feige Rochel
HON	Meir and Sarah

ITZIKOWITZ	Beremiche and family
ITZIKOWITZ	Joseph and family

JANKELOWITZ	Gute and family
Jekel & Beile	
JELOWITZ	Meir and family
JOSEPH	Lea
JUDEL	family

KAPLAN	Chaie
KAPLAN	Tova
KARABELNIK	Benjamin and Esther
KARABELNIK	Leibe and Nechama
KARABELNIK	Rachel, husband and children
KATZ	Azriel
KATZ	Basse and Elke
KATZ	Michle
KATZ	Mosheand family
KATZ	Roche Tille and son Leib
KERL	Elijahu and family
KOHEN	Feitel and family
KREINGEL	Joseph and family

LEVINSON	Frume and family
LEVINSON	Sarah and family
LEVINSON	Rav Shmuel and family
LEVINSON	Taube
LEVINSON	Two daughters of Avraham and Pere
LEVITE	Benzion and family
LEVITE	Chaim and Sheine

LEVITE	Mordche Ber
LINDE	Zipe and son Eliezer
LONDON	Shimon Reuven and family
LURIE	Leib and Feige
MARKUS	Dvora
MEIEROWITZ	Avraham and family
MEIEROWITZ	Eliezer and Sheva
MEIEROWITZ	Nechemia and family
MENT	Shmuel Chaim and family
MILSTEIN	Meir and family
MOGILEVSKY	Benzion and family
MOVSHOVITZ	Eide Gitte
MUSALIN	Gershon andPnina
NAPARSTOK	Moshe and family
NAPARSTOK	Nissen and family
NAPARSTOK	Shmuel and family
NAVARON	Nissen and family
NOCHOMOVITCH	Hinde and family
NODEL	Izchak and famiuly
NODEL	Jecheskel and family
NODEL	Sarah Lea
NODEL	Sepe and family
OLSHWANG	Avraham Meir and son Moshe
PALUKST	Itzchak Leib and Sara Rifka
POSSEL	Jacov Leib and family
PRESS	Benzion and family
PRISMAN	Chana Peshe
PRISMAN	Eleizer and family
RABINOWITZ	Aba and family
RIVKIN	Rifka and husband
ROSENHEIM	Baruch and family
ROSENHEIM	Kreine and family
ROSENKOWITZ	Chana Lea

ROSENKOWITZ	Kroshe, husband and children
RUDAIZKY	Basse
RUDAIZKY	Leib and family
RUDAIZKY	Nissan and family
RUDAIZKY	Shalom Izchak and family
SAFIR	Dobe and family
SAFRANSKY	Blume and children
SAKS	Aron and Chana
SAKS	Dr Bendet and family
SAKS	Gute
SAKS	Nachman and family
SAKS	Simche and family
SALZMAN	Meir Reuven and family
SALZMAN	Shmuel Zvi and family
SEGAL	Sheina Zire and family
SHAPIRO	Baruch and family
SHAPIRO	Israel Ber and family
SHAPIRO	Izchak and family
SHAPIRO	Mones and family
SHAPIRO	Pessach and family
SHEFTELOWITZ	Jacov and family
SHIFRE	Feige Chazes
SHMILING	Rachel and children
SHMOLE	Basse and family
SHMOLE	Meine and family
SHUR	Rav Joseph and family
STRASS	Joseph and family
TOLMAN	Rav Jechiel and family
VERKUL	Frume
VUNDILLER	Rav Shmuel and Sheine
WACHTVOGEL	Zise and Benzion
WELVELOWITZ	Aba and family
WISHNEVSKY	Rav Izchak and family
WOLFOWITZ	Aron Idel and family

ZAUBER	Itzejanke and family
ZAUBER	Moshe and family
ZELKER	Alter and family
ZWICK	Rochel
ZWICK	Zvi and family

Footnotes

1. Ephraim Oshri, The Destruction of Lithuania (Yiddish). New York and Montreal. 1951. p. 251.

2. Lithuania (Yiddish) (eds. Dr. M Sudarski. A Katzenellenbogen and Y Kissin), New York, 1951. Vol. I. p. 186.

3. He was probably arrested by the Communist regime after the Soviet occupation in June 1940.

4. According to some testimonies, the Russians were the ones who set fire to the town while retreating from this part of Lithuania. Other survivors testified that the fire was caused by a German air mid.

5. It was the instruction of the Lithuanian collaborationist committee of Riteve.

6. They were concentrated in Oginski's. estate.

7. Rabbi Shmuel Fundlier.

8. The persecutions of the Jews in Riteve began on 22–23 June 1941, immediately after the arrival of the first news about the German invasion.

9. Other survivors testified that the Russian set fire to the town while retreating from this part of Lithuania.

10. They were accused by the Lithuanians of being Communists.

11. Small shtetl in the Memel district. The Germans set up several labour camps in Heidekrug and the surrounding arca.

12. According to other testimonies, the whole community, men, women and children, were evacuated together Vishtevian and Telz.

13. About 10 kilometres from Telz.

14. All small shtetlakh located in the districts of Telz and Taurage.

15. For more details see the introduction on 'The destruction of the Riteve community.' According to the testimony of a Lithuanian farmer, taken by Selwyn Singer in June 1992, three young women managed to escape from the pit. The farmer was then 12 years old, yet he vividly remembers how the earth–filled with the bodies of about 3,500 women

and children – swelled, the pit opened, and German soldiers came and poured corrosive chemicals into it.

16. The inscriptions on commemoration sites built in the Soviet Union after the war bear no mention of the fact that most of the victims were Jews. It is only now, after the collapse of the Soviet Union, that new inscriptions are being introduced with the correct details.

17. Other survivors testified that this period was much longer–about 10–14 days. See for instance testimony by Shaul Shenker, YVA. M–1/Q/1322/136 testimony by Ethel Levinson–Friedman in this book.

18. The first victims in most of the Jewish communities in the ex–Soviet territories in general and in Lithuania in particular were those who were accused of being Communists.

19. A small shtetl located in the Telz district.

20. Shavli. a major town in northwest Lithuania, with a population of about 5,000 Jews before the Holocaust, became the third largest ghetto in Lithuania, with about 8,000 Jews (following Vilna with 20,000 and Kovno with 17,000). When the Jews of Riteve were killed, the ghetto of Shavli was still living through a period of relative calm, which lasted until its liquidation in July 1944.

[Page 168]

Chapter Ten

A South African Returns to the Lithuanian Shtetl

by Mendel Kaplan

My father was born in Johannesburg in 1906, but lost both his parents at a very early age. His mother, who was Rose Karabelnik from Krakinovo, died in 1913 when my father was 6 years old; and his father, Menachem Mendel (Max), who was born in Shadove, died in 1923. My mother's father, Isaac Bloch from Riteve, died in 1919 and only my mother's mother, Rochel, born Groll, also from Riteve, survived to become the link between her grandchildren and her shtetl. So, while we knew vaguely of Shadove through cousins of my grandfather, and even more vaguely of Krakinovo, we had learnt a great deal about Riteve.

My grandmother had spoken of the 'blotte' or mud streets and of the Porilz in whose fields she collected chestnuts; and of the Beit Midrash or school to which she could not go because only males studied – she paid her brother to teach her his lessons. She told the story, related in this book, of the Poritz Oginski, father of the Poritz she knew. Offended by some Jews, he had removed all the holy objects from the Beit Midrash and had ordercc pigs to be driven into it. afterwards turning it into a dwelling for his tenants. Some years later, in 1859, he had fomented rebellion against the Russian government. Knowing he was going to be arrested, he committed suicide. It so happened that this event took place on the eve of Purim. The Jews regarded this as G–d's will and, thereafter, celebrated not only the death of Haman at Purim, but that of the Poritz Oginski, too. My grandmother did point out, however, that his son permitted the building of a new Beit Midrash on a different site from the one his father had desecrated.

So Riteve was part of our memory and, in fact, my grandmother and her large family all came to South Africa and all lived in the little village of Parow. My grandmother's father, Israel Groll, after whom I have my middle name, was born in 1845 outside Riteve on a farm in Pastravinska, and died in Cape Town in 1922. I think that, by the mid–1930s when I was born, there was nobody left in Riteve whom my grandmother had known personally. Even before that, my mother did not remember any letters passing to and from Riteve. She could not recall that her mother mourned for any family members who died in the Holocaust. The people that the family in South Africa should have mourned were probably not born by the time my grandmother left Riteve. She did not even know who they were. And to me, growing up in Parow in my own environment, Riteve was like a world chat existed in another universe.

[Page 169]

Outside the synagogue of Vilna

The return to a Lithuanian shtetl by a South African Jew, not only bom in South Africa, but whose parents were bom there too, was inconceivable over most of my lifetime. For one reason, there was no relationship between South Africa and most East European countries. For another, there was a long distance in time, culture and history between the Lithuanian shtetl of my great–grandfather and today's industrial environment.

Then, during the 1980s. Jewish communal commitments enabled my family and me to visit Eastern Europe on a regular basis for some five years on behalf of the World Jewish Congress and Jewish Agency. I remember a visit in 1983 to Tichocin, on the border between Poland and Lithuania – because of its situation it gave me a feel of what Lithuania must have been like. I thought to myself that this was the sort of countryside that my grandmother had come from; the horses pulling ploughs in the fields and the wonderful old synagogue. I had no hope then of going there, but this made me determined to do so.

The World Jewish Congress was able to organise the first Jewish meeting in Eastern Europe in Budapest in 1987 and further contacts were cemented when its offices for the Jewish Agency for Eastern Europe were opened in the same city in 1988. These meetings created a personal relationship with the prime minister and members of the government of Hungary and an increased willingness on their part to act as a bridge between East and West.

[Page 170]

The Forest of Ponery (Ponar). Young trees grow where 80,000 Jews were killed in 1941. This was one of a number of Holocaust sites visited

The changes in Hungary, together with Glasnost in the Soviet Union, allowed Edgar Bronfman, Simcha Dinitz and myself to pay an official visit to Moscow in November 1988. This, together with other initiatives, led, and will lead, to a greater involvement of Israel and Diaspora Jewry with the Jews of the Soviet Union. It allowed a massive opportunity for 'operation redemption' in terms of the reconstruction of Soviet Jewish life and 'operation exodus' – the ability to persuade those who emigrate to live in Israel. In November 1988, the minister of culture suggested that I could get permission to visit Lithuania. (I was not a Catholic, and it was Catholics who were giving the Soviet Union problems at that stage!) And so, in June 1989. apart from communal opportunities, the new era also allowed my wife, my elder son, David, and me to visit Lithuania – which we did the following month.

After receiving our visas in Budapest, we flew directly to Riga for a programme of four days in that city and four days in Vilna – with an opportunity to visit the shtetlakh meaningful to our family in between. It was not so much a geographical exploration, but more like peeling off layers from an onion as our journey became a sort of time machine. Layers of the more recent past had to be peeled away before we could perceive something of what we really yearned to see: the Lithuania of the shtetl and to walk in the footsteps of our antecedents and feel something of the life style they had experienced.

[Page 171]

We wondered to what extent we could realise our dream. At the outset, we had no direct links with anybody in Lithuania or Latvia – other than with the leaders of the Latvian Jewish Cultural Society, whom we would meet in Riga, and their Lithuanian counterparts in Vilna. However, as I was leaving London for Budapest, my wife informed me that Abe Galaun, a relative in Zambia, had met a man of our family who had survived the Holocaust and was living close to Riteve. This man would be able to guide us in our search for the past. And, through a totally random incident, we met him: Alexander Judelis. It was through him that we became entwined in the world of our great–grandfathers. But first, to get to this world, we had to peel off three levels of time which kept interposing themselves between the shtetl of the late 19th century and the world of the present 20th century.

I feel, therefore, that a true understanding of our experiences is best captured by looking at our journey in an attempt to work through the layers of time which separated us from the world of the shtetl. The layers we had to peel away were, firstly the Lithuania and Latvia of today; secondly the Holocaust which still overwhelms any Jewish experience; and thirdly, the high point of history of the Baltic States, which came between the two world wars – the independence of Lithuania, Latvia and Estonia. And only after we had peeled off these layers, we soon realised, would we grasp the life of the shtetl – if there was anything left to grasp.

Lithuania and Latvia of 1989

Any newspaper of today gives evidence of the major changes facing Eastern Europe. Those of us who have visited it since 1989 are amazed at the almost monthly changes taking place. This was reflected particularly, as early as 1989, in the openness of society, their questioning of their political and economic principles and a desire for immediate change and independence. The Baltic States led the demand for at least economic independence and greater regional freedoms. A symbol of the change in 1989 was the alteration in street names to those which were current before 1939. So in Vilna, despite the now sparse Jewish population, you today have Gaon Street and Jew Street as they used to be before the Soviet take–over. When we visited in 1989, Jews had recently been officially permitted to open a Latvian and a Lithuanian Jewish Cultural Society with its own board of directors and authority over Jewish matters.

I was met in Riga by three leaders of the Latvian Cultural Society who acted as guides and hosts during our visit. One of my hosts, Gregory, took me to a meeting of their board in Riga in the reclaimed Jewish Community Centre Building. It was built in 1913 by the Jewish community and had recently been given back to them to use as offices and a meeting place. Changing conditions had already allowed Gregory to reidentify with his Jewish past. The Latvian Society was publishing a magazine in Russian with a distribution of 50,000, was doing research on the history of Latvian Jewry and, possibly most important of all, was busy try ing to establish the first Jewish day school to be allowed in the Soviet Union.

[Page 172]

Outside the Jewish community Centre building in Riga, erected in 1913, with a group of the Jewish Cultural Society

In Jurmala, a seaside resort near Riga, we visited 30 people who had come from all over the Soviet Union to spend their summer vacation learning Hebrew and studying our religious sources. Everybody at the 'diboor', as they called this gathering, was enthused with a desire to learn Hebrew and his or her religion. And this was in a world where one could not get kosher food and where religious practice was almost impossible.

A week later, in Vilna, the leaders of the Lithuanian Cultural Society invited members of the community to meet me. With only one day's notice, over 200 people attended and our discussion focused mainly on the problems of Aliyah to Israel. It was a miracle in that day and age in the Soviet Union that such a meeting could take place. This was the Lithuania and Latvia of 1989, bubbling with new–found nationalism, demanding independence from Soviet control and, with the ability of the Jewish community to rebuild some form of cultural community experience, to re–establish a Jewish school system, openly to learn Hebrew, practise the Jewish religion and plan Aliyah.

[Page 173]

Should one leave the issues of the moment and peel off another layer of time, the remnants of the Jewish community of the Baltic States and their leaders were wholly immersed in the events of the Holocaust. There was very little interest in what had occurred before, because there was no point in rekindling memories of a world that had disappeared altogether. So, to get to that world, we had first to go through the process of the events that had overtaken the Jewish community so tragically in June 1941 and which led to its almost complete destruction.

We had started on our trip to the world of the shletl from Riga and were making our way towards Shavli. We had a minibus with a Lithuanian driver and were accompanied by two Latvian Jews, a father and son. The father was a reasonably well–off scientist and the son was a student from Vilna who had been studying with a man from Rostock at Jurmala. With Jill, David and me, we were a party of six. As we were on our way to Shavli, the driver told us that he had been bom and brought up in Joniskis. We were travelling through this town when he said that he wanted to show us something. He turned off into a forest road and, after a few hundred metres, stopped and took us to a memorial which had inscribed on it: 'Here perished 493 Soviet Citizens – victims of Fascism.'

He then said: 'When I was 8 years old, I was playing in a tree and I noticed Lithuanians, who had been fed a lot of vodka by the Germans, who then drove hundreds of Jews from our village into this forest. The Germans had arranged for loud music to be played and then they instructed the Lithuanians to shoot the Jews. And I saw all the Jews shot and then buried right on the spot.' As he paused and we absorbed this horrific event, the young man from Vilna. who was 18, said: 'Yes, my family was among those who lie buried here.'

There was no moment in which we were not made aware of the events of the Holocaust. In Riga, we had been taken by Gregory to the site of the Choral Synagogue where, he informed us, on 4 July 1941 the Nazis had burnt the synagogue with hundreds of Jews inside it. On 4 July 1988, the first small tablet with a Magen David, recording the event, was unveiled on the site. From the synagogue he took us into the forest at Rumbulas where the Jews of the Riga ghetto had been slaughtered. As we visited each small shtetl we were reminded of the Holocaust: there were, at the most, only a handful of Jews in them and, sometimes, none at all. At Telz we visited the forests in which 30,000 Jews had been killed – the men on one side and the women and children on the other. Some years later, a small stone tablet was erected to record this horror. I was particularly conscious of this event because it was to the Forest of Telz that our family from Riteve had been taken and it was in the Forest of Telz that Lithuanian remnants gather on 4 September every year to remember the communities destroyed.

When we reached Vilna, we were taken to the Forest of Ponery where, in the foundations of oil tanks. 100,000 Lithuanians, of whom 80,000 were Jews, had been killed by the Nazis. Their remains were set on fire in order to cover up the atrocity. In no instance was a victim of Fascism anyone other than a Soviet citizen.

[Page 174]

I visited the minister of foreign affairs in Lithuania with Mr Moshe Aaronson, a member of the Lithuanian Jewish Cultural Society. I explained that the anti–Semitism of Soviet society shown by the lack of understanding for the Jewish suffering in the Holocaust through omission on the memorials of any Jewish link, was unacceptable. He promised that memorials would be set up in Yiddish and Hebrew and that appropriate references to the Jewish victims would be made – as has now been done. Approximately 134 memorial sites would be marked and 434 cemeteries would be cleared and tidied up. Much of this work has been done. The Riteve cemetery which used to be what we call 'bush' in South Africa, is now not only cleared, but is also fenced.

Lithuania between the World Wars: 1918–1939

Is it possible after viewing these honors to persuade any members of the community to pierce the veil into the world that existed before the Holocaust? Only very slightly. In Telz, I was fortunate to meet members of two or three Jewish families living there: Mr Shapiro and Mr Schmuliwitz. Alexander Judelis, who had joined our party, pointed out the house in which he had lived before the war as well as the house of Rabbi Bloch whose son was his chavrusah. And, ultimately, we found the building that housed the famous yeshiva – now used as a cinema. Alexander remembered that there were 110 students before the war, of whom 30 were qualified. (He was talking of the yeshiva and not the mechina or the teachers' seminary.)

We found a synagogue operating in Vilna, in Kovno and in Riga. Wc attended a Friday night and a Saturday morning service which took us right back to the pre–war years. The reader of the morning service and the additional service had exactly the same intonation and musical tone as we have in South Africa today. Unlike the Soviet Union, religious intolerance came to the Baltic States only in 1940 and all those attending the service had had some form of religious education. In Vilna and Kovno, the interiors of the synagogues reminded us of those in South Africa in the period before the Second World War.

Our first venture into finding the tracks of the past was to pick up memories of the years between the wars. We visited Radviliskis where Jill had been given the address of a house in which her grandmother's family had lived before the war. She had been told to go to the railway station, turn right and find the fourth house on the left – a face–brick building. We did this and came to a wooden building. We were about to give up the search when our young Lithuanian fnend said he thought that we were in the wrong street. The correct one was the street facing the railway station and he was proved right. The fourth house was exactly as it had been described to Jill: face–brick with an A–frame roof. It was now a vegetable shop. This had been the home of Jill's great–grandmother and her children.

[Page 175]

Standing outside the once famous yeshiva at Telz. Left, heads of two of the last three remaining Jewish families in the town, Mr. Shapiro and Mr. Schmuliwitz

My wife, Jill, stands with our elder son David, right, outside the house in Radviliskis where her mother's family lived before the war.

[Page 176]

My second cousin, the late Alexander Judelis and his wife, Leokadija, right, were our guides as we explored the shtetlakh in which family members had lived

This scene in Telz is typical of our journey; the minibus parked in a wet street next to a muddy pavement – the 'blotte' (mud) that my Bobba Rachel had so often told us about – as Alexander and Leokadija indicated places to us. It rained or drizzled most of the time. The house behind them is where Alexander lived at Telz and they are pointing to the home of the famous Rabbi Bloch, head of the yeshiva.

The successful conclusion of this search was topped off by an incredible event that happened a few days later in Vilna. In the hotel elevator, I was carrying my talit when a small man entered and spoke to me in Yiddish. He asked me where I was from and I replied: 'Johannesburg, Jerusalem.' He said he was from New York, but had been born in Radviliskis. I told him that my wife's family, the Goldstucks, came from there. He collapsed and said that we must be related. I replied, 'Not to me, but maybe to my wife.' He told me: 'You know, I was in Radviliskis looking for the house in which I grew up – the Goldstuck house. It was near the railway station.' I said: 'You made the same

mistake as us: you turned right and looked for the fourth house on the left.'
He could not believe that he had met a member of his family in the elevator
and we discovered that he had lived in the very same house as Jill's
grandmother – his aunt's sister. And also, of course, his aunt, too, although
he never knew her.

In Biers, a little shtetl in which my wife's grandfather was born, we stopped
outside a church on a Sunday morning and tried to find anyone with any
recollection of a Jewish past. One of the congregants hurrying into the church
told us of an old man who might have some memories. We went to the
apartment building indicated and found the old man's wife there. She said she
would show us what had once been a synagogue.

[Page 177]

**This is an old picture of Shadove, obtained 20 years ago from the late
Sarah Broer, my Grandfather's cousin**
**The twin spires of the Catholic church, still in existence, may be seen in
the background**

As she climbed into the minibus, I asked her if she spoke Yiddish and she replied: 'How can a Jew not speak Yiddish?' She took us to the shtibuls that existed before the war and were now homes and also to a neglected grave site where the only gravestone upright and legible was that of her father. She told us that when they had returned from Siberia after the war, she had heard that her husband was in Vilna. Her father had said: 'Children must not grow up without their father' and they had proceeded to Vilna to find him. However, en route her father was shot by Lithuanian bandits. She returned to Biers and was joined by her husband and her children. She said: 'The street through which we are driving had only Jewish homes. The village was 60 per cent Jewish – but that was before the war. Now there are a tobacconist, two teachers, my husband and myself. That is the totality of Jewish life in Biers.' The cemetery of Biers was much like other cemeteries: overgrown; gravestones indecipherable. It was impossible to find memories of the past – even the recent past. However, in discussions with the minister of foreign affairs, he approved a project to reconstruct the old cemeteries of Lithuania.

These were shreds of memories: there were too few people left for vivid ones. It was then possible, having gone through the period of today and experienced the pangs of the Holocaust and peeled off the last, very thin layer – that of the elements of Lithuania between the two world wars – to attempt to find the life of the shtetl.

[Page 178]

My son David stands outside a typical house in Shadove – compare this with the photograph on the previous page. This house stands above the stream, unchanged from the sort of dwelling in which his great–grandfather might have been born.

Life in the shtetl

We were approaching Shadove for which we had very little direct source material. We knew that it was the shtetl in which my grandfather, Max Kaplan, had been born in 1876. We knew thati his cousin, Sarah Broer, had lived in the house in which he had been bom before she left for South Africa. We knew that she had written that Shadove had a main square with a Russian Orthodox Church and that from the square, there led three roads: the one to Shavli in which was the Roman Catholic Church; one to Ponevezh in which was the shop of the German chemist; and one to Keidan which was lined only by wooden houses except for two brick buildings that had been owned by Jews.

Well, we stopped at the Roman Catholic Church which dominated the village as we entered via the road from Shavli to Shadove. We found a Roman Catholic priest, quietly spoken, who remembered that he was at school with Boraks. Katzes and Kaplans before the war. The Jews, he said, lived all around the village, especially the main square. He knew where the synagogue had been – today, it is an open parking ground. He suggested that we walk along the path behind the church to some fields and find an old man who would tell us more.

We walked along this path and crossed a wooden bridge over a stream – the stream in which Sarah Broer had said the village people did their laundry. Not only did the stream still exist, but the house above it in which the old man lived had no running water – only wells. We could not find this scion of the village as unfortunately he had broken his arm the day before. But this village had been maintained as a timewarp of the shtetl era. We walked in the same fields in which Sarah had walked as a child 90 years ago. with the houses unchanged and the stream still used for laundry.

[Page 179]

The farmhouse at Pastravinska where my great-grandfather, Israel Groll, was born
– a photograph taken by a relative, Abe Galaun

We walked past the Roman Catholic church into the town square and there was no longer a Russian Orthodox church – it had been burnt with the synagogue during the Stalinist period. Next to the empty space where the synagogue had been was the house of the rabbi; behind that was the house in which Sarah had lived and behind that was the well, still in use. which her family and my grandfather's family had shared with the rabbi. The houses along Keidan Street which Sarah had described were still wooden ones, but there were the two brick houses among them: one of them a library and the other still a home. You could sense the world of the shtetl. Little had changed since the birth of my grandfather – except that there were no Jews. A shtetl which had had a population of over 50 per cent Jews was now a little village of around 3,000 people, lost in time and, to a large extent, lifeless in terms of the energy and distinctiveness of its Jewish soul.

From Shadove we visited Krakinovo whose shtetl world centres on the remnants of two synagogues, a town square and a river which still rushed past an overgrown cemetery. It was celebrating its 580th year and brought back memories from an old photograph of the marriage of my grandmother's sister in that shtetl over 80 years ago. Otherwise, there was no sign of its Jewish past, no memory of anyone there and no concern about what had been.

[Page 180]

A farmhouse at Shadove

The shtetl came alive to us through Alexander Judelis. And it was a miraculous discovery to find a close relative who had survived the war. He was the grandson of David Groll, the youngest brother of my great–grandfather, Israel Groll. The older brother, Israel, had moved in the 1870s from the farm on which he was born in Pastravinska, outside Riteve, to the shtetl of Riteve. His young brother, David, had remained on the farm, succeeding his father, Abba, as the farmer. After his wife's death. Israel Groll had followed all his children to South Africa where they had settled not long after the turn of the century. My grandmother, Rochel Groll, had married in Parow and had transferred the shtetl of Riteve to Parow, making her home the venue for services until the shul could be built. She created a family atmosphere which included over 50 members in Parow – an atmosphere, as I now discovered, she had experienced in Riteve.

David Groll remained on the farm in Pastravinska and fathered five children – two settled in South Africa just before the Second World War, one went to Israel and two were killed with David by the Nazis in 1941, together with the rest of our family – except for one grandson. This was Alexander who had joined the Russian forces in 1941, had been wounded three times and given the Order of the Red Banner – the highest honour in the Red Army – and who had then returned to Riteve. After restarting his father's timber factory, he was sent to Leningrad University to study forestry. He rose subsequently to be head of the forestry division of Lithuania and was awarded the Order of Lenin for services rendered – the highest award in the Soviet Union.

I stand right with Alexander and Leokadija Judelis outside the now decrepit gateway and lodge of the former estate of of the Poritz at Riteve

[Page 181]

Alexander welcomed us to his home and we spent four hours with his wife and son building bridges across 50 years of emptiness and then through a period of common ground. Alexander showed us his wounds and said: 'I was convinced that the entire village of Riteve had been wiped out including every member of my family. I got drunk in the forests on vodka for three months and then decided to'start anew.'

He took us to Pastravinska. where his grandfather and my great-grandfather had been born. The farmhouse had remained exactly the same; if anything it seemed to him a little smaller! The barn with a calf was the same, as was the well which supplied the farmer with his water. The farm was occupied by a Lithuanian who had worked with the family in the timber factory 60 years before. He had carried Alexander and his sisters in his arms when they were born. He knew Alexander's grandfather and his parents intimately. He was a direct link to the operations of the farm which had not been changed since Abba Groll had started it in the 1840s. We asked him about perestroika. He said that Lithuania was a land which had suffered under many conquerors and many changes. He did not believe in the magic of Gorbachev. He said: 'Wait and see.'

Alexander took us a few kilometres to the shtetl of Riteve and into the town square with its Catholic church. Facing the church had been the shops of the Jewish traders. On one comer of the square, on the road to Plungyan, had been the shop of a relative, Ura Groll. Leading off the square was a smaller street which housed the Beit Midrash, the synagogue, the rabbi's house and the school to which Israel Groll had sent his children. There was nothing left except the Beit Midrash, now used as a cinema. The road had led over the bridge past my great–grand– father's house to the cemetery. We visited the cemetery, which was overgrown. The only inscription I could read was that of a man buried in 1936 – the year in which I was born.

[Page 182]

A family group taken at a later visit to Pastravinska

The well may be seen on the right–hand side and the house on the left–hand side. Since it has become possible to visit Lithuania, many families like ours have been able to make then nostalgic journey to our roots, although always overshadowed by the tragedy of the Holocaust.

However, near the Beit Midrash were the houses of the Groll and Sacks families and the street which led to the grounds of the Poritz, the palace of Oginski. We entered the neglected gateway and saw what had once been a beautiful lake in the forests in which my grandmother had collected chestnuts. Oginski's palace still stood and was used as a school – next to the building was a dairy which had existed since time immemorial. Above the dairy were the foundations of a windmill which the Poritz had built to provide electricity to the village. My Bobba remembered that Riteve had electric lights before Kovno and here were the remains of that miracle. Riteve had the remnants of a beautiful little shtetl – the Poritz, after all, had given it a lake, forests and a park. The Jewish people had their houses on either side of the square and the synagogue. While the shtetl was recalled through the memory of Alexander Judelis and the words of my Bobba. it was left, of course, without the soul of the people who had built, developed and given it the dynamism of a period long past.

[Page 183]

The surviving soul of the shtetl

The year 1989 was my first, unforgettable visit to try to find the life of the shtetl. There was another memorable one from 9–19 June 1992 when 39 members of the family and close friends, all South African–born and all with roots in Lithuania, toured it together following a more extensive route than on our first visit. The tour included, for example, a visit to Memel (Klaipeda), from which some emigrants had embarked on the journey which would take them to South Africa.

Taking part on this tour were my late mother, Jesse Kaplan, and her elder sister, Janie Kushlick, the two daughters of Rochel Bloch, born Grail, who had carried on the traditions passed onto them by their mother. There came a moment at the farm at Pastravinska when a drink from the well was offered to us. And there, on the video taken of the trip, you can see my mother and Aunt Janie sipping the water with a look of wonder on their faces. Did they realise then, perhaps, as I appreciate every time I see it, that the well of the spiritual waters of the shtetl has not run dry; that it carried on from one generation to another in a different country? Our finest tribute to those who died in the destruction of the Jewish community in Lithuania in 1941 is to be faithful to the traditions they passed down to us and to strengthen the centre of Jewish life – Israel.

[Page 184]

Appendix 1

From: Ha–Melitz, No. 128, June 24, 1900.

A list of names of about 100 donors from Riteve, who collected 26.20 roubles for a fund for the hungry in Bessarabia.[1]

Rabbi Yaffe, M. Itzikowitz, Dr. Linde, Leib Levite, Ze'ev Grod, Issar Hirshberg, A. Saks, l.B. Saks, Nachman Averbuch, Tuvie Devorah, Nachimovitch. M.D. Levite, Meir Hon. M.Z. Friedman. I.B. Hirshowitz, H.I. Mosinson, M.L. Maoschivitz, I.L. Palukst, David Levinson, Yechiel Saks, l.M. Averbuch, M.A. Heiman, Nachman Saks, Ze'ev Kahn. Bendet Groll, Moshe Schwartz, Yosef Scheraz, Zisman Averbuch, D. Talmud, Hinde Tubiles, Keile Saks, Rachel–Leah Schnieder, Yitzhak Gershon Berman. Eliyahu Zinger, Sh. V. Aharonson, Sh. Klugman, M. Garin, Nissan Wein, I.B. Shapira, Zusman Yeroslaiski, Meir Zaks, Rachel–Leah Davidovitch, Sarah–Feige Rudaizky, Sarah Bea, Yechezkel Groll, Aharon Zelker, Itzhak Yabetz, P.I. Yabetz, Baruch Shapira, Sh. R. Shapira, Leah Levite, P. Orwin, Chaya Saks, Neta Levite, Channah Saks, Ester Graf, Moshe Segal, Dov Wolf Biraki, Ya'acov Saks, M.I. Segal, Moshe Averbuch, l.M.Tubiles, Michael Ber Ya'acov, l.D. Milner, P. Pmolei, Leah Miller, Ze'ev Talman, Arieh Leib Krom, Leah Sergei, I.A. Hirschowitz, Simcha Saks, B. Hendler, M Makus, Yitzhak Galvin, Shechna Saks, Mane Wolf, Gitl Abelevitch, Eliezer Meierowitz, Sarah Glugman, Devorah Jankelowitz, Itzhak Gratz, Israel Tietz, Yosef Segal, Beile Kahn, Abba Rabinowitz, H.K. Prisman, Sh. Levite, Avraham Geniss. Lipman Sirat, Meir Lasovski, A.B. Averbuch, Yitzhak Meierowitz, P. Meierowitz, Wolfowitz, Zalman Klevonski, A.G. Mindel, Zvi Fig, Maiete Saks, Bezalel Buchman, Dov Saks. Aharon Saks, P.M. Fishelewitz, Yechiel Baruch, Cohen, P.M. Markus, Chaim Levite, Alte Hering, Eliyahu Dov Markus.

Footnote

1. The Bessarabia region is located between the rivers Prut and Dniester near the Black Sea. It was part of Moldavia until 1812, when it was annexed by the Russians and remained part of the Russian Empire until 1918. Jewish communities were found in Bessarabia is early as

the 16th century. Their numbers increased rapidly after the Russian annexation and, by the end of the 18th century, there were more than 200,000 Jews living in Bessarabia, most of them in Kishinev and its district. After the early 1880s the economic situation of Bessarabian Jewry deteriorated. This was a result of the 'Temporary Laws', which were published by the Russian cabinet in 1882. The laws prohibited the Jews from living in villages and restricted the limits of their residence to the towns and townlets. As a result, many Jews in Bessarabia were deprived of their livelihood, all the more so in the wake of the agrarian crisis in Russia. The difficult economic situation caused great hunger and many impoverished Jews emigrated overseas. The fact that about 100 households in Riteve donated even a modest sum is additional proof of the feelings of national solidarity that prevailed in Riteve.

———

[Page 185]

Appendix 2

They Died For Israel – Some Obituaries

These five obituaries, not in order of date of death, were included at the end of the original publication. Not all those concerned were born in Riteve, but were children or grandchildren of people of Riteve who made Aliyah. Their inclusion demonstrated the close ties of their relatives to the shtetl, feeling that these young people 'belonged' to Riteve although they had never known it.

MR

These are the sacrifices of Riteve Jewry on the altar of the homeland, in the days of the riots and during the War of Independence.

Saks Yizhak, son of Israel and Minna

Born in Riteve in 1926, Saks Yizhak emigrated to Israel with his parents in 1936. He was a student at the Haifa Technicon and active in the Haganah. At the beginning of the battles in 1948, he was mur– dered by the British on the road to Beit Oren, near Haifa.

Yehuda Friedman

Born 19th of Heshvan 5701 – 20.11.1940
Fell 29th of Av 5722 – 29.8.1962

Yehuda Friedman had a happy and loving childhood, the childhood of a healthy kibbutznik. At the age of 16 he became interested in scientific subjects, which were his special pride. His favourite pastimes were hiking and sport.

[Page 186]

He volunteered to join Golani and. after completing his basic training, was transferred to a reconnaisance unit. This was followed by a section commanders' course and then an officers' course. He attained the rank of second lieutenant and served for four months as platoon commander.

Yehuda belonged to the division of the army which guarded the settlements, folds, roads and borders in the Hulah Valley. He ventured to the highest cliffs of the Golan mountains. He fell in the line of duty in a border incident, not far from his kibbutz. The words of his father, a son of Riteve, read next to the open grave were moving: 'Yehuda! Young lion!'

A shrubbery named after him fulfils the commandment which guided him: With all your soul and with all your might' – without deviation, you even fulfilled with all 'your soul'. And gave your body and soul for the sake of our safety.

Shraga Ballin, son of Tova and Yirmiyahu

Born 30 April 1928

**Saks Yizhak, son of Israel
and Minna**

Shraga Ballin was found by a member of Kibbutz Yagur who was serving in the Jewish Brigade in a camp controlled by the Americans. He had survived after endless sufferings and after the death marches in the Giroli mountains. When he was miraculously rescued from the claws of the Nazis, he weighed 27 kilograms and, because of his weakness, had been hospitalised in the camp.

He was killed on 27 May 1951 in Wadi Sarar, a military camp of the Israel Defence Force. He died as a sergeant of the camp, from a fractured skull and brain damage.

[Page 187]

Yaron Landsman, son of Hadassah and Yechezkel, grandson of Rachel Tilla and Aron Katz

Born 4th Kisleve 5711 – 13.11.1950
Fell 28th Sivan 5729 11.6.1969

A light mane of hair, eyes maybe blue, maybe green, maybe gray, looked out of a sunburnt face. This was his appearance – unforgettable. Yaron – his voice like his name was clear and strong, warm and resonant. He held a beautiful tune, his voice warbled in his throat. In his childhood, when he was told a story, he would listen intently and dream and want more – as if stories were all seeds which were sown in his tender soul and which later grew into strong plants.

In the Jordan Valley, a desolate burning place of the pursued and the bereaved, mottled with small mounds of dust along the sides of the road, a place where every green bush spits fire and every crevice in the rock is a refuge and hiding place, in this valley between the olive and carob trees, encircled by a ring of hollowed–out rocks, he fired his last shot. Clutching his machine gun, Yaron fell.

Mira Birger z"l, daughter of Dvora and David Birger, granddaughter of Avigail and Dov Levite

Mira Birger z"l specialised in helping families with terminal diseases and was recognised at Hadassah Hospital in Jerusalem as an authority on this painful subject.

As a graduate of the School of Social Work of the Hebrew University, her aim in life was to help her fellow human beings. She worked in the Social Work Department at Hadassah Hospital while continuing her studies. She wrote articles about the mental state of the sick and their difficulties in adapting to their environment, after their release from hospital.

In 1969 Mira was awarded a bursary from Hadassah and travelled to the United States where she did her Masters degree. In the first year she was involved mainly with the problems of the elderly who suffered from chronic illnesses. Unfortunately, her humanitarian plan was cut short by hatred. On Friday 28th Tammuz 5735 – 4.7.1975 – she chanced to be in the vicinity of Zion Square in Jerusalem, where she was critically injured by the explosion of the 'refrigerator bomb' planted by terrorists. On Monday 31st Tammuz 5735 – 7.7.1975 – she was laid to rest in the cemetery on the Mount of Olives, Jerusalem.

[Page 188]

* * *

It is thanks to young people such as these that the Israeli nation can dwell securely in their land forever.

That is our consolation – in their departure!

And that the awaited peace shall come!

Their memory will be blessed

———

[Page 189]

Glossary of Jewish Terms
Used Frequently in the Book

A. The synagogue

Minyan – a prayer quorum, made up of no less than ten Jews who are past their Bar mitzvah and are allowed to read in the Torah.

Bima – the podium in the centre of the synagogue, on which the reading from the Torah, placed on a high table, is performed.

Talit – a prayer shawl.

Mincha and **Ma'ariv** – the afternoon prayer, called after the afternoon sacrifice in the Temple; and the evening prayer, following sunset, called after the Hebrew word for evening, 'Erev'.

Chazan – the cantor in the synagogue, who leads the public's prayers. The cantors personal variations became the source of various styles of Jewish music.

Shammas – the synagogue's attendant and keeper.

Gabbai – the synagogue's treasurer.

Shema Israel – the beginning of the 'Hear, Oh Israel, our Lord is G–d, our Lord is one'. It has become the essence of Judaism in one sentence (and is therefore said before death) and a code word for Jews who have forgotten or never known any– thing else, such as Soviet Jewry.

B. Study

Cheder – was meant for younger boys. The Cheder Metukan was the modern one, where girls too could study, and the door was opened for knowledge in general. Talmud Torah – the study of the Torah and also a kind of elementary school for boys, based on religious studies.

Yeshiva – if the cheder is a sort of beginners' school, and the Talmud Torah is the elementary school, then the yeshiva is the highest school, where the young men study under the supervision and guidance of the great rabbis.

The Lithuanian yeshivot flourished continuously from the end of the 18th century until the Holocaust.

Kollel – after their marriage, Torah students continue their studies in kollalim.

[Page 190]

Beit Midrash – while the synagogue served for prayers, ceremonies and holidays, the Beit Midrash ('House of Studies') was the place of studies for the adults, who spent much of their time there.

Mishnah – commentaries (Midrashim and Agadah) and laws (Halachah), on and of the Torah, as organised around CE 200 by Rabbi Yehuda Hanassi in Galilee, in six orders divided into 60 tractates. It is called in short 'Shas', an acronym of Shisha Sedarim, the six orders.

Talmud and **Gemara** – the Yerushalmi (of Jerusalem) Talmud, composed in the Land of Israel, was sealed in the 4th century and the Bavli (of Babylon), composed in Bavel (now Iraq), in the 6th century, the Bavli being the fuller and larger of the two. The Talmuds include in their turn commentaries and laws of and on the Mishnah. Gemara is a wider term that includes the two Talmuds.

Zohar (the Book of Splendour) – the central work in the literature of the **Kabbalah** (Jewish mysticism). The book is a collection of several sections that include short Midrashic statements (rabbinical commentary on a biblical text), homilies and discussion.

Ein Yaacov – a collection of legends and homilies from the Talmud, assembled by Rabbi Ya'akov Ibn Haviv, Halachist and a communal leader in Salonika at the beginning of the 16th century.

C. Rituals

Mitzvot – deeds that a Jewish person above 13 has to perform or to refrain from doing. There are 613 Mitzvot, divided into 365 to refrain from and 248 to perform. Their number is equal to the days of the year and to the number of the body's sinews (365) and its organs (248).

Shulchan Aruch – this is the most important book of Halachah (Jewish law), com– posed by Yosef Karo in the 16th century. Its importance lies in the fact that it divides the vast material into sections and subsections, clearly and concisely Kiddush – the blessing over the cup of wine (or grape juice) on Fridays and the eve of Holidays to mark the entrance of the holy (Kadosh) Sabbath and the Holidays.

Mikveh – a ritual bath, where it is a custom for some men to wash in order to be purified for the Sabbath and Holidays. Women immerse themselves in the Mikveh at the conclusion of their menstrual cycle.

Shabbat Nachamu – the Sabbath following the Ninth of Av, on which the Haftara starts with 'Nachamu, Nachamu' (be consoled) from the prophet Yeshayahu, Chapter 40.

Sephirat ha–Omer – counting of the Omer: a Pentateuchal injunction to count 49 days from the first offering of the Omer – a sheaf of corn – in the Temple. The counting starts from the 16th of Nissan until Shavuot (Pentecost). On each day the

[Page 191]

counting must mention both the number of days and the number of weeks. The days of the Omer ard also characterised by semi–mourning customs. It is a very old tradition, normally associated with the deaths of the disciples of Rabbi Akiva. The solemnisation of marriages as well as haircutting and the playing of musical instru– ments are prohibited during these days.

Kleizmorim – folk musicians.

Chevra Kadisha – 'a Holy association' that took care of burials.

[Page 200]

Index

IMPORTANT NOTE: Please note that the page numbers here are the page numbers in the original translation, of which this book is a reprint. For an index using this books page numbers go to page 278.

C

[Page 202]

INDEX for this book's page numbers